Estate Planning for the Healthy Wealthy Family

How to Promote Family Harmony,

Affirm Your Values,

and Protect Your Assets

STANLEY D. NEELEMAN, J.D.

CARLA B. GARRITY, PH.D.

MITCHELL A. BARIS, PH.D.

ALLWORTH PRESS
NEW YORK

08   07   06   05   03   5   4   3   2   1

Published by Allworth Press
An imprint of Allworth Communications, Inc.
10 East 23rd Street, New York, NY 10010

Cover design by Derek Bacchus
Cover photo by Digital Vision
Page composition/typography by SR Desktop Services, Ridge, NY

Library of Congress Cataloging-in-Publication Data
Neeleman, Stanley D.
    Estate planning for the healthy wealthy family : how to promote family
harmony, affirm your values, and protect your assets / Stanley D. Neeleman,
Carla B. Garrity, Mitchell A. Baris.
        p.   cm.
Includes index.
    1. Estate planning—United States.   2. Family—United States.
I. Garrity, Carla B.   II. Baris, Mitchell A.   III. Title.

KF750.N44   2003
346.7305'2—dc22

                                                              2003018963

Printed in Canada

CONTENTS

Acknowledgments

S ometimes a book grows from interesting conversations, insights from colleagues, novel questions posed by clients, admiration for another's creative ideas, personal struggles, issues that defy resolution, even tragedy and loss. This book grew, not as a book the authors decided to write, planned together, or ever even imagined, but from those moments and life experiences that accumulate into treasures that we fail to recognize at the time.

Many individuals provided these moments and experiences; we simply put the pieces together. Jim Bye was the first—a man of exceptional intellect and acerbic wit, who questioned and challenged our beliefs and assumptions about values-based estate planning. Despite our desperate efforts to refute his critique of our initial analysis and conclusions, Jim stood his ground, invigorating our thinking with dissenting viewpoints. We had other enlightening and stimulating dialogues with Don Hopkins, John Warnick, and Carol Lay, attorneys who are without equal in their understanding of the complex and multifaceted process we refer to as *estate planning*. We discovered the profoundly inspirational and wise writings of John Levy. Just how we found John is beyond our recall. His work is not published nor can it be found in the library, bookstore, or on the Internet. It is available only from John himself, and if you write or call him, it is yours for the asking. Stimulated by his insights on the influences of money on relationships, we began to write.

The outstanding team of financial advisors at Northstar Investment Advisors, including Tony Taylor and Fred Taylor, listened and then listened some more, and one of them, Bob Van Wetter, picked up his pencil and out came remarkably creative ideas for the children of this world. The next step led us to our daughters, Alyssa, Megan, and Amy, whom we questioned about their values and the origins of their values. We found that they were challenged to make sense of the marketing pitches that targeted them in their schools, on the computer, through the media, and, poignantly, through the peer culture. Of our children, only Carla's son, Mark, is a parent. Mark was enlisted to read our early thoughts. He read, he criticized, he elaborated, and he spurred us on. He liked the material, and it provoked his own thinking about raising a child and planning an estate. Thank you, Mark, for affirming the importance of values, for having them, believing in them, and for transmitting them to Beren.

Then others walked unwittingly into our ever-widening perspective. After all, estate planning is about more than planning an estate—it is about relationships in life, those formed through business ventures, marriage, friendship, family, and, yes, loss, whether through death, divorce, or just through acrimony. Charlie Butcher, an atypical businessman and amazingly accomplished, spent hours reading and conversing with Mitch, and yet more thoughts fell into place. The Family Business Institute welcomed us as observers at their monthly meetings, as an interdisciplinary team cogently tackled tough decisions for family-held businesses. Lunches were seasoned with mouthfuls of sage comments that Russ Oliver kindly provided year after year.

Thanks are due to Alex, Mitch's wife and consultant, not only for her patience and encouragement, but for her steadfast financial know-how as well. And our gratitude goes to Mitch's son, Matthew, who followed his graduation from college with seminar experience to shape his ideals into action. He brought ideas back to us about socially minded charitable giving and more. Thanks, Matthew.

Stan's colleague, Larry Farmer, a recognized expert in the techniques of interviewing, counseling, and reflective practice, opened our eyes to the shortcomings of estate planning professionals in helping clients to articulate and pursue their values-based objectives. Particularly valuable were his insights into the tendencies of experts to define and resolve a client's problem based on an initial assessment of objective indicators, rather than a searching effort to determine the client's true concerns and objectives. Thanks also go to members of Stan's immediate and extended family, who steadfastly refuse to let success in business and the professions blind them to the things that matter most.

The one person who dedicatedly stands behind all of this—actually, she sits for long hours in front of a computer screen, her fingers nimbly entering our words while her mind astutely catches every unexplained idea, confused thought, unclear logic, and misuse of grammar—is Sandra Rush. Sandy, thank you, and may a forest grace your yard by the time we run out of words.

Foreword

Broadly defined, *estate planning* is the process by which you, as a person of means, with the assistance of your professional advisors

- Clarify, prioritize and articulate your values;
- Gain perspective on the utility of wealth as a resource to be employed in the service of those values;
- Formulate and articulate specific objectives with respect to the accumulation, preservation, and disposition of your wealth; and
- Select and implement the means necessary to accomplish those objectives.

Those who write and practice in the field of estate planning too frequently assume that we all have the same objectives with respect to wealth: (1) to accumulate all we can during life, and (2) to pass as much as possible on to our children at death. That assumption completely overlooks the significance of our diversity of perspectives on the role of wealth in our own and our children's lives, and inevitably leads to excessive focus on the selection and implementation of tax-reduction and other wealth-preservation strategies.

Although it is true that most of us indeed would like to have more money, few of us see any value in the pursuit of wealth for its own sake. Wealth, as we know, has no value apart from the purposes to which it is applied. In Aristotle's words: "Wealth is evidently not the good we are seeking, for it is merely useful and for the sake of something else."[1] The "usefulness" of wealth is inherent in its power over the development, management, consumption, and disposition of personal and community resources. If that power is exercised "for the sake of something" that is truly important to its owner, its potential for contributing to an authentic state of happiness and personal well-being is readily apparent. Thus, a more appropriate formulation of our objective with respect to wealth might be to accumulate all we can, consistent with and in furtherance of our values.

It is also true that many of us would like to confer a financial legacy on our children. However, not everyone holds that view. Indeed, according to a recent survey, only 48.4 percent of the heads of all households believe it is important to leave an estate for their children.[2] And for many of us who do, our purpose is not simply to enrich our children; rather, it is to endow them with the power to consume and manage financial resources to appropriate ends, based on our individual judgments as to what is in their best interests. We realize that the responsible exercise of those powers can enrich and give meaning to our children's lives, while at the same time promote the economic well-being of the larger community. We also know that the misuse of that power can engender in our children laziness, aimlessness, arrogance, greed, extravagance, and a disposition to control and manipulate others. Fortunately, the risk that the powers inherent in transferred wealth will be abused by our children can be minimized through the formulation and implementation of an estate plan specifically tailored to our respective values and our children's unique needs, circumstances, attributes, and abilities.

The key, then, to effective estate planning is to formulate and pursue objectives that are informed and shaped by our own unique mix of values and circumstances. Those with expertise and experience in estate planning can provide invaluable assistance in discerning and articulating their clients' values and objectives as well as selecting and implementing appropriate planning strategies. However, they should not be permitted to sell an ill-fitted, "off-the-rack" plan by impressing the planning process with their preconceived notions of what is in their clients' best interests.

This book offers guidance and support not only in achieving personal empowerment, and identifying and communicating values but also in rearing and grounding well-functioning children who, as whole individuals, are less likely to embrace negative values or be diverted from their positive strivings by the dazzle, allure, and temptation of family wealth. The ensuing chapters are arranged into three primary parts: Part I, Your Values and Your Estate Plan; Part II, Building an Estate Plan for Your Family; Part III, Facing Dangers and Seeking Fairness. These discussions address themes of the impact of wealth at each stage of life, and, as such, some readers will use this book as a reference text, selecting chapters relevant only to their circumstances. Other readers might read the chapters sequentially, finding templates for formulating or modifying their estate plans. The proffered observations, principles, and suggestions are the product of collaboration across disciplines, blending the elements of principled estate planning, community-minded charitable pursuits, pro-social relationships, and sound child-development principles.

The principles and case examples contained in this book are intended to provide a framework for shaping the reader's own perspective on wealth as a means of accomplishing values-based objectives. We recognize that the values to be served will differ from reader to reader. We also believe, however, that there exists an array of values to which most people aspire. Among those shared aspirations are integrity, self-reliance, dependability, industry, education, prudence, preservation, compassion, justice, intimacy, and civility. In our effort to develop a meaningful context for discussion, we have made liberal reference to these notions. In doing so, we do not intend to suggest what the reader's values *should* be. The central theme of the book is that wealth can serve as a unique and effective medium for expressing, validating, and refining core values, whatever they may be, and in so doing can serve as the means by which one's values become one's legacy.

STANLEY D. NEELEMAN
CARLA B. GARRITY
MITCHELL A. BARIS

Your Values and Your Estate Plan

CHAPTER ONE

The Values-Based Estate Plan

A respected and knowledgeable attorney described an experience in which an eighteen-year-old arrived at his office enraged that his grandfather had left him a legacy in trust rather than outright. The young man wanted his money, and he wanted it immediately. He spouted angry and rude epithets at the attorney, whom he blamed for inducing his grandfather to create the trust that denied him ready access to what was rightfully his. His rudeness and expectation of unencumbered wealth, as well as his obvious lack of appreciation, may well have been foreseen by his grandfather and likely accounted for his decision to impede the young man's access to his legacy through the use of a values-based trust. In structuring his grandson's legacy, this grandfather was guided by his own moral compass and not by his grandson's expectations. Thus, he not only protected the legacy from his grandson's youthful sense of indignant entitlement, but also taught him a valuable lesson regarding the responsibility that attends the ownership, management, and disposition of wealth.

Some may see the grandfather's action as an inappropriate attempt to control his grandson's conduct "from the grave." However, only misplaced emphasis on the grandchild's expectations can justify that view. As the rightful steward over his own wealth, the grandfather was free to apply it to ends he alone deemed worthy. And, as an autonomous individual, his grandson was free to accept the legacy on his grandfather's terms or to decline it if he found the terms unacceptable.

The grandson's defiant reaction to his grandfather's entrusted legacy likely was due, at least in part, to his immaturity. However, it may also have been a consequence of his grandfather's failure during life to teach his grandchild the principles the legacy was intended to impart. In other words, perhaps it was the grandson's dashed expectations that account for his hostile reaction, rather than the arrangement itself. If the grandfather had taken the time to explain to the grandson his reasons for establishing the trust, perhaps the grandson would have been more accepting of his grandfather's intentions and gained a better understanding of the principles that moved his grandfather to structure the legacy as he did. In the realm of families and wealth, there is no substitute for open and honest communication.

THE MEANING OF VALUES

For present purposes, a *value* is a normative principle that informs and shapes thoughts, desires, feelings, choices, and behavior. A value is not merely a preference for one thing over another, such as a Ford over a Buick. A preference is a matter of taste and style and is subject to change. A value, rather, is an enduring and essential attribute of character. Examples of commonly held values that are particularly relevant in estate planning include:

- **Integrity**—honesty, sincerity, authenticity, dependability, stewardship, and personal responsibility
- **Security**—self-reliance, self-determination, self-actualization, prudence, health, education, comfort, acceptance, power, and prestige
- **Beneficence**—philanthropy, gratitude, respect, tolerance, generosity, compassion, service, and justice

The guiding values are "commonly held" only in the sense that few would challenge their status as principles that contribute to good character. Differences between individuals abound with regard to both the meaning and relative importance of those principles. For one person, *security* may just mean having a steady job; for another, it may entail presiding over a successful business empire. Moreover, the components of a particular individual's value system inevitably will change with experience and maturity. A young entrepreneur's consuming desire for self-reliance and prestige may well give way to a commitment to philanthropy during his twilight years. Or, an aggressive investor who suffers substantial losses may gain a new appreciation for prudence as a more certain path to financial security.

THE RELATIONSHIP OF VALUES TO ESTATE PLANNING

If you exercise personal choice in the development, management, consumption, and disposition of personal and community resources in harmony with your core values, you likely will experience a sense of self-fulfillment and personal well-being. Conversely, if you pursue and apply wealth to ends that violate your values, you likely will feel unsettled, duplicitous, and out of balance.

Consider, for example, the elderly woman who was persuaded by her advisors to deplete her assets through gifts to her children in order to qualify for nursing home assistance through the federal Medicaid program. In recommending that strategy, her advisors likely assumed that preserving her estate for her children was more important to her than maintaining her financial independence. Contrary to that assumption, her deep commitment to the principles of self-reliance and personal responsibility far outweighed her desire to confer an economic benefit on her children. The employment of a strategy that produced an outcome that was the antithesis of that commitment was an affront to her integrity and left her feeling diminished and disillusioned.

If your estate plan is to serve its essential purpose of enhancing your own and your family's sense of well-being, its objectives, as well as the techniques employed to achieve those objectives, must be formulated and validated with reference to your values.

CLARIFYING AND PRIORITIZING VALUES

If your value system is to serve effectively as the framework for the formulation of your personal estate plan, you must first clarify and prioritize its components. Most of us are only vaguely aware of the standards and concerns that compose our own personal value systems, and few of us have consciously attempted to resolve the tension that inevitably arises when those standards and concerns conflict.

Many of us unthinkingly embrace as our own an array of normative standards to which we assume most caring and intelligent people in the larger community adhere. Accordingly, unless you are among the few who have had occasion to reflect deliberately on what really matters to you, you likely will find it difficult to define your "legacy of values" without some degree of guided introspection. In that regard, you might want to compare your values with those attributed to Americans by observers from other cultures.

Dr. Robert Kohls, the former executive director of the Washington International Center, a contract agency of the U.S. government that helps nonWesterners adapt to life in the United States, has commented extensively on perceived differences between Western and nonWestern values.[1] Among the values he identifies as uniquely American are the following: (1) personal control over the environment, (2) prudent use of time, (3) equality of opportunity and class mobility ("lifting oneself up by the bootstraps"), (4) competition as the best means to superior performance, (5) privacy and personal space, and (6) materialism—the seemingly insatiable desire to acquire new and replace old "things." Dr. Kohl finds no little irony in the fact that Americans believe so strongly in individual autonomy and uniqueness and yet unthinkingly embrace a value system rooted in conformity. Implicit in Dr. Kohl's observation is an invitation to each of us to acknowledge and examine the cultural influences that shape our professed value systems and then to choose only those values that truly resonate with our own inner yearnings. Only values that are authentically and uniquely our own are relevant to the process of gaining for ourselves and transmitting to our children an understanding of how wealth can contribute to our sense of fulfillment and well-being.

To bring clarity and order to your personal value system, you may find it useful to reflect on the circumstances and experiences that have informed and shaped your hopes, fears, and perspectives, particularly as they relate to wealth and its purposes. The following questions, based in part on Scott C. Fithian's more comprehensive list of questions designed to reveal one's financial philosophy,[2] are offered as a means of stimulating and focusing your thinking in that regard:

- What are your family's ethnic and cultural origins?
- What did your parents do for a living?
- Were your parents affluent or poor?
- What challenges did you encounter as a member of [an affluent] [a poor] family?

- Were your parents concerned with maintaining or improving their social standing?
- Did your parents aspire to a higher standard of living than they were able to afford?
- Which of your parents made the financial decisions?
- What were your parents' most cherished values?
- Did your parents conduct their lives in harmony with those values?
- To what extent did your parents' attitudes with respect to the accumulation, preservation, and disposition of wealth shape your own?
- Are you envious of your more prosperous acquaintances?
- What attributes of your character account for your financial success?
- In what ways does your wealth contribute to your family's well-being?
- What would you change in order to enhance your family's well-being?
- To what extent are your attitudes with respect to wealth informed by your religious beliefs and convictions?
- Do your attitudes with respect to wealth differ from those of your spouse or children?
- Are there elements of your relationship with wealth that you would not want your children to emulate?
- Is your standard of living about right? Too extravagant? Too miserly?
- To what extent is your standard of living based on your desire to impress your acquaintances with your financial power and achievements?
- What is your view of welfare and other government assistance programs?
- Do your spouse and children spend money in ways that anger or disappoint you?
- What is your assessment of your children's ability to apply their financial resources to appropriate ends?
- Are you concerned about the negative influence inherited wealth might have on your children's well-being?
- To what extent are you inclined to devote your income or wealth to community or charitable causes?

MEMORIALIZING YOUR VALUES

In light of their crucial importance to the planning process, you would be well served to memorialize in writing those of your values that are relevant to the development of your estate plan. The writing might be styled as a "mission statement" or "value statement," and should be reviewed and altered from time to time to reflect changing circumstances and perspectives. The following excerpt from one family's financial mission statement illustrates how core values can serve as a framework for the formulation and implementation of a comprehensive estate plan:

Statement of Purpose. Our primary purpose is to ensure that the financial resources accumulated through our common effort are preserved and employed as a means of instilling and magnifying in individual family members the following values: (1) stewardship—**responsibility and concern for the interests of others; (2)** enterprise—**creativity, initiative, and willingness to take prudent risks to foster self-reliance and add value to the larger economy; (3)** personal growth—**recognition and development of personal aptitude and abilities; (4)** integrity—**honesty, sincerity, and trustworthiness; and (5)** community—**interdependence that fosters security and aggregates strength. We intend to be guided by those same values in administering all of our financial affairs.**

You may want to enlist the services of a professional advisor who is sensitive to the importance of values in estate planning to assist you in developing your personal mission or value statement. In any event, you should give copies of the statement to your advisors with the instruction that it serve as the embodiment of the principles that will guide the formulation and implementation of your estate plan. You also may want to give copies to members of your family, particularly if you intend to dispose of your wealth in a manner that is contrary to their expectations. If you make the members of your family aware of the principles that informed and shaped your estate plan, they will be more likely to understand and accept the plan as a genuine expression of your desire to apply your wealth to rational and virtuous ends.

A reflective and honest appraisal of your responses to the foregoing questions will reveal a normative framework for the formulation of specific estate planning objectives and indicate the strategies and techniques appropriate to the implementation of those objectives. It may also reveal a measure of dissonance in your relationship with your wealth. For example, you may find that, despite your firm conviction that your wealth is not the measure of your worth, you maintain a level of consumption that can only be explained as an attempt to impress others with your financial prowess and social status. That insight may well motivate you to moderate your consumption in favor of applying your wealth to more productive ends. It may also serve you in your effort to fortify your children against the popular myth, carefully cultivated by the commercial media, that the capacity to consume high-quality goods and services is the measure of a happy and meaningful life.

FORMULATING YOUR VALUES-BASED OBJECTIVES

The clarification and prioritization of your values with respect to your wealth will shape and define your specific planning objectives. The relationship between values and objectives is illustrated by the following examples:

- If self-sufficiency and financial security are among your core values, you likely will seek to enhance your wealth through a conservative program of savings and investment, rather than pursue strategies that place your existing assets at risk.
- If you believe your children should "earn their own way," you likely will structure their inheritances in such a way as to provide them with appropriate incentives to engage in meaningful work.

Representative Values-Based Objectives

Although your particular objectives will be unique to your own values and circumstances, they likely will include one or more of the following:

- Exposing and dispelling popular myths that distort and exaggerate the role of wealth as the measure of a happy and meaningful life
- Instilling in your dependents an understanding of the role of wealth as a resource to be employed in the service of values
- Fostering in your dependents the attitudes, knowledge, and skills necessary to enable them to achieve financial independence
- Accumulating and preserving sufficient wealth to achieve and maintain a comfortable standard of living for yourself and your dependents
- Providing for competent management in the event of incapacity
- Avoiding unnecessary medical and funeral expenses

- Transferring assets to your successors in a form that accounts for their disparate needs, circumstances, and capacities and is calculated to develop and reinforce positive attributes and virtues
- Applying additional resources in support of charitable and community causes
- Minimizing the potential for disputes among your successors over the disposition of your estate
- Minimizing the expense of transferring assets to your descendants

Objectives Pertaining to Transfers of Wealth to Children

In planning for the transfer of wealth to your children, you should begin by evaluating the effect this will have on their physical, emotional, relational, and spiritual well-being. You should carefully consider the needs, maturity, experience, and capabilities of each child and tailor a financial legacy uniquely suited to that child.

An approach that takes into account the unique attributes and circumstances of the children may well result in a distribution plan that forgoes objective equality for subjective fairness. Consider, for example, a family with two children—one a schoolteacher and the other a highly compensated business executive. A plan that allocates more of the estate to the former obviously would not be *equal*, but it would be *fair*, in the sense that it addresses the children's relative financial needs and validates the teacher's choice of a socially productive (although not lucrative) career.

Of the values manifest in American culture, none is more ingrained and cherished than equality. In the family, that value often is reflected in the strong inclination of parents to divide their wealth equally among their children, irrespective of differences in financial need and maturity. It also is manifest in the attitude of entitlement that children often exhibit with respect to their parents' wealth. Children all too often assume they have a birthright to an equal share of their parents' estate, to do with as they please, regardless of their benefactors' values and expectations. That same attitude may account for the resentment and even anger some children feel toward parents who encumber their estate with trusts or other devices that impose restrictions on access and consumption.

INFORMING THE CHILDREN

It is almost always advisable to discuss your estate plan with your children. And it is essential that you do so if you plan to allocate your estate to your children in other than equal shares. The authors are aware of numerous cases in which family harmony has been severely strained because children misconstrued their parents' motives in providing for unequal treatment. In one such case, a parent allocated a smaller share of her estate to a child who had enjoyed considerable financial success as a trial lawyer. When, after his mother's death, that child discovered that he had been "short-changed," he was deeply hurt and blamed his siblings for turning their mother against him. Several years have passed since his mother's death, and that son's relationship with his siblings remains frosty.

In another case, the parents had the wisdom and foresight to discuss their plans with their children in advance. The circumstances were similar in that they were inclined to favor the poorer of their two children with a larger share of their estate, but were reluctant to do so for fear of engendering family disharmony. In sharing their feelings with their well-off child, they began by affirming their love for her, expressing their pride over her accomplishments, and mentioning their concern that the poorer child's share of their estate would be insufficient to ensure her financial well-being. Not surprisingly, the well-off child herself suggested that they allocate a larger share to her less-fortunate sister. They then discussed with the poorer child their intent to leave her a larger share of the estate in order to enable her to pursue her less-remunerative but socially productive career. That discussion left the poorer child with a greater appreciation for her parents' values and with a feeling of being neither favored nor diminished in their eyes.

If a family has managed its financial affairs in an open and cooperative manner, parents likely will find it easy, gratifying, and ultimately rewarding to discuss their plans for the disposition of their estates with their children. Children who have been schooled to view wealth as an instrument for achieving objectives that are grounded in a common value system will be eager to participate in a process leading to the formulation of strategies calculated to ensure the continuing pursuit of those objectives upon and following their parents' deaths. Children who have been party to family decisions allocating family financial resources in a way that takes into account differing needs and circumstances are not likely to insist on equality of treatment or to misinterpret inequality of treatment as inequality of parental love.

Although likely more difficult to initiate, full and frank discussion of the parents' estate plan is even more important in a family that does not have the advantage of shared objectives and values concerning financial matters. In the absence of such discussion, children are more likely to regard any disposition other than outright and equal as "unfair." That perception in turn may lead to hurt feelings, sibling resentment, and family discord.

Parents sometimes are reluctant to discuss their estate plans with their children. Often that reluctance stems from the fear of creating a forum in which simmering rivalry and resentment may become manifest. However, more often than not, such occasions, when conducted in a spirit of goodwill and conciliation, actually have the effect of healing old wounds and strengthening family relationships. In any case, such a discussion is so vital to avoiding a family rift over what might otherwise be viewed as disparate treatment under the parents' estate plan that it is well worth the risk of evoking hostile feelings. At worst, the hostility will be directed toward the parents, leaving the children with little reason to blame each other for the perceived unfairness of the parents' estate plan.

CHAPTER TWO

How Do Money Myths Torment Families?

The myths of the power of money proliferate throughout our culture. Ironically, money is viewed as the ultimate healer, yet at the same time money is viewed as the ultimate destroyer. Myths are created and perpetuated such as:

- Money destroys and corrupts people.
- Growing up with money will take away your motivation.
- Wealthy people have more privileges in our society; the rules don't apply to them.
- If only I had a "little" (or a lot) more money, I would be happy.
- If only I would win the lottery, my problems would be solved.

Many metaphors are incorporated into our language:

- Right on the money.
- It's like money in the bank.
- If you're so smart, why aren't you rich?
- Everybody has their price.
- Money talks!

CULTURAL IRONY

How can such dissimilar, even opposite, themes run through our culture simultaneously? The answer, to some extent, rests on the reality that the function of money itself is an enhancer of whatever traits and values the individual already possesses. Money alone does not make a life or ruin a life. We are all aware of the irony of happy poor people and unhappy rich people. This is hardly a new notion. "Many who seem to be struggling with adversity are happy; many amid great affluence are utterly miserable," wrote Publius Cornelius Tacitus in Ancient Rome around A.D. 100[1] We can learn from philosophers who have struggled with this idea since ancient times: money is a multiplier of those personality traits that exist within us.

IS MONEY HAPPINESS?

Money is not happiness, nor does it necessarily bring contentment to those who possess it, yet we are led by the media, determined to shape our cultural directives, to believe otherwise. The promise of fulfillment lurks in every ad. "Whoever said money can't buy happiness isn't spending it right," a Lexus ad instructs. Unfortunately, our values may be influenced and ultimately shaped by this commercialism. A new scent will bring fulfillment, love, attractiveness; clothes make the man; and children especially believe the newest toy offers whatever self-enhancement is implied in the ad. The myth of money as healer is fueled by advertisers urging the consumer to believe that style, image, companionship, self-worth, and even contentment can be purchased. Interestingly, however, psychological research demonstrates that once a certain hierarchy of need is met and a certain level of material comfort is obtained, more money fails to enhance, motivate, or reinforce. It should then be no surprise that lottery winners, for instance, feel no long-lasting happiness in spite of their increase in wealth.[2] At best, a "temporary jolt of joy" is all they experience.[3] In fact, studies find that the wealthiest people are not significantly happier than those with average incomes.[4] Nevertheless, many persistently yearn for more money, holding steadfastly to the idea that their happiness would be enhanced if they only had more.

Nowhere in social science research findings can more money be found to translate into more happiness. As has been pointed out, the research shows, in fact, that after one has attained a certain minimum level of comfort, which varies from individual to individual, more wealth simply fails to be motivating or gratifying. Psychologist Abraham Maslow for instance, in his well-known hierarchy of need gratification, suggests that once basic needs are met, most individuals aspire to a higher order of need gratification involving a level of self-actualization that includes spirituality and community-focused pursuits to attain fulfillment.[5] Thus, as material possessions are gathered beyond the point of basic need satisfaction, no greater sense of well-being or personal fulfillment will result. "Once comfortable, more money provides diminishing returns on happiness."[6]

Yet many people continue to strive for more material wealth because cultural alternatives are not available. Ads do not hype self-actualization and meaningful contribution to others; they promote consumerism. Success, in our culture, continues to be measured by financial milestones rather than acknowledging that social responsibilities, artistic and cultural contributions, and playing a supportive relationship role are also measures of success. Contentment may be elusive for some. There is no direct pathway; although money appears to pave the way, it is not that simple. Material possessions do bring at least a short-lived sense of increased pleasure or well-being, but they are not in themselves capable of satisfying higher-order needs.

For those with wealth to pass on to their children, fears may loom large that their children will fail to develop a work ethic or even a desire to be contributing members of society. Among our shared cultural values is the persistent belief that children of wealth, especially those of the second and third generation, are inept squanderers weaned with a "silver spoon." The larger society often scoffs at these individuals, ascribing fraudulent status to their claims of having struggled or even having had legitimate problems to overcome at all. ("He cried all the way to the bank.") This may be an even greater uphill struggle for the children of high-profile parents due to their visibility and success.

MONEY AND SELF-CONCEPT

The contradictory money myths that pervade society are shackles that can bind. Each individual benefits from stepping back from presumptions and considering the power of money in his or her own life. The pervasive danger is unwittingly to "buy" into the notion that self-worth is tied to net worth. Money represents opportunities and options; it must not represent a quantified sense of oneself. Examining the themes of the generation in which one grew into adulthood helps to expose the money myths and attitudes that society perpetuated and likely were internalized by the individual. For example, the thirties and forties were a period of frugality, savings, and deprivation for many families. By con-

trast, the seventies saw the advent of the "me" generation, characterized by society's sanction of self-indulgence; for some, indulgence
meant rejecting the prevailing values, whereas for others, it meant
accumulating or collecting anything one's heart desired, be that multiple material possessions, multiple marriages and divorces, assets, or
career changes.

By the eighties and early nineties, money seemed easy to come by.
The media proliferated with messages that promised the good life
defined by material goods. Young adults amassed fortunes and often
possessed greater net worth by their mid-twenties than their parents
had managed to accumulate in a lifetime. Then the tides shifted with
the fall of the dot.coms in the late nineties. Later, the tragic events of
9/11 ushered in uncertain times. Anxiety over uncertainty began to
reflect in people's attitudes toward wealth and its accumulation and
disposal. Personal security, retirement savings, pensions, and careers
evaporated for many. Savings dwindled and the freedom from anxiety
that wealth once promised faded.

Thus, each individual is affected by these generational themes. Often
such generational differences can manifest as conflict and misunder-
standings within families. The older generation, preparing an estate
plan, has no doubt experienced a different relationship to money than
the younger generation preparing to inherit. One may resent the other
if values are not shared, and concerns may grow about the meaning of
inherited wealth. The older generation may view the younger generation as failing to appreciate the social responsibility that comes with
wealth. They may see little sense of stewardship and too much ideal-
izing of celebrities and sports figures that model lavish spending and
self-indulgence. Some may even assume that good values and the pursuit of money are inconsistent goals, that pursuing wealth is degrading
or inherently antisocial. One man who left a low-paying, high-prestige
university faculty position for a better-paying job with a multinational
corporation stated that he had "crossed over to the dark side." Money
itself or the pursuit of it may indeed be corrupting; however, it is not
the money per se but the individual's attitude toward and relationship
to it that defines its effect or lack of effect on the individual.

Popular culture, the economic themes of each generation, and the
buying power of money not only generate values but also perpetuate
myths. A person's contribution to a marriage may be valued in financial
units, not in contributions of time, energy, or nurturing. A person may

be denigrated for failing to accumulate wealth when so many opportunities to "lift oneself up by the bootstraps" abound. In a land of opportunity, it is believed that anybody can "make it." If happiness is indeed "money in the bank," then cultural insight can be gained by understanding the notion of "buyer's remorse." Once a large sum of money that has been accrued is spent, the wide range of options and windows for opportunities that having the money represented become closed forever. The process may well leave the buyer let-down, or at best ambivalent and questioning the wisdom of his or her longed-for purchase.

Why, then, is the spending of long-saved money only marginally satisfying? It is because "the exercise of money's purchasing power entails . . . a loss of promising power."[7] Thus, ironically, spending money does not give unremitting joy any more than does letting the wealth accumulate in a bank account. In exploring these issues, it becomes apparent why wealth alone does not contribute much at all to an individual's personal sense of value, fulfillment, or happiness. Yet, preserving all possible wealth to be passed to the next generation is too often the sole goal reflected in planning one's estate. Nonmonetary values that contribute to life's meaning and purpose, that help to define wealth as opportunities and options, may be overlooked entirely. Wealth alone is neither good nor bad; it is an instrument that must be shaped and defined to further one's core values. Until those values are articulated and prioritized by the individual, the danger exists that they will not be one's own but those perpetuated by pervading societal myths. An estate plan can act as a repository of personal values. It can be formulated with a view to compelling conformity with one's strict sense of values, or it can be constructed to provide opportunities and options as a gift not of wealth but of pathways with which to build a meaningful future.

CHAPTER THREE

The Role of Money in a Happy, Healthy Family

I f it is so well understood that money can't buy happiness,[1] why is it that when asked what would most improve the quality of life, most of us answer "more money"?[2] The only way to harmonize those apparently inconsistent perspectives is to acknowledge a fundamental distinction between "quality of life" and "happiness."

Prompted by the commercial media, many of us assess the quality of our lives with reference to the volume and grade of the goods and services we consume. This notion of quality appears to evolve from the physical, psychological, and social gratification commonly associated with material abundance. Because the capacity to consume more and better goods and services is measured and limited by the amount of money at our disposal, it is not surprising that many of us, therefore, believe that more money will mean more "quality" in our lives.

We have all experienced a social event in which we encountered one or more individuals who distinguished themselves by their wealth. Perhaps they mentioned the yacht or helicopter they own, the fact that they set sail this coming week on the QEII, or the new Prada shoes purchased that very afternoon. Recently, when arranging an out-of-town appointment, one man said, condescendingly, "I have my private plane at my disposal, so of course it will be no problem to be there on time."

THE CONCEPT OF HAPPINESS

Happiness, unlike a "quality life," is not an inevitable outcome of a high level of consumption of premium goods and services. To be sure, one who wants for adequate food, shelter, clothing, and health care is not likely to be happy. But beyond that basic level, consumption contributes to happiness only to the extent that it enhances the elements that comprise that elusive state of happiness itself.

Clinically, the term *happiness* encompasses a complex mix of psychological, emotional, and spiritual attributes that defies precise description and tends instead to vary from person to person. Attempts to identify the elements of happiness commonly allude to such equally ill-defined feelings as peace, joy, contentment, security, and self-sufficiency. For present purposes, perhaps all that need be said about happiness is that it is the sense of well-being and personal fulfillment that comes from living life in harmony with one's core values. In the words of Ralph Waldo Emerson in his work "Self-Reliance": "Nothing can bring you peace but the triumph of principles."

The things money can buy, regardless of amount and quality, cannot, of course, ensure that one will live life in harmony with his or her values. In that sense, money surely cannot buy happiness. Indeed, if one pursues and applies wealth to ends that violate his or her core values, that person may well experience a sense of diminished well-being. The negative consequences of the misuse of wealth fill the gossip columns in newspapers and neighborhood grapevines. One young man who had access to enormous family wealth used his assets to drink, carouse, underwrite parties, and offer housing for unsavory drifters. One evening, driving his distinctive custom-made sports car, he crashed into a well-known and well-loved, high-profile public figure, which catapulted his plight into the headlines.

Despite the illusory link between wealth and happiness, the accumulation, management, consumption, and disposition of wealth are not vain endeavors that should be cast aside in favor of more virtuous activities. Indeed, active, measured, and prudent involvement in financial matters provides a rich and varied context in which one's core values can be expressed, validated, and refined. In that sense, money and the things it can buy at least facilitate the pursuit and attainment of happiness.

In a nutshell, the functional essence of money is power over the development, management, consumption, and disposition of personal and community resources. If that power is exercised in a manner that enhances personal growth, its value as an agent for both enriching the quality of life and contributing to an authentic sense of well-being and personal fulfillment is readily apparent.

SHEILA'S EXPERIENCE OF WEALTH

Sheila came from a family of five siblings who all struggled with financial and medical problems. Over time, Sheila grew wealthy from working with and ultimately marrying a successful entrepreneur who rode to success on the crest of the dot.com craze. With her wealth, Sheila funded housing for one sibling, financed a divorce for another, and paid for a complicated life-enhancing surgery for a third. She felt enormously fulfilled personally that she could effect these outcomes for those she loved with wealth she herself participated in generating.

Proper perspective is the key to pursuing, managing, and applying wealth to worthy ends. If a person sees wealth primarily as a means of experiencing the self-indulgent pleasures associated with consuming high-quality goods and services, he or she likely will save little, borrow excessively, and, in the end, be dependent upon and controlled by wealth. As the old Roman proverb states, "Money is like seawater: the more you drink, the thirstier you become." If a person believes that attainment of wealth is the critical measure of success and self-worth, he or she likely will pursue it obsessively, hoard it anxiously, and, ultimately, curse it mournfully. In neither case are financial endeavors likely to yield any appreciable benefit in terms of fostering a genuine sense of well-being and personal fulfillment.

One who views wealth as a resource to be employed in the service of values will define and validate financial objectives with reference to those values. Such an individual will not spend time accumulating additional wealth if to do so will leave insufficient time to pursue more important objectives. Rather, a balance will be found between saving and consumption that best serves immediate and long-range values-based priorities. This person will seize opportunities to use wealth to enhance the personal growth and well-being of family members as well as to address community needs.

RAISING HAPPY, HEALTHY CHILDREN

To raise a child with the capacity to enjoy life, a foundation must be built of relationships, personal integrity, contribution, purpose, and a sense of belonging. To raise a child in an atmosphere of wealth with the prospect of inherited wealth requires building strength of character to combat possible guilt and self-esteem issues that often afflict similarly situated individuals. One very accomplished young attorney, upon completion of law school, was selected over her classmates for a most desired clerkship. Her envious classmates became bitterly resentful and loudly announced throughout the law school that rather than properly earning her way with hard work, she had been selected because of the wealth and status her family held within the local community. Although hearing this characterization no doubt hurt her, this young woman had pride in her personal accomplishments, achievements, and attributes; she knew full well that she herself had earned what was offered to her. Children growing up with wealth must be raised to develop the courage to be assertive regarding their own strengths and accomplishments. Instilling such qualities of character in children assures the perpetuation not only of family wealth but also of a legacy of solid family values for the next generation and beyond.

Philosophers have long struggled with the concept of human contentment. Aristotle synthesized four basic dimensions as essential to human fulfillment, each directed toward the attainment of a different goal. The first is the intellectual dimension, which drives toward truth. The second is the aesthetic dimension, which strives for beauty. Next is the moral dimension, which aims at goodness. Finally, he defined the spiritual dimension, which drives toward unity.[3]

Presently, a growing body of psychological literature in the area of contentment identifies elements of happiness that after all these centuries correspond closely to Aristotle's ideas. A summary of these essential elements follows.

- **An ability to immerse oneself in an activity.** This means a personal and intense involvement with a pursuit that is meaningful to an individual. The pursuit might be physical, mental, interpersonal, spiritual, or emotional. For one individual, this might mean an artistic endeavor; for another, a mathematical or engineering feat; for yet others, a marathon to be run, or a journey to be made, or perhaps a book waiting to be conceived, or the joy in giving to and supporting others. It is a passion for an endeavor that brings one personal fulfillment. Integrity, a personal sense of competence, and self-acceptance grow through pursuit and accomplishment derived from such active involvement. It should be stressed that this element of fulfillment cannot come from observation or passivity, but from activity, energy, and investment of one's own time and self. This includes not just a focus on the outcome—the material reward—but the awareness that "getting there is all the fun."

- **A balance in life among the physical, mental, interpersonal, spiritual/emotional pursuits, work, and play.** All of these realms of life are important. An isolated, narrow, or obsessive involvement with only one area rarely brings joy. Balance, flexibility, and a capacity to move between realms of enjoyment we now know define individual pleasure and fulfillment in the long run.

- **Sharing the joy with others.** Actively pursuing a goal brings joy; sharing the significance with others brings greater joy. Writing music that no one ever hears or ever praises it with an "I love it," robs the composer of the completion of the fulfillment cycle. Fulfillment does not happen in isolation. Humans are intrinsically social. A sense of belonging to a larger group is intrinsic to contentment. Sharing with others, coaching, teaching, and learning together provide the basis for the interrelational aspect of happiness. D. Myers, a psychological researcher in the field of contentment, stresses how important it is for people to establish a sense of belonging.[4] As an example, he cites strangers who meet even so briefly as on a two-week cruise often parting with addresses and promises to write and stay in touch. Traditionally, children end summer camp by exchanging addresses, or end the school year with vows in the yearbook to stay connected. Participation in and identification with a group with norms, beliefs, and ideals— be it family, community, workplace, charitable, political, or spiritual—is essential. Knowing appreciation, bringing joy to others, giving back, building teams, and belonging to a family that supports and encourages individual and group generativity—these experiences bring happiness.

Money cannot substitute for any of these realms, but it can provide the opportunity for the pursuit of all of them. Years of hard work at a career, a sudden business windfall, a lottery win, or an inheritance will provide such potential. However, it is the building blocks or foundation for enjoyment itself that parents must establish in their children. Without these underpinnings, a child may try to buy his or her happiness only to find it has no price.

Many wise parents ask themselves or trusted others, "How much is too much for my child to have?" Basically, a concrete answer can now be seen as irrelevant for that child or adult who has the capacity for contentment. For the individual who lacks this capacity, wealth may be corrupting or lead to wasteful expenditures without direction or context in desperate pursuit of hopeless fulfillment. It might be used to buy possessions, image, or status instead of developing the foundations of personal integrity, balance, and solid relationships with others.

CHAPTER FOUR

Our Children: Building Values

Greed entices and rushes in to fill the void for those who lack capacities for personal integrity—that is, self-involvement integrated with a multiplicity of roles and activities, balanced with relationships and a sense of belonging. The myth that money will shore up any of these deficiencies is the basis of so many of the commercial messages advertisers glibly peddle. Daily we are bombarded with promises that products can confer on their purchasers desirable attributes—attributes that, in reality, require cultivation and effort to obtain. The easiest solution for those with the means is to turn to materialism for self-fulfillment, and marketers rush to meet the demand. The greater an individual's sense of emptiness and isolation, the more vulnerable that person is.

THE MARKETING PLOY

The marketing process, manifested by advertising, is ubiquitous, yet it takes greater hold of some than others. Many who become the victims of marketing ploys believe the promises. Marketers exploit first those who are easiest to convince, yet they are also able to seep into the psyches of those sophisticated consumers who insist they are unaffected by advertising. Jean Kilbourne, in *Deadly Persuasion*,[1] describes the way advertisers even co-opt our idea of independence from advertising and repackage these notions in such a manner as to pitch their products right back to us. "When Apple reprints an old photo of Gandhi, or

Heineken ends its ads with the words 'Seek the Truth,' or Winston suggests that we buy cigarettes by proposing (just under the surgeon general's warning) that 'You have to appreciate authenticity in all its forms,' or Kelloggs Cereals identifies itself with the message 'Simple is Good,' these occasions color our contact with those words and images in their other, possibly less promotional applications."[2] Kilbourne shows how advertisers manipulate and entice all of us into falling prey to their products, some of which are addictive, unhealthy, and even toxic to children, adolescents, and adults. Advertisers shape our values and redefine our cultural directives in powerful yet subtle ways.

Increasingly, children have become hapless victims. The amount of money Americans spend on toys and amusement for children is equal to the gross national product of some reasonably large nations.[3] Corporate marketers cultivate the identified "nag" factor in children to get to their vulnerable parents. Children nag and parents buy. "The ads teach that buying is good and will make them happy. They teach that the solution to life's problems lies not in good values, hard work, or education, but in materialism and the purchasing of more and more things."[4] So, well-intentioned parents ask, "If I can afford these toys, should I indulge my child?"

RESISTING THE ALLURE OF ADVERTISING

Although families cannot limit the reach of many marketers, they can resist their influence by teaching their children what values their family holds for cultivating capacities for fulfillment. As long as these values are identified and supported, then the acquisition of material possessions or products will not be viewed as a solution. By directly decoding and interpreting the messages inherent in the ads, parents are empowering their children to resist them. Notice how grocery stores frequently put sugary cereal and gums and candies at either eye level or at the check-out counter to encourage nagging and impulse buying. Parents can tell their children, "Let's look when we go into the store at what the marketers are trying to entice us into buying." On the other hand, when a child has more toys than can be played with, no toy becomes special or meaningful. Remember the children's story, "The Velveteen Rabbit,"[5] where the toy that is loved the most becomes real? Loving a special toy develops one aspect of the capacity for later attachment and commitment to others, to purpose, and to perseverance. When there is an overabundance of toys, they become expendable. One toy replaces another toy and yet another.

RESISTING MARKETING MESSAGES

Jacob Needleman, in *Money and the Meaning of Life*,[6] relates a poignant vignette from his own childhood:

> . . . when I was . . . eight years old . . . , I visited [a friend's] house. . . . My eyes nearly leaped out of my head when I saw what he had there. Every toy I had ever dreamed of . . . [was] . . . neatly arrayed on wide shelves all around the room. Not one of them was broken, and that fact startled me. . . . Every toy of mine sooner or later broke or wore out, if only because I had to extract all the joy and meaning I could from it before finding the energy to beg, really beg, my parents to buy me a new one. Subconsciously, I must have felt that [my friend] never really knew the intensity of that kind of desire.[7]

A child who gets every new toy as soon as it is available loses the joy that comes with waiting and anticipating. Lost as well is the sense of personal investment and accomplishment that comes with waiting or saving to contribute toward the purchase. Remember the days of collecting bubblegum card packs and opening each packet hoping for the much-needed card that would complete your collection of that set? Remember what it felt like to open each packet, chew the gum, and look at the treasured card found inside. Occasionally, that card was the one you needed or the one a best friend needed. The excitement, enthusiasm, and joy felt wonderful. Would it have felt so special if mom or dad bought fifty packets at a time to maximize the chances the desired card would be there? While they might have fulfilled a momentary wish, they, in turn, would have taken away the excitement of waiting, anticipating, and investing one's own time and effort into the process. There is a psychological meaningfulness in wanting, working, and waiting that builds that sense of joy in what one can accomplish on one's own, which no amount of money can simply buy.

Witnessing and attending to advertising that exhorts consumers to gluttony also sows seeds of greed. Children raised in this atmosphere run the risk of never feeling satisfied, yearning for yet another purchase to fill their desires. The opportunity to obtain what is wanted through their own efforts has been denied to them. As parents, it is important to remember that toys teach the rudiments of life: yearning, striving, collecting, possessing, attaching, sharing, maintaining, discarding. The question, then, is not "Will I spoil my child?" if the desire is gratified, but whether the desire can be satisfied without compromising the child's growing capacities to feel a sense of integrity, balance, and relationship. Being mindful of priorities and goals helps to put a single consumer decision into context. One well-intentioned dad asked, "Will I spoil my child if I buy her a car for her sixteenth birthday?" The answer is now obviously not a simple yes or no. The answer depends on the meaning that car holds for that child. Did she contribute to its cost? Did she look forward to having it or long for it? Or, on the other hand, did she ever request it? Is she clear on her sense of responsibility to maintain it, to pay for insurance and gas? Will she feel a sense of personal accomplishment in ownership? The answer depends on the responses to these questions as well as the history of attitude toward consumption and self-reliance the family has built for this daughter.

Interestingly, fads play an important role in the lives of children. Certain toys become part of peer culture. Having the newest toy and being aware of current movies and television shows build a sense of belonging. Children should not uniformly be deprived of these cultural equalizers and the opportunities offered for identification with their own generation. We live in a generation-stratified society of "boomers, gen-Xers, millennials," etc.—and each individual needs to connect with others who are coping with similar developmental and era-specific issues. Yet marketers use gimmicks that exploit the psychological vulnerabilities and needs of children to belong and fit in at different developmental stages. When a popular movie is released, action figures, T-shirts, and other gadgets follow in stores, supermarkets, and restaurant promotions. The joy of categorizing and collecting during middle childhood is recognized by the marketers, so there are likely to be many incarnations of a particular character or object to entice a child to spend in order to acquire the entire collection.

For parents of wealth, there are no natural, built-in limits. The new toy is affordable; in fact, the entire collection is immediately within reach. Chances are, children realize this and pester to have more and more. Parents who are tempted to give in should think back to their own childhood experience of collecting something, and discuss and determine with the child what value this fad is promoting and who is profiting. The child needs to know that the resources for the collection are finite or will accrue over time, such as saving allowance for it.

The following strategies can help parents to subvert greed:

- **Build relationships and connections to each other.** The psychological building blocks of character strength come from attachments and connections to people. Employing nannies and other child-care helpers is fine, but the core elements of parenting must be done by the parents themselves. A nanny does not in most instances have the lifelong commitment to a child that a parent has. Attachment to at least one consistent special somebody, especially a parent, who will be there throughout the growing-up years is essential for trust, self-esteem, emotional regulation, and independence. Money cannot replace relationships. They are the most crucial building blocks of all. *The Golden Ghetto*[8] tells the author's personal story of growing up emotionally impoverished in a home of affluence. She would have traded in a heartbeat her many material possessions and succession of nannies for the warmth and nurturance of a caring and involved family.

- **Teach from an early age the pleasure in giving to others, sharing with others, and, finally, experiencing life from another's perspective.** This is far more than giving to charities. A child who cleans out his old toys and places them in a bag that is delivered to a charity never experiences firsthand the awareness of how others live and experience life. Talk together about what type of giving feels right for your family. Most of all, build a plan for how to actively participate in the giving process. Volunteer time, if possible. Participation builds empathy, which is a cornerstone for healthy moral development.

- **Be alert to danger signs that your child has too much too easily.** These include:
    - No one toy has special importance.
    - A collection is built only to be discarded and a new one started.
    - Interests don't last, and when they start to involve effort, a new one is wanted.
    - No toy is cherished enough that your child wants to take it to bed or be certain to have it along on a vacation.
    - Little interest is displayed in the impact the child's behavior has on others. The child thinks only of his or her own pleasures.
    - The child has little or no capacity to wait or plan ahead for something desired, constantly wants immediate gratification, and nags more than usual.

- **Define the values you want for your child and teach your child how to obtain these values.** Look for the promises in the ads of quick, easy fixes in place of personal investment or dedication. Do you really gain faithful, good friends because you have the newest fad? Do these kinds of friends last over time?
- **As a family, develop an interest, hobby, or activity that drives your family's time.** Don't let marketers fill your calendar and define your interests—you define them.
- **Teach your child to recognize marketing ploys.** Children as young as early-elementary-school age enjoy this activity. Dissect the ads together. See if together you can identify the tactics used to prey on vulnerabilities. Look for the following ploys:
    - The product is presented in association with desirable attributes such as attractiveness, popularity, an adventuresome lifestyle, etc.
    - Provocation is used to get publicity.
    - Repeat customers are built up through an emphasis on having all or the newest models in the collection.
    - Affiliation with others is promised. The product can be traded or used to build popularity.
    - Obsolescence is planned. The child is told this model will be phased out soon. A desire is built to have the originals and the other forms soon to be released.
    - The price for one is affordable, but an entire product range is offered so the child fails to recognize the overall expense of buying multiple units.
    - The product is multimedia. It plays on a favorite movie or television series and connects to toys and action figures, fast-food products, logos on clothing, etc.
- **Look around the world your child or teen inhabits and point out the ubiquity of advertising.** Ads appear in many surprising places today—on school buses, on clothing, and on Channel 1, the TV feed that is brought directly into the classroom to teach current events. Point out the obvious as well, how certain products are sold around the world—Coca Cola, McDonalds. Are they selling substance or image?
- **Empower your child to make choices and stand up to persuasion.** Talk together about how much that toy or item is really of value versus just desired because of the persuasion or promise of fulfillment offered by an ad. Consider how a

T-shirt with a few choice letters or a logo is triple the price of one without the designer name. Agree to wait for a period of time to see if it is still as desirable. If it is, develop a plan for how to buy it after an agreed-upon waiting period.

- **Don't shut off the television, computers, or movies; instead, watch them with your children.** See what they are experiencing, join in, and talk about the messages. Place limits, of course, on what is offensive to your family's values and beliefs, but don't delude yourself into believing you can shut off the messages entirely with a "V chip" or other means of physical restriction. The media will find your children through school, peers, and other influences whether or not they view television or videos. One savvy weight-management program encouraging permanent behavior change has children and teens bring in ads promoting quick and effortless weight loss. They compare the outrageous promises, knowing full well that it is only through hard work and perseverance that weight loss and sustaining a healthy body weight can be attained.

When children display characteristics of greed, parents need to emphasize and plan activities that involve personal effort, affiliation with others in a goal-focused peer group, and the capacity to tolerate frustration. If these activities are not successful in developing the desired character traits, it may be important to seek professional help, especially before these self-serving values shape into lifelong personality dimensions.

CHAPTER FIVE

How Parents Model Values

In the last generation, we have become increasingly aware of the significance and complexity of the family as a social and economic entity. Families do not just generate and disperse wealth; they perpetuate values and skills, and model them for future generations to live meaningful and contributory lives. Many business and financial advisors have noted that those who acquire wealth by inheritance often suffer from a sense of guilt and diminished self-worth that becomes magnified through successive generations. A likely explanation for that phenomenon is the failure of parents to adequately prepare their children for their challenging role as stewards of family resources. Obviously, such preparation goes beyond providing children with experiences in money management. It requires the careful inculcation of the values, attitudes, and skills that will enable them to at once bear the burden of stewardship and realize their full potential as human beings. In that regard, the allocation of their "attention and emotion will have a greater impact on their children's life than . . . the allocation of funds."[1]

Parents who articulate, model, and instill core values beyond net worth take away the stigma associated with inherited wealth for their children. To attain this, contributions of value must be expected from every family member beginning in early childhood and continuing through adolescence and into adulthood. The message must be imparted that when a family member is not contributing by developing his or her talents and abilities, the family itself is not in balance. Thus, family members would do well to attend each other's events, performances, and competitions to offer support and encouragement. The objective should be to develop a sense that a family is a team and convey this message to *each* of its members. Time is a resource, and so are intellectual stimulation, interpersonal engagement, commitment, respect, and attention. Thus, contribution is made not just through monetary earning but through contributing skills and talents, academic pursuits, networking, and community giving; all of these are of value to the family. Families are as strong and effective as the individuals who compose them. Each family member is unique and must assess and develop his or her unique talents to contribute to the family's overall well-being. Our media culture, as well as the legal and financial system, would have all families believing monetary worth and those who contribute directly to it are all that matter. Those families who value and cultivate the unique talents and abilities that their children possess, including artistic and athletic, as well as social virtues, such as kindness, compassion, and support of others, raise children to be adults capable of carrying on the family's true legacy.

The foundation for a sense of contentment and fulfillment starts very early. Building joy through relationships, mutuality, and empathy comes first from the family. A danger of wealth is that interpersonal services that are indispensable foundations for the parent-child relationship may be bought. Being loved and cared for by parents has no substitute. Without this bond, the capacity for sharing joy with others throughout life will be compromised. Personal involvement starts early with opportunity, support, and permission to find one's own direction. Wealthy parents have the means to provide opportunity, but this must be combined with encouragement for self-actualization. It is risky when an agenda that may not fall within a child's passions or talents is written for the child by the parents or predetermined by the nature of the family business. Each individual must be free to pursue his or her own passions with the family's encouragement and blessing. Balance comes from exposure to multiple possibilities.

Opportunities to experience physical, mental, spiritual, interpersonal, and emotional pleasures early enable a child to find these pursuits again later in life. Valuing each individual during the growing-up years teaches the importance of finding one's own direction. Placing greater value on one area than on another compromises the synergy and harmony that is one of the foundations for contentment. One may even inadvertently plant the seeds for the pernicious sort of sibling rivalry that sometimes plays out in wealthy families when a parent dies. It is the family that models, teaches, and shapes individual capacities in each of their children that heads off destructive resentments later.

Parents, especially those with family-owned businesses, often have plans for their children that may not be consistent with the children's interests. One man, at forty-eight years of age, was tormented by his distress around a family commitment made when he was in his early thirties. The youngest of five, he made the commitment to sustain the family interest in a multistate chain of successful retail stores. Each of the other siblings had been encouraged to join the family business, but none had elected to do so. As the youngest sibling, this man was the parents' last remaining hope, and he felt no option but to fulfill this family obligation. By age forty-eight, he felt joyless, despairing, and resentful that he had sacrificed decades of his life for this family commitment while his siblings pursued their own interests. He kept this well-meaning but foolish commitment, unable to tolerate the guilt that resulted when he contemplated pursuing other options.

WHAT MONEY CANNOT BUY

Family wealth offers privilege, opportunity, and special decisions. You have the means to buy the newest toys or fashions, but should you? You have the capacity to hire nannies and caretakers, but what is the balance point? How much do your children need *you*, their parent? Four essential parental tasks, which cannot be allocated to others, will predict success and fulfillment in children of wealth and privilege.

Building a Parental Bond of Caring

Providing for an infant's basic needs, such as feeding, bathing, sleeping, and playing, establishes the first relationship bond. Later, during the school-age years, someone special needs to be there to validate academic, athletic, artistic, and community interests. Parents must give careful thought to which tasks they are willing to delegate, keeping in mind the critical importance of the parents' direct involvement in these tasks to the emotional growth of their children. Having the means to hire others to perform what may be labeled "low-level" tasks of child care can lead a family to cut corners in this way, so that parental time can be prioritized. This can be an early pitfall because developmental psychology teaches that future relationship potential is based on first establishing a relationship with one special caretaker who comforts. Usually this is one or both of the parents during the infancy and toddler years. There are no "low-level" maintenance tasks in infancy and childhood, when direct interaction with the child is involved. These tasks are the very building blocks of trusting connections between children and parents.

The Inheritance Project[2] published a poignant remembrance of losing a special attachment figure when that special person was not the parent:

> Nanny left the summer I turned five. I could almost cry now because it was so horrible for me. . . . It wasn't just that she left, it was that suddenly I realized all those people who spent more time with me than anyone else could leave because we paid them. And if we didn't pay them, they would go. I concluded that they could be fired if they did something I didn't like. I would run around screaming that I was going to fire them. Can you imagine how insulting that was to have a little child screaming, "You're fired!"?

Active Involvement in the Child's Self-Esteem Building

Children build pride when their parents acknowledge their accomplishments. What parent has not heard the familiar call for attention of the elementary school–aged child, "Watch me, Daddy. Watch me, Mommy." Children must receive external praise and encouragement from those who matter the most before they can begin to feel proud of their own accomplishments. Those moments of parents cheering at the swim meet, coming to teacher conferences, driving for a community service, or applauding at the holiday recital are the events in a child's life that contribute to building a positive self-image and sense of self-worth. These are the rudiments of self-esteem building. It does not feel the same for the child who has no parent there to cheer, notice, support, and share the moment. Missing these opportunities to directly participate in your child's young life creates an emotional distance difficult to bridge later on.

Participation in Solution Seeking

If all of your children's needs are met before they realize they have them, there is a risk that nothing will gratify them. It is important for children to grapple with problems. If the solution to a problem is not the product of personal effort, it has little meaning and value. When parents anticipate and gratify material and social needs, through their buying power without ever discussing or involving the children, they have deprived their children of the opportunity to build skills for problem solving. There is a balance to obtain here. All of us want to give our children every advantage, but keep an eye on the bottom line. Yes, give rewards, but don't let the rewards be so ever-present as to lose their reinforcement value.

THE DANGER OF OVERINDULGING CHILDREN

One family of wealth was ecstatic when finally a son, David, was born to their marriage after years of trying to have a family. This son wanted for nothing. He was enrolled in tumbling, soccer, and swimming lessons during his preschool years. Proudly, his parents attended his events, praising him and cheering him on. Yet, David was only moderately successful. Rarely did he hit or kick the ball with precision, and soon he lost interest in these activities, refusing to continue attending tedious practice sessions. Undaunted, his parents would find a new athletic event, equip him with expensive new gear, and start anew, believing that the right sport to capture David's interest and into which he could marshal his efforts had not yet been found. They failed to cultivate efforts to overcome personal frustration and engage his own self-disciplinary efforts to improve. The ultimate, embarrassing moment of this overindulgence did not come until years later. Around age twelve, David wanted to participate as a hockey goalie. He had learned to skate and play early in life, but had neglected to train rigorously. Again, David was given the finest of costly equipment, and his parents, without fail, woke him and responsibly drove him to the practices weekday mornings in the pre-dawn hours for the training sessions, heaping on praise. Eagerly, they arrived for an early-season game. David held his own as goalie for the first period of play, but, becoming somewhat overconfident, he allowed several goals to be scored in the next period of play. The crowd, even though primarily comprised of parents, jeered and booed. Fury overtook David. He menacingly lifted his hockey stick and impulsively hurled it directly into the crowd nearby, injuring an onlooker. David's parents were horrified as they realized David's frustration tolerance and personal sense of tenacity for problem solving had not been cultivated.

Immersion in an Activity

Develop joy in the pursuit of activity. Take your children along to the things you love to do, explain and model the joy of participating in this activity. Provide multiple opportunities for your child to find meaningful activity. In the early school years, expose your child to a variety of activities. Help your child explore and find a niche. By middle childhood, your child hopefully will have settled on favored activities and a pathway for accomplishment. Provide opportunity to explore but not opportunity to exploit or feel entitled. Do not terminate your child's participation in an activity because he or she is not the best. Teaching staying power and hard work is critical. Let your child earn with his or her own effort some part of what is needed. A personal investment builds pride in accomplishment. Hard work yields results.

Family wealth means a wider array of choices and, therefore, extra effort because there are no material limitations, which narrow options for other families. Money may appear to temporarily take away adversity and the pain of coping. In the long run, it can buy opportunity but alone it cannot buy self-esteem or coping skills. These are internal qualities the family must cultivate in the child with awareness and deliberateness.

MALADAPTIVE COPING STYLES

Unhealthy coping styles do sometimes come from situations where there is considerable family wealth. These styles tend to fall toward the ends of a continuum, with "Hide It" at one extreme and "Flaunt It" at the other.

Flaunting wealth is many parents' greatest fear for their inheriting children. They fear their children will define themselves by wealth, objects, or consumption. An aura of wasteful disregard may develop in which everything appears to be expendable. At worst, this may even extend to people and relationships. Appearance and outside trappings may become all that count. Think of the wealthy dilettante decked out in high-end, expensive ski equipment who barely has the skill level to get off the lift. This level of absurdity is embarrassing and yet it exists in the experiences of all of us. Those children who relish the money, flaunt it, and buy their way through life are often lacking in any true definition of who they are separate from their wealth. They are terrified of losing it or being separated from it in any way. It is a sad scenario that parents hope to avoid, but unwittingly can create.

One eight-year-old girl, when drawing a picture of her family, colored her mother and father away at their jobs and other activities in which they participated. Each one was on a separate page. Finally, when she drew herself, she drew her ballerina costume, without herself in it, her big stuffed safari lion that her grandmother bought for her, and her cassette player and headset. She neglected to ever include a representation of herself in the drawing, as if she were defined solely by these possessions.

At the other end of the continuum are the children who hide their wealth, believing that others will not respect them because they did not earn their own money. There is at times an attitude of disrespect for wealthy heirs in our society. They may be negatively labeled by perhaps envious others as "trust funders," or lately as "trustafarians," and viewed as indolent, lazy, pampered, personally irresponsible, and unaccomplished. Therefore, even those heirs with solid character and a record of personal achievement may feel they have an uphill battle to prove to potential employers, peers, and dating partners that they are not inept or inferior. Some fear being valued only for their money or used by others. Others fear being targeted or exploited for their money or valued only for their wealth and not for their possibly solid contributions in other areas. The making of the family money may have been the height of achievement—the ultimate measure of success—in the family legacy. The burden of achieving at the level established by successful, older family members may be enormous and overwhelming to some.

In addition to the children who flaunt wealth, and those who accept their family's wealth but hide it from others, yet another group of children resolutely rejects family wealth. In struggling to define themselves, they do not want money to be a defining factor. They may resent some of the values, or lack of values, in their family. They may feel manipulated or controlled "with strings attached." Perhaps problems were solved with money rather than with communication, family support, and interactive problem solving. Perhaps the money was illegally or immorally obtained. Perhaps desired objects could be acquired without working to earn them. Toys may have been so plentiful that nothing became special. Some of these heirs report that the family home itself created isolation and remoteness with its palatial size. No room was the family's congregation point, no bathroom had to be shared with siblings or others, and a separate playroom, or even playhouse, contained all the toys.

One depressed college student described an endless battle with unfulfilled yearnings and sadness. He described growing up as the third child—a nondescript position, as he saw it, in a family with four children—in a wealthy southern California neighborhood. His memories of his mother were those of her socializing, drinking, and never being available to him. His home was massive, but a sense of loneliness, isolation, and emotional impoverishment pervaded his childhood. He recalled one incident in which his dad berated him for a poor grade on a school report in middle school, and after repeated degrading remarks, rolled up the report itself, hitting him on the side of his head with it, saying, "Maybe this will knock some sense into you." At nineteen, this young man was bitter, negative, and cynical. He found little humor or joy. Sadly, his privileged but humiliating upbringing had robbed him of optimism to believe he would ever feel fulfilled.

These extremes represent maladaptive coping with family wealth, but they can be prevented. Family wealth is visible and evident to the developing child, and it must be acknowledged and integrated in a balanced way into a sense of self and identity. At risk is the possibility that money itself can build self-centeredness. The world often does treat wealthy individuals with deference, and a sense of entitlement may grow from this special treatment. It will take extra effort on the part of parents to impart the core values that lead to strong character.

Talk together as a family and decide how to:

- **Distinguish your family's uniqueness by defining each person's values.** These will be based on the talents, skills, and interests of the individuals in your family. Having fun or leisure time together is important; so is contributing by developing talents and skills from an early age.
- **Acknowledge that belonging is critical to a sense of well-being.** It is intrinsic to feel a sense of togetherness with others, whether through family, church, support groups, camps, cruises, or reunions. If the family is not available to provide that critical sense of belonging, then peers, friends' families, or even cults, factions, or charismatic leaders will fill that void. It is human nature to connect to others. Decide how much your family will provide those connections that contribute to growth, acceptance, positive regard, and encouragement for its individuals.
- **Develop each individual's self-worth.** Set a model for consumption that is in line with your value structure—a sense of preservation, not wasteful consumption. Teach your children

your values by what you model. Consume all you need to support your own values, even extravagances, but not more than that. Consumption is not wasteful as long as it is spent furthering the priorities you defined. Extract meaning from your wealth.

Values are thus instilled in children by parents who demonstrate, model, and live their values on a day-to-day basis, thereby creating positive childhood experiences. Certainly intrinsic factors within each child, as well as external circumstances, contribute to shaping values; not all factors are within parental control. However, as children continue to grow, gaining self-esteem and confidence as the recipients of their parents' appropriate focus and merited praise, they tend to internalize and become personally committed to a similar set of ideals and standards.

CHAPTER SIX

Teaching Children and Young Adults about Money

Parents of wealth can and do raise children who are accomplished, motivated, and resourceful. Although parents worry that knowledge of family wealth or of a trust fund may rob their children of an incentive to work, children who inherit may be even more likely to start businesses, work toward personal goals, and grow their wealth faster than others. "For most people, it's just a wonderful experience," is how John Levy, wealth consultant, encapsulates the impact of inherited wealth.[1] Accomplished children who enhance their lives with family wealth did not just "get lucky"; they had parents who established for them a strong sense of family relationship, expectation, support, and value and taught them important lessons on the proper relationship between wealth and true contentment. There is no guarantee that any child will grow into an adult who handles money wisely, but children raised with expressed money values, as well as concurrent family emotional support and a strong sense of place in their communities, are in the best position to assume the responsibility of wealth when it comes their way. The process of cultivating this wisdom begins in the early years.

Family wealth neither should nor can be kept secret from children. Children are sufficiently aware to recognize that their family is more affluent than others. They know if their home is significantly larger

---

Thanks to Robert Van Wetter, a principal with North Star Investment Advisors in Denver, Colorado, who joined in the preparation of this chapter.

than their friends' homes, if the family car is more luxurious, if their family vacations are to more exotic places, if their family is able to purchase the newest and most expensive consumer products. Parents who attempt to hide family wealth risk injecting an air of deception and dishonesty into their relationships with their children (i.e., "what you see is not how I say things are"). Children benefit from knowing the truth. Children who know they are valued enough to be entrusted with truth gain a foundation of personal responsibility. They may then go on to build integrity by knowing they can be trusted. These are the children who grow into the adults who are the best prepared to view money as opportunity rather than as a free ride.

This does not mean children need to know the precise amount or quantity of family wealth, especially when they are young. When an intelligent child asks, as many do, "What is my IQ score?" wise parents do not reveal the precise number, but may say, "You are bright enough to accomplish whatever you would like in life." A similar answer is appropriate when a child asks how much money he or she will inherit or have someday: "enough to accomplish what you would like with enough left over to confer the same benefit on your own children." The child understands that the money does not signify carte blanche, but comes with the expectation that the child will be a good steward of the family money. Money values start early and solidify based on relationship experiences children have as they move through stages of development. Sound money values do not develop in a vacuum and cannot be taught in isolation from the individual's family and community.

Parents generally are reluctant to share specific facts regarding their net worth with their children. Many are concerned that the children's awareness of family wealth will rob them of motivation. Most parents dearly want to build their children's character on a foundation, not of net worth, but of virtue, merit, and self-esteem, and free of a sense of entitlement, narcissism, or self-centeredness. In essence, parents fear their children's identity might become defined by money.

Additionally, some parents will not discuss their personal financial circumstances with their child because they don't want to be held to promises. Too early a declaration about wealth can be a mistake. Parents do not know what their future will bring—who their children will marry, if they will divorce, where their careers are headed. It feels safer for some to postpone transferring wealth to their children until those uncertainties are resolved, and, in the meantime, to avoid raising their children's expectations regarding the amount of wealth they are likely to inherit. Change is rapid and rampant. As marketers intrude and as privacy is increasingly lost, the last things most people want to reveal is more concrete information about their assets. Moreover, many fear that high net worth combined with high visibility make a family vulnerable to victimization and exploitation. For example, one father did not want his daughter's school picture in the local newspaper with her last name. He had earned enormous wealth with a company that gave him a high profile and thus feared for her safety if the family name were to be identified with her picture.

There is another fear that drives parents not to talk about money with their children. Society seems too focused on "making millions." There is an aura of importance, adulation, and respect for those in possession of their millions. The media focus on money. Game shows prioritize what viewers value. Game shows that give away large sums of money draw more primetime viewers than other shows. As parents, we don't want our children's self-image shaped by money; we want them to achieve on their own.

Fear of children being abducted, of liability suits, of irresponsible individuals attaching themselves to the family—all of these fears create an aura of secretiveness about revealing wealth. For these reasons, it is generally not prudent to spread word of one's net worth to neighbors, business associates, friends, or distant relatives, but what about to one's immediate family—one's children and spouse? Growing up with wealth and being prepared to deal with it, to have built the character to manage it effectively, and to use it as an enabling tool rather than being dependent, groveling, manipulative, or entitled is the aim parents have for their children, their spouses, and for themselves.

BUILDING TRUST (AGES BIRTH TO 4)

Building attachment in the early years sets the foundation for relationships throughout life. Trust in others is developed as parents respond to the cries and manifest needs of infants, toddlers, and preschoolers. Direct caretaking activities such as feeding, holding, and comforting young children create this bond of trust. Parents are typically the first with whom the child learns to build a relationship of trust. This trust expands through early years of life into a foundation for communication, self-confidence, and the capacity to struggle tenaciously with a problem to see it through to completion.

INTEGRATING MONEY VALUES WITH MONEY MECHANICS (AGES 5 TO 12)

These are years of building competence and a sense of self-worth. The manner in which parents model, communicate, and place value on character traits shapes the child's future. The following areas teach important lessons about the emotional meaning of money:

- **Allowance.** No matter how wealthy their family is, children need to develop perspective on the utility of money. Money is a finite, quantifiable resource. If it is all spent, there is no more of it. Giving an allowance teaches this concept. It also provides a sense of ownership and personal responsibility. If a child spends his or her entire allowance, there is no more until next week. Money is earned, valued, accumulated, and preserved for desired things and activities.

- **Setting limits on wishes and needs.** As discussed in chapter 5, there is value in anticipating and learning to wait. If nothing is special, there is little of value. Immediately gratifying every material need takes away a child's opportunity to wish for something. Wishing and waiting are the foundations for long-term goal-setting and working toward something desired. It sets the tone for persistence and stamina in steady pursuit of long-range goals. Children benefit from savings and from the passage of time. Seeing their money grow as interest compounds underscores and quantifies these values. Waiting until a birthday for a bicycle is a value-building experience. For younger children, timing could mean saving for a not-so-distant future treat, such as a toy on Saturday.

- **Exploring the notion of expensive.** Children aged five to twelve are also ready to learn the meaning of the word *expensive*. It is important to teach this concept at this stage of development. Expensive items may be defined as the ones for which a child must save or wait. What is expensive in your family? *Expensive* is variable and subjective for each family and for each individual. For some families what may be easily affordable and normal is too costly and out of range for others. Convey a sense of being fortunate by comparison. Standards vary, but parents must somehow teach this lesson. It is helpful as well to teach the relative value of material things to your children through comparison; for example, a teddy bear or stuffed animal costs more than a bag of holiday candy.

- **Sense of giving back.** There is a finite number of things any child needs. Children benefit from learning to give as well as to take. They must be taught to both share and donate things while they are still young. Nurturing others is a value in life that builds generosity later. Knowing that others will use and enjoy the things being given away builds more meaning and value to giving. Allow your child to participate in selecting to whom gifts should be given or to whom usable toys or clothes should be given. Children learn even more if they participate directly in delivering them, if possible. A gift of community service in the form of time, energy, or knowledge is of enormous value as well.

    Donating often sounds appealing to a young child when first discussed. However, at the moment of actually parting with his or her things, a child may balk or renege. Gavin, a four-year-old boy, agreed to give the toys he outgrew to a shelter for homeless mothers and children. As the other children excitedly staked their claims to his former toys, he burst into tears and yelled, "Mine, mine," much to the horror of his well-intentioned father, who was determined to begin his son's legacy of charitable giving. Later, when Gavin got home, he regained his composure and proudly announced, "I gave my little-boy toys, Mommy, to children who had no toys." By stirring up emotionality, it gave more meaning to the act of giving and receiving than if his parents had simply given the things to charity. It enhanced for him what he had retained as well as what he gave away.

- **Gift giving is a skill to cultivate well.** Children need to be taught while they are still young the lifelong joy that results from giving gifts that carry meaning. You can help your child consider the interests and possible special needs of the person who is to receive a gift. Think about who that person is and what brings that person happiness. Parents appreciate hand-made gifts from their children, which represent an investment of time and creativity rather than cost. A young child can paint a flowerpot, design stationery on their own with stickers or on the computer with graphics; a creative preschooler can turn pipe cleaners into hundreds of creations. If a friend is having a birthday or a neighbor is ailing, enjoy brainstorming together to think of what unique gift will brighten that person's spirits.

- **Giving is also a means of working through trauma.** Children who learn to give early in life will know how to draw upon giving as a personal resource later if necessary. Whenever there is a tragedy, our only recourse is to pour out gifts of resources, time, and expressions of caring. In these instances, giving is healing for both the donor and the recipient and should be cultivated as such. Many family foundations and charities have been established as families have channeled their own grief into a charitable cause.

BUILDING AN IDENTITY IN THE LARGER SOCIAL WORLD (AGES 12 TO 15)

By early adolescence, teens become astute observers of differences. They notice differences in competencies, in lifestyle, and in wealth. This is the age of building a sense of self, based on recognizing who is like you and who is different. Defining your own identity by wealth, instead of values, is a risk. Parents should discuss with their teens the characteristics for which they want to be recognized and valued.

This is an important age at which to engage in honest discussions about money and self-worth. A sense of family heritage and pride needs to be interwoven into a sense of financial responsibility. Where did and where does money in the family come from? Respect for money and an awareness of the specific costs of maintaining a comfortable lifestyle takes a more serious tone during these years. Adolescents are ready to assume some active involvement in money management. They are now ready to know they will someday receive some sort of an inheritance without necessarily knowing specific amounts and that making money grow and work for them is a family responsibility.

Consider using the following in dealing with early adolescents:

- A fixed allowance by which freedom, and opportunity for mistakes and successes, are granted and not interceded. Give a reasonable monthly stipend and remain available to consult in its management but resist making the final decisions or bailing out mistakes.

- Opportunities to earn additional income through jobs in the home that do not include routine household responsibilities, as well as work in the community.
- Active involvement in money management through:
  - Checking and savings accounts.
  - Credit cards with prescribed limits.
  - Real or mock investments—a small investment portfolio of different stocks or shares in a mutual fund to begin to learn investing principles and to see that they themselves may be effective in generating or losing wealth in their own portfolios. Log onto *www.smg2000.org*, where children can play a simulated version of Wall Street trading. Or consider the real thing and place some funds into Stein Roe's Young Investor's Mutual Fund, where the stocks are ones of high quality but also of high appeal and interest to this age. Check on them regularly. It will become boring unless adults play, too.
  - Investment in or research of stocks of companies that produce products and services your child uses or values, such as retail clothing, computers, disc players, or music and entertainment. One enterprising mom tried this with her daughter and watched her interest in a high-visibility, prestigious clothing manufacturer diminish along with the stock's value. This approach may help to stimulate interest in the under-concerned child.
  - Participation in planning and budgeting for a family event, such as a vacation, holiday, or even weekly food shopping.

SHAPING FOR ADULTHOOD (AGES 15 TO 18)

Children who will inherit money need the chance to learn, communicate, and make mistakes while they are still young and living at home. "Parents need to balance the risk of wasting part of the inheritance against the children's development as responsible adults."[2] The goal at the late adolescent stage is to shape dignity and self-worth, not to foster long-term dependency or to turn adolescents into beggars and connivers. Multiple opportunities exist for parents to continue to teach the values of wishing, earning, and being responsible:

- Earning money through a job
- Setting up a retirement account

- Spending money—budgeting for a car and its insurance or other desired items
- Charitable giving

Understanding the different types of professionals in the money field, such as a stockbroker, financial planner, investment advisor, certified public accountant, and estate-planning attorney, is well within the grasp of these older adolescents. Being included in some of the parents' discussions with these professionals is helpful as well.

THE COLLEGE YEARS (AGES 18 TO 22)

Although children are legally emancipated at age eighteen, few are ready to inherit or to manage a large amount of family money at this age. Easy money—and even easier debt—can come into your child's life at age eighteen. The young adult will receive offers of credit cards, debit cards, and possible inheritance money as well. Even though this is the age of beginning financial independence, for many it rarely corresponds to the beginning of emotional independence. Receiving too much too early may derail a young adult from defining a sense of career identity and direction. Money may, in fact, interfere with working out important issues that involve motivation and initiative.

Characteristically, people of this age try out, and then accept or discard, various life choices. Choices one makes in interpersonal relationships, career directions, and personal identity are often later shifted, redefined, and tried again. Most parents wish for their children to define identity by issues of character, such as personal accomplishment, academic achievement, obtaining other desired goals, and valued relationships. Young adults with too much money at their disposal may come to define themselves by their money, their privileges, and their possessions, or they may conversely come to worry that they are valued by others only for their capacity to bankroll rather than for themselves and their capabilities. Although some money may be imparted, keep it manageable enough that your young adult has the opportunity to define new directions and solidify his or her sense of character. This is a high-risk time to derail, as young adults are defining their careers and life choices as well as possibly making decisions about commitments and relationships. Too much financial independence can shape choices that might better be deferred until later.

TRYING OUT RELATIONSHIPS

Life-partner commitments are difficult in one's late teens and early twenties. From the divorce statistics, it is apparent that most individuals are not ready at a young adult age to commit to a long-term relationship. This is a time of trying out relationships but not making permanent commitments such as marriage and parenthood. Typically in this day and age, most young adults take this time and opportunity to understand and evaluate their own goals and desires as well as those of their partners. They are also working out issues of give-and-take, priorities, and compromises of sharing money and of sharing in a relationship.

Discuss with your son or daughter what it is like to share living expenses with others (i.e., college apartments, roommate situations, etc.). Talk openly about the hazards—being taken advantage of, paying more than his or her fair share, being asked for a loan, running short one month, overspending, etc.

As these good and difficult moments happen, discuss them. What lessons were learned? How is sharing accomplished without evolving into exploitation? How do you say no to a best friend who wants a loan? What do you do about a roommate who eats all of the food you bought or never contributes his or her fair share?

Ray had a roommate, Matt, who was charming and could legitimately play on sympathies because he had lost both parents early in life. Matt started by asking Ray for a loan of clothes or money for food when they were out as well as other simple requests. As these were granted, they grew into larger requests, such as multiple loans in excess of $500. The culmination of this evolving exploitation occurred when Matt showed up at the home of Ray's parents requesting an expensive stereo system that he knew Ray stored there. Matt said he had permission from Ray to have the stereo. At this point, Ray's parents called their son, found he had given no such permission, and the nature of this alleged friendship was brought into question.

Teach your young adult that others may not be able to "share and share alike." Thus, approach roommate situations with a realistic degree of self-protection and caution as trust is built across many circumstances and over time. Therefore, think through the wisdom of putting all expenses—phone bill, utility bill, lease—in his or her name alone. He or she should insist on equality, or at least some sort of fair apportionment, in sharing expenses.

FINDING MEANINGFUL WORK AND A FULFILLING CAREER (AGES 23 TO 29)

One of the goals for young adulthood is choosing a career that brings fulfillment and shapes skills while matching an individual's interests and temperament. Hopefully, that career will eventually provide earning potential and/or meaning to match that individual's lifestyle choice. Although many by this age are launching into professional careers, some twenty-three-year-olds still lack a long-term vision and the steps that may be involved in getting to it. In fact, there is a growing population of young adults who move home after college and find it difficult to locate jobs or define careers.

Discuss hopes, dreams, and passions with your son or daughter. Ask, "What do you think would be the most exciting thing about being a doctor, software developer, teacher, CEO?" Use their answers to identify their present skills and talents as well as those necessary for different career paths. Talk about further required education or skill training to pursue different career directions.

Encourage self-support at this age to build work experience and to narrow and bring focus to longer-term career options. Self-support at this age builds self-esteem, a sense of competency, and independence, which are of great value even if the current work is not along a chosen career path.

Set long-range goals first, then work backward. Ask, "What do you envision doing ten years from now?" "What is your ideal job?" "Do you know someone whose career looks appealing?" This can help in the short term in finding job experience that might have value later. If your son or daughter can respond, you are ahead of the game. If they cannot think this far ahead, define shorter goals. For example, ask, "How about five years from now?"

TRYING OUT POSITIONS IN PREPARATION FOR ADULT COMMITMENTS

This is an age of idealism, self-indulgence, activism, and even austerity for some. Young adults are learning about who they are. Most don't proceed in a linear, sequential style. They will meander off-course, they will learn by trial and error, and mistakes will happen. Money styles are being tried out as well—too much money can commit the young adult to a position or a lifestyle even before he or she is ready to make such a commitment.

- Teach value for money spent—how to get your money's worth.
- Set budget limits that require young adults to live within their means. If they are not self-supporting, be sure they understand what their own lifestyle actually costs.

- For those who are not fully self-supporting, limit the money at their disposal—some money outright (i.e., allowance or budgeted living expenses) and some additional money that must be earned.
- Do not completely bail out mistakes. Hold them accountable to at least a reasonable percentage of mistakes that are made.
- Continue to work on long-term investments and investment strategies: IRAs, when started young, can accumulate substantial amounts over time, thanks to the power of tax-deferred growth; teach how long-term investments may generate income without sacrificing principal.

TRYING OUT FINANCIAL INDEPENDENCE

Parents should never pass up an opportunity to teach their sons and daughters about financial responsibility. Young adults view managing money as a sign of independence and maturity. Discussing financial issues with them shows that you see them as responsible. All adults today are faced with many temptations to spend what they don't necessarily have. Credit card issuers, in their quest for new customers, are targeting younger and younger borrowers. Fourteen percent of American college students are carrying credit card balances of $3,000 to $7,000, and 10 percent owe amounts exceeding $7,000. [3] As long as they are more than eighteen years of age, any student can get a credit card without parental permission. Plastic cards, whether for a debit or credit account, can be wonderfully useful tools for establishing an independent credit rating when handled with understanding and responsibility.

CHILDREN WHO COME BACK HOME

Most children are eager to emancipate and take their place in the world, but some return home after years away working or attending college. In American culture, which emphasizes individual autonomy and emancipation, this may be viewed as unhealthy or regressive. Parents may feel they have failed in teaching independence or they may feel exploited financially or emotionally. Interestingly, in other cultures, returning home is not looked upon in this fashion. In fact, many generations of one family may live together, forming a supportive and a nurturing environment. Each family, therefore, must honestly examine its own personal beliefs and feelings about this issue and not feel influenced by the larger culture. When a young adult returns to the parents' home, both legal and moral issues arise. Legally, children are emancipated at age eighteen, and a parent is not obligated to provide support. Morally, most parents do not withdraw financial support from their children at age eighteen. Few eighteen-year-olds can sustain a job with sufficient income to meet basic living expenses. While attending college or working at a first job, many parents continue their son or daughter on their health care insurance plan and help with automobile insurance or other necessities. The path from home into full emancipation and independence is not a smooth or linear continuum; most children gradually ease into adulthood by using their parents for support in a variety of financial and emotional ways, including moving back home to obtain specified goals for specified time periods.

If, however, a parent feels used in a fashion that is not promoting progress toward independence, dialogue and guidelines may need to be established. For example, some young adults return home with a child of his or her own following an unsuccessful marriage or an unexpected pregnancy. Parents may be expected to provide babysitting for an infant while their own child finishes an education or develops job skills. This is a negotiable point, as parents are not legally obligated to provide this. Before such an arrangement is established and a precedent set, parents must address this issue with their own grown child and establish clear expectations and guidelines. What might be acceptable in one family may be abhorrent in another. Parents must examine their own expectations of their children. Feeling used is very different from feeling that temporary help is needed to establish independence and progress toward a goal. Some children, for instance, return home to save financially for a down payment on a home or to pay off a student loan. Often they are working full-time and clearly progressing toward a long-term goal. Many parents are delighted to help in those circumstances and seldom express concern that the arrangement will become permanent. The underlying issue is what the stated purpose is, the expectations from the child moving back home, and the time frame for pursuing the stated goals. Typically, families who have not talked together about these issues are the ones for whom resentment, misunderstanding, and conflict build. After the arrangement has been established, it is difficult to begin the process of dialoguing. Talking first and moving in later is the sequence more conducive to honesty, support, and goodwill.

CHAPTER SEVEN

The Impact of Wealth
on Husbands and Wives

I t is taboo in our culture to talk specifically about our own wealth. In fact, it is more difficult for most of us to conduct an open and honest discussion about our earnings and net worth than to talk about any other topic, including sex. Perhaps this is because it feels intrusive and depersonalizing, and exposes us to the risk of categorization and unfair judgments and comparisons. People do not want their self-image or the esteem of others tied to their earnings or net worth. In reality, for most of us, money comes and money goes. Earnings and net worth fluctuate, especially in these days of job market uncertainty and volatile financial markets. A person might respond to a question regarding their worth only to find the answer is different a few months later. There are many stories of titled families in Europe who lost their own wealth, retained their titles, and struggled with identity. There are analogous old-money families in the United States.

This creates a puzzling paradox. Though the media focus constantly on generating and consuming wealth, disclosing the details of personal wealth is considered tasteless and offensive. It is culturally acceptable to seek, attain, and even flaunt financial independence; but few want to risk disclosure of how much wealth they actually have. It is no wonder, then, that even for husbands and wives, money may be a private matter, difficult to bring to the light of day.

POWER BALANCE WITHIN MARRIAGE

A young adult who is ready for marriage wants to know that the prospective partner is trustworthy, honest, and not an exploitative "gold-digger." But money is power, and the key issue to resolve in marriage is power balance. When one spouse dominates the other through control, resentment builds—sometimes to the point of abuse. This extends, of course, to control over money. "At virtually every stage of marriage the issue of money is the No. 1 cause of fighting that leads to divorce," says Howard Markman, the author of *Fighting for Your Marriage*.[1] Yet most psychologists feel that the underlying issue is not the money per se but the emotional issues attached to money. "Money can be a metaphor for control and power."[2] If this is the case, then a marriage in which two spouses each control widely varying levels of wealth would seem to be at especially high risk. On the other hand, the survival of a couple's marriage depends more on their characters, emotional strengths, communication skills, and shared values and dreams than on their willingness to combine their respective assets in a common pool in which each has an equal interest.

Happiness in marriage first and foremost derives from nurturing, trust, communication, compassion, and understanding. The manner in which money issues are managed sets a precedent and forges a direction for other power inequities within the marriage. Only some of the issues within a relationship revolve around money; however, the way money issues are resolved may set a symbolic tone for the resolution of other issues relevant to decision making and power balance in the marriage. "Money is valuable, love is priceless."[3] Marriages that are successful in managing substantially discrepant wealth or earnings have some features in common:

- **Each person is individuated from his or her family of origin, is fully functional on his or her own, and has self-respect and respect for the partner.** He or she is entitled to discretionary spending of choice. Retaining individuality, and hence independent say in personal spending, is an essential component of partnership today. Two generations ago, this value was not as universally held. Marriage in the last generation has shifted from the paradigm where the man is the primary or sole wage-earner and the woman raises the children while remaining at home. In those days, the union often existed out of necessity and social pressures and expectations more than choice. Currently, this is rarely the economic premise of marriage. Today's marriages are not based on obedience. Today, people write their own wedding vows, usually involving mutuality, equality, and independence.

For example, Bryce was dumbfounded and dismayed that his wife, Meg, had filed for a divorce. When he described his admiration of and attraction to Meg, Bryce focused on her beauty, her lavish spending on accoutrements to adorn her beauty, and the wealth he offered that made all of this possible. Bryce failed to comprehend fully that underlying his support of her lavish lifestyle was Bryce's wish to make Meg dependent and reliant on him; he felt that by means of his wealth he was able to provide her with an abundant lifestyle that would be the envy of every woman. Meg, however, after a while, found herself stifled and gradually developed independent interests that did not necessarily overlap with Bryce's interests. One of these, working for humane treatment of animals, cut across social classes and kept her away until late at night attending meetings and arranging fundraisers. Bryce resented this and ultimately forbade Meg from participating. This set into motion a downward spiral. Bryce simply was unable to grasp that the more he insistently objected to her participation in animal-rights pursuits, the more it would feel like he was denying Meg her individuality and a means for self-expression. Meg continued to pull away. Bryce continued to be baffled, believing that by his standards Meg had been provided with everything she needed to be happy.

In many families today, both spouses are gainfully employed but at different levels of compensation. Thus, regardless of the wealth the couple brings to the marriage, disparities in wealth often arise. This may continue to be especially troublesome for the partner with less wealth. This sets the stage for a "strings attached" relationship to money; it feels diminishing and humiliating to those on the receiving end.

The law, unfortunately, upholds this notion by not attributing monetary value to the uncompensated contribution of a spouse. This may be remedied in a divorce, but to remedy this within an existing marriage will require gifts between spouses, such as through the establishment of joint accounts. Chapter 10 explores interspousal transfers.

- **There is a shared vision of a future together and faith in the couple's ability to make joint decisions.** It is far more important to share values than money. The value of a relationship is not in the extent of the wealth of the individuals, but in all of the contributions the individuals make to the relationship. Valuable contributions are made to relationships that are not material; these include support of others, nurturing, labor, creativity, thoughtfulness, accomplishment, pride, and kindness. All of these are contributions that family members make to the well-being of a family.

  For example, one couple sought marital counseling when the husband grew increasingly unhappy and even embarrassed by his wife's lack of personal achievement. Yet, she was very accomplished in enabling the success of others in her family. Her stamina, resourcefulness, and dedication to and joy in maintaining the well-being of family members were completely disregarded by him. Her contribution was through these virtues, but he had looked only at dollar value. The family is not only an economic entity; it is also a social unit, and each member contributes in his or her own way to its functionality. Marriage is an economic and emotional foundation for performing life's functions together. It is a union for joint betterment and will have a unique signature to which the two unique individuals who compose it conform and accommodate.

- **There is a capacity to be expressive of one's own feelings and views, and there is confidence that joint and mutual resolution of problems can be obtained between the marriage partners, even if that resolution results in agreement to disagree or be different.** Certain issues will be defined by life circumstances regardless of whether they are discussed. Planning for a future together is based on being able to shape and initiate jointly formulated couple's resolutions to address these circumstances irrespective of the origins of wealth or earnings. "Our culture is changing, of course, as women move into the workplace, but there are still strong biases against the man who marries a rich woman."[4] Men still see their role as primary provider, and they often struggle to redefine themselves in a positive light if this role is altered within their families. Society as well tends to regard negatively and cynically a man who fails to fill the role of primary provider for his family. At the same time, a wife may resent that she is carrying a heavy share of the financial burden.

WHEN THE WIFE IS WEALTHIER

Ellen, who had more earnings and inherited assets than her husband, Greg, invited him to participate in managing her assets and the overall financial planning for the family. Greg refused, declaring that the money was not his and he wished to have no part of it. As the years passed, Greg continued to refuse any participation, leaving it to Ellen to make all major decisions regarding investments, savings, household expenditures, and planning for the children's education expenses. Although Ellen had attempted to include Greg in decision making, Greg increasingly felt threatened, humiliated, and excluded. Unfortunately, Greg appeared to have little insight into the role he played in his growing resentment. Eventually, it developed into outright hostility and rejection of Ellen for what he labeled as her selfishness, willfulness, and unwillingness to involve Greg in decision making.

Money planning and talking are essential to resolve underlying issues. In the reverse scenario, women with less income resent being made to feel dependent, belittled, or beholden to men who provide all or a disproportionately large share of the family income. It is especially difficult when those men demean or manipulate women or children by attaching behavioral or attitudinal contingencies to their access to the family's financial resources without discussion, negotiation, and mutual agreement.

Successful couples have an optimistic attitude regarding their ability to arrive at joint solutions to problems. Gail and Darrell were an engaging couple in social situations. Each displayed a wonderful sense of humor that carried them together through many challenging circumstances. In addition, they loved athletic pursuits, shared many critical values, and cherished their children. Dual career professionals, they were comfortable financially. One problem, however, tainted their relationship and threatened their marriage. Each tended to anticipate that the other would judge and condemn him or her whenever external pressures mounted that required joint problem solving. Each felt the partner would think he or she hadn't done enough. Each held high goals personally. The manifestation was fighting, defensiveness, and intense bickering over issues of even the smallest consequence. Over time, they questioned if they could go on together given this atmosphere of defensiveness over implied or falsely perceived accusations. Somehow this couple had no faith that they could mutually problem solve, and over time they lost the capacity to listen to each other's issues without feeling that blame was being cast on them.

Planning a future together is another dimension of a successful marriage. Couples who create a viable marriage have generally talked about core financial issues prior to marriage and can continue throughout the marriage to discuss, redefine, and resolve the following issues:

- **Ways of handling money.** Is one a spender and another a saver? How will money be managed? Money decisions extend beyond mere money mechanics. One individual may write the checks, but major buying decisions should be made jointly. What defines a major purchase needs to be decided jointly in advance of such purchases and revisited and redefined later in the marriage. The solution may be as simple as "yours, mine, and ours" bank accounts. There is not one right way to handle marital assets. One size does not fit all. Couples need to work out a means to satisfy their own individual sense of fairness and comfort as well as the needs of the marriage, the household, and the children's futures. Again, some individual discretionary spending needs to be permitted for both spouses.
- **Individual needs and joint needs.** When there are two incomes, how will they be handled? Who will pay what? Who will save and invest? Which assets will be saved and invested and which assets spent? Again, couples need to speak to their individual needs as well as joint goals.
- **Goals of the marriage.** Marriage is a balance of children, extended families, friends, community/charitable pursuits, home, travel, education, business, earning, spending, savings, and consumption. Many opportunities present themselves to reflect the family's unique goals and values.
- **Standard of living.** Unequal wealth going into a marriage can create strong differences about how to define a standard of

living. The wealthier spouse may be accustomed to a higher standard of living. The less wealthy spouse may feel certain items and services are luxuries, not necessities, or may even feel embarrassed by a standard of living vastly beyond what defined his or her childhood living circumstances. Many feel that marrying into wealth or other "sudden wealth" situations will isolate them from their former friends, peers, or relatives. These differences may be worked out through identification of the problem, acknowledgment, discussion, and resolution through compromise or mutual agreement to allow the one who feels the strongest to call it his or her way with the understanding that there will be reciprocation and balance in other decisions at other times.

One discrepancy that may bring great discomfort to a marriage occurs when cultural and social upbringings have been disparate. One spouse may have vastly more education; one may have more worldliness; or one may be more knowledgeable of "social graces." Although these may be acceptable between the spouses, both sets of in-laws could create difficulty by vehemently announcing their embarrassment and rejection of the other spouse's attitudes, behaviors, family traditions, and expectations. A couple in this situation needs to expect and be ready to handle this criticism if it comes their way.

Overall, those who enjoy long-term marriages characterized by sizeable wealth differences:

- Show a capacity to jointly problem solve and share in the confidence that they will continue to be able to jointly problem solve
- Have shared interests and basically agree about goals for themselves and their children
- Are functional and independent as individuals
- Respect each other and the contribution each makes to the marriage, tangible or intangible
- Have achieved independence and autonomy from their own parents' "apron strings"

PRENUPTIAL AGREEMENTS

Gone is the era of being swept away by romance. Marriage as an economic entity makes major expenditures, produces and consumes goods and services, and may well incur substantial amounts of debt. As such, marriage is far more than romance. Good marriage partners function as good business partners, with an articulated understanding of financial goals and priorities, with openness and accountability, all the while being mindful of the bottom line. A prenuptial agreement tailored to the couple's unique values and circumstances allows the couple to be actively involved in defining the principles and guidelines that will govern their financial relationship, rather than passively accepting the presumptions and rules defined for and imposed by others. By marrying, a couple becomes subject to a binding contract imposed by the state, which prescribes the way in which money and property is to be shared in the event of divorce. A couple can disengage that contract and define their own legal relationship with respect to financial matters through the use of a prenuptial agreement. A prenuptial agreement at its best serves as a written financial plan formulated by and for the couple. Topics typically addressed by a prenuptial agreement include: (1) identification and management of separate and marital property, (2) allocation and use of separate and marital income, (3) disposition of separate and marital property upon termination of the marriage by divorce or death, (4) responsibility for separate and marital indebtedness, and (5) specification of support and living expenses.

Some couples may be reluctant to enter into a prenuptial agreement because they view contemplation of divorce as the antithesis of their idyllic expectations. Their reluctance also may be based on the view that a prenuptial agreement reflects a lack of mutual trust. Others readily accept the reality of today's world in which more than half of all marriages terminate in divorce. Contemplating the end of a marriage before it has even begun may seem like forecasting its doom, yet it may be the smartest and safest emotional, as well as legal, decision two individuals can jointly make. Actually, a prenuptial agreement enables a couple to deal with potential sources of disagreement before the wedding and sets a tone for better communication about finances during the marriage. It also serves to protect individuality, clarify the couple's respective views on wealth, and, ironically, may in the end thus provide a disincentive to divorce.

Certain scenarios are so ambiguous and fraught with pitfalls that a prenuptial agreement may actually preserve the marriage when conflict and upsetting situations arise. These may include:

- Individuals with extensive wealth or significant wealth discrepancy
- Those with children from a previous marriage
- Anyone marrying a person with spendthrift tendencies, such as gambling, drug or alcohol addiction, shopping, high-risk investments, etc.
- Anyone marrying a person with current debt or a past history of accumulating debt

Some may wonder how to bring up the subject of a prenuptial agreement in a fledgling relationship without damaging it. The truth is that discussing wealth, earnings, relative contributions, and spending expectations helps couples to address the issues of individual needs versus couple needs within the relationship. So often when couples are discussing or arguing about allocating their joint resources, they invariably are discussing the basic issues of supporting the values the couple holds for each of the individuals versus the values the couple holds for the marital needs, a most worthwhile topic for discussion.

One couple, for example, recognized their need for an outside facilitator to help them with decision making with respect to the issue of sharing inherited assets. When the couple first married, the husband was not wealthy but the wife had received a large inheritance from a grandparent. Nevertheless, she worked and brought in a small amount of income, which she shared with her husband. The husband, on the other hand, took on the task of primary financial support of the family, gradually built a thriving business, and contributed the lion's share of it to the family's financial well-being. The wife's parents, meanwhile, continued to make annual gifts to her, which she viewed as her own individual assets. Her husband, however, saw her money as rightfully belonging to the "ours" category. The wife felt that the money given to her by her parents held special emotional meaning and that she had the right to earmark it for something meaningful to her. Her husband became bitter. He felt that she participated freely in making decisions about his earnings, but that he did not have the same privilege with the money she received by gift. In a lively discussion, which finally opened up with professional help, this husband was able to ask his wife how she intended to use the wealth received by gift from her parents. The wife revealed that she was saving it for his son from a former marriage to enable him to attend an expensive private college he had dreamed of attending, qualified for academically, but lacked the financial means to attend. This couple always held the best intentions for each other, but because of their implicit taboo against discussing money and finances, they had been unable to fully trust one another.

Creative features can be built into a prenuptial agreement that do not necessarily lead to and maintain the often contentious notion of individualized ownership of all assets. A concept being used frequently today, and even being adopted as a legal mandate in some states, is that of "vesting" as the relationship matures over time. Essentially this means that each spouse becomes vested in a greater proportion of the assets of the other spouse on a graduated basis. The more years of the marriage, the greater the mutual trust and shared history, the greater the vesting. Many jurisdictions mandate that a spouse is fully vested after ten years of marriage. Some couples elect in their prenuptial agreements to prolong the full joint-ownership process of assets for twenty or even thirty years of marriage.

Another possibility is for the wealthier spouse, or that spouse's family, to make a sizeable gift to the less wealthy spouse in order to assure some measure of financial independence to that person and a greater balance of financial power within the couple's relationship. For example, one family of considerable means gave $1 million to their future son-in-law to assure he not only had sufficient independence but also the opportunity to invest in and grow his own economic well-being over time.[5]

Some couples maintain, or think they must maintain, joint accounts; many others decide in their prenuptial agreement that each will maintain separate accounts and spending habits, but that neither will make a unilateral decision regarding a major expenditure over a certain, predefined amount. This assures that substantial expenditures as determined by the couple, such as the purchase of the family home, private school tuition, or expensive luxuries, will be jointly decided.

Although bringing up the issue of a prenuptial agreement still sounds to some like inviting conflict and struggle, it really may ask the relevant question, "What comes first—the marriage or the individual?" The answer for long-term relationships is the dominance of each at different times. In a strong relationship, the desires to sustain together and to be supportive of individual needs are equally important. The process of melding together as a couple is not just assuming all will be well because we have now tied the knot. Couples always need to maintain a solid sense of individuality as well as a solid sense of union. Strong and lasting marriages acknowledge this; excessively dependent ones are saddled with standards and mandates of what a marriage must, should, and ought to be in the arena of individual versus couple interests and expectations.

Couples in strong relationships become more invested in each other and in the relationship emotionally as time goes by, and may manifest this in reality by becoming more invested financially in each other over time as well. A prenuptial agreement may assure that each individual, and the couple together, have the opportunity to redefine restrictions and antiquated laws. A prenuptial agreement additionally is thus a means to individualize the rules. Laws are written to govern all. Relationships, however, are unique. A prenuptial agreement may be viewed as a means to define both individual and joint financial and economic futures and to determine that the law is shaped to the partner's understandings and desires in support of the unique relationship.

In fact, it may be a red flag if one partner feels afraid to bring up and fully discuss these issues before marriage. Perhaps this is a relationship in which communication is strained. If this is the case, professionals can help to guide a couple in a discussion that takes into account planning for their future emotional and financial joint well-being. It may take resourcefulness to find such a professional. As accountants and financial planners, most typically, tend to talk comfortably about money goals, relationship counselors can facilitate discussions about the communication process itself. Finding one professional who can integrate creative money-management ideas with communication skills, one with blended disciplines, even in these times, remains difficult. Chapter 18 discusses this issue at length.

If a marrying couple has missed the opportunity to enter into a prenuptial agreement, it does not mean that they must accept local law as the sole source of their rights with respect to marital income and property. Under the laws of most jurisdictions, couples already married have considerable latitude in defining and redefining the financial aspects of their relationships by means of a *postnuptial agreement*. A postnuptial agreement is suitable for a couple who intend to either stay married or to separate and want to strengthen their relationship by resolving difficult money issues before such issues preempt the stability or civility of their relationship.

Postnuptial agreements are enforceable in most jurisdictions. However, some impose limits on the ability of a couple to predefine their maintenance and property rights in the event of divorce. Others condition the agreement's enforceability on satisfaction of minimum net worth and other requirements.

Finally, marital agreements will be binding only if they are the product of good faith negotiations, with each partner having knowledge of all the relevant facts and an understanding of the agreements' effect with respect to legal rights he or she would otherwise have. A party to a marital agreement can make informed and intelligent choices only if he or she is fully aware of the financial circumstances of the other party. At a minimum, at the time an agreement is drafted, each party should provide the other with a current full-disclosure financial statement. If a spouse owns assets that are difficult to value, it is advisable to have the value determined by an independent appraiser. In order to fully understand an agreement's legal consequences, each party must seek the advice of independent legal counsel with experience in drafting marital agreements. It is not uncommon for a marital agreement to be declared unenforceable on the ground that the parties were not represented by separate counsel. The fees incurred in employing two attorneys may be money well spent when compared to the cost of litigating issues arising from an unenforceable or unclear marital agreement.

Building an Estate Plan
for Your Family

CHAPTER EIGHT

The Fundamentals of Estate Planning

This chapter addresses the fundamental financial and legal principles, processes, and devices from which the means necessary to accomplish your values-based estate planning objectives derive. It provides a basic framework for understanding and evaluating the strategies and techniques described subsequently.

THE COMPOSITION OF YOUR ESTATE

The subject of estate planning is your *estate*. Broadly defined, your estate is the amalgam of *personal* and *financial capital* that accounts for your capacity to control and consume goods and services.

Personal capital comprises the inherent and acquired attributes that enable you to produce income through personal services. These attributes include intelligence, character, self-discipline, physical well-being, social prowess, work skills, and general and specialized knowledge. Planning with respect to personal capital generally entails the formulation of strategies for developing and enhancing personal attributes and ensuring the availability of alternative sources of income in the event of physical or mental disability.

Financial capital includes savings, investments, business assets, and personal-use assets. Financial capital generally yields *income*: bonds and bank accounts pay interest; stocks yield dividends; commercial real property generates rent; a patent produces royalties; and a personal residence provides rent-free lodging. Financial capital also may produce *gain* or *loss* as its value increases or decreases due to the passage of time or changing economic circumstances. Planning with respect to financial capital generally seeks to increase value, enhance yield, prevent loss, and provide for the orderly transfer of ownership during life and at death.

BENEFITS OF OWNERSHIP

Ownership of financial capital confers three fundamental entitlements: *management*, *consumption*, and *disposition*. Only if you become so physically or mentally impaired that you lack the capacity to make responsible decisions can you be deprived of your right to manage, use, and dispose of your property as you see fit. In that event, absent proper planning, your family may have no alternative but to petition the court for the appointment of a *conservator* (also called a *property guardian*) to manage your property on your behalf.

To protect against the possibility that you will outlive your capacity to manage your property effectively, you can give to a family member or trusted acquaintance *power of attorney* to act on your behalf in the event of your disability. The use of a power of attorney for that purpose obviates the need for a court-appointed conservator. The utility of a power of attorney as a safeguard against disability is discussed in chapter 9.

LIFETIME GIFTS

Inherent in the right to *dispose* of financial capital is the right to give it away, either during life or at death. Lifetime gifts generally are advisable if you have more than enough to maintain your desired standard of living. The principal advantages of lifetime gifts include the pleasure of giving, the economic benefit to the recipient at the time of greatest need, and the potential for significant income and estate tax savings. Disadvantages of lifetime gifts include the threat they pose to the giver's sense of financial security and the detrimental affect they may have on the recipient's initiative and self-sufficiency. These and other considerations pertaining to the advisability of making lifetime gifts are discussed in greater detail in chapter 10.

TRANSFERS AT DEATH

Items of financial capital that are owned at death pass by one or more of the following means: *testamentary disposition, revocable living trust, beneficiary designation, joint tenancy,* and *intestate succession*. Familiarity with the salient features of each of these means of transmission is essential to understanding each as an appropriate component of your estate plan.

Testamentary Disposition

A *testamentary disposition* is effectuated through a *will*. A *will* is a document by which a *testator*: (1) directs the disposition of property owned at death; (2) prescribes guidelines, procedures, and standards for administering the property pending its distribution; and (3) nominates a *personal representative* (also called an *executor*) to oversee the administration and distribution of the property. A will also may name the person who will serve as the guardian of the testator's minor or disabled children. A specimen form of a will is included as appendix A.

Capacity to make a will is determined by the law of the state in which the testator resides. In most states, the testator must be at least eighteen years old, of *sound mind*, and under no *duress* or *undue influence*. Generally, a testator is considered to be of *sound mind* if he is aware of the nature, value, and extent of his assets, can identify the members of his family, and understands the effect of the will on the disposition of his assets. A testator is considered to be under *duress* or *undue influence* if external pressure or influence deprives him of free will and causes him to make a disposition that is contrary to his true desires.

A will is effective only if the testator signs it in strict compliance with prescribed formalities. Most states require the will to be: (1) signed by the testator or by another in the testator's presence and at his direction, and (2) signed by at least two other persons, each of whom watched the testator and the other witness sign the will. A testator may amend his will at any time by means of a *codicil* signed with those same formalities. The testator may revoke the will by any action that clearly manifests his intent to do so.

The validity of a will is established following the testator's death in a judicial proceeding called *probate*. In the course of the probate proceeding, interested persons are given the opportunity to challenge the will's validity. If the probate proceeding confirms the will's validity, it is *admitted to probate* and given legal effect with respect to the disposition of the testator's *probate estate*. Generally, the testator's probate estate is composed of all of his property, regardless of its nature and location. However, it does not include assets that, by reason of the form of ownership or the existence of contractual arrangements or beneficiary designations, pass directly to the testator's successors. Examples of such assets include insurance proceeds, property held in a revocable living trust, and property held in joint tenancy. Those and other *nonprobate assets* are discussed in later sections of this chapter.

At the time a testator's will is admitted to probate, the court appoints, and issues *letters testamentary* to, the *personal representative* (also called the *executor*). The letters testamentary authorize the personal representative to marshal the testator's assets, pay debts, expenses, and taxes, and distribute the probate estate in accordance with the terms of the will. In some states, the personal representative's actions are subject to the court's continuing supervision. The court's involvement frequently prolongs the process and increases legal and other expenses. The delay and added expense associated with the administration of the probate estate account for the widespread use of alternatives to wills as the means of transferring assets at death.

Revocable Living Trust

A flexible alternative to a will as a vehicle for disposing of property at death is a *revocable living trust* (RLT). A *trust* is a relationship between a *settlor,* a *trustee,* and one or more *beneficiaries* with respect to property. The settlor establishes the relationship by transferring property to the trustee, subject to the provisions of a written *trust agreement.* While the trustee holds *legal title* to the trust property, he is duty bound to administer and distribute it to and for the beneficiaries only as authorized and directed by the trust agreement.

A *living* trust is a relationship established by the settlor during life. It is to be distinguished from a *testamentary* trust, which is established by the settlor pursuant to the terms of a will and comes into existence only upon death. A living trust is *revocable* if the settlor retains the unrestricted right to reacquire the trust property or amend the terms of the trust agreement. A specimen form of a revocable living trust is included as appendix B.

The agreement that governs the administration of a revocable living trust need not be admitted to probate to be effective. Accordingly, unlike a will, it does not become a matter of public record. Also, because the trust property is not included in the settlor's probate estate, the trustee is able to distribute it to the settlor's successors without the delay, expense, and public scrutiny associated with probate administration. The significance of these features for planning purposes depends on the laws and procedures governing the settlement of estates in the jurisdictions in which you reside or your real property is located. If the settlement process is expensive, time-consuming, and open to the public, you should consider using a revocable living trust to reduce costs, expedite the process, and preserve your privacy.

Even in those jurisdictions where probate avoidance is desirable, a revocable living trust is not for everyone. In evaluating the suitability of a revocable living trust to your particular situation, you should consider the following disadvantages and drawbacks:

- In some jurisdictions, the additional expenses incurred in establishing, funding, and administering a revocable living trust may actually exceed those incurred in transferring assets by will, especially considering the time value of money.
- The settlor must learn to deal with assets in a formal and cumbersome manner: the settlor's assets must be transferred to the trust; the trustee must deal with the assets in the name of the trust; and persons dealing with the trust may demand evidence of the trustee's authority.
- The settlor must keep additional records and exercise vigilance to make certain that subsequently acquired assets are properly transferred to the trust.
- If someone other than the settlor serves as trustee, separate federal and state income tax returns may have to be filed on the trust's behalf.
- Avoiding probate administration through the use of a revocable living trust may offer less protection against creditors' claims. At the beginning of the probate process, the personal representative gives notice to creditors. A creditor who does not file a claim for payment within a prescribed period, often as short as two months, is legally barred from pressing the claim. That procedure generally does not apply to bar claims a creditor may assert against the assets of a revocable living trust.
- The transmission of real estate property through a revocable living trust may result in the loss of title insurance coverage.
- The transfer of encumbered assets to a revocable living trust may accelerate the due date of the associated indebtedness, thus depriving the settlor of the benefits of a favorable interest rate.
- A revocable living trust qualifies as an eligible shareholder of a corporation subject to tax under subchapter S of the Internal Revenue Code only during the two-year period following the settlor's death. If the trustee fails to transfer the stock to an eligible shareholder within that two-year period, the corporation will forfeit its tax-favored status.

Beneficiary Designation

Certain contractual arrangements with third parties may call for payments directly to designated beneficiaries upon death. Examples of such arrangements include annuities, life insurance policies, retirement plans, individual retirement accounts, *payable on death* (POD) bank accounts, and *transferable on death* (TOD) securities accounts. Amounts payable under such arrangements are not subject to administration as part of the probate estate and generally are not subject to the claims of creditors. They thus pass to the named beneficiaries without the delay and added expense often associated with probate administration.

Joint Tenancy with Right of Survivorship

If you own a fractional interest in property, you are party to a *cotenancy* with the other owners. There are two basic forms of cotenancy: *joint tenancy* and *tenancy in common*. Each confers on the co-owners equal rights to manage, enjoy, and dispose of their respective interests in the property. The forms differ only with respect to ownership succession upon the death of a cotenant. In the case of joint tenancy, the deceased tenant's interest in the property automatically passes to the surviving tenant, while in the case of tenancy in common, it passes as part of the deceased tenant's probate estate. Thus joint tenancy is an appropriate form of ownership if the co-owners are willing to let the order of their deaths dictate which of them has power over the property's ultimate disposition.

A parent may be tempted to place her property in joint tenancy with one of her children for the sake of convenience in dealing with the property during her life and to avoid subjecting the property to probate administration after her death. Generally, such an arrangement is inadvisable, for the following reasons: (1) its creation may have adverse gift tax consequences, (2) it may expose the parent's property to the claims of the child's creditors, and (3) the child may be unwilling to share the property with his siblings, contrary to the parent's expectations.

Intestate Succession

Property that is not subject to disposition by will, revocable living trust, beneficiary designation or right of survivorship passes by *intestate succession* to the estate owner's *heirs-at-law,* as determined by the law of the state in which the estate owner was residing at the time of death. Under the laws of most states, a decedent's heirs-at-law include, prioritized in the order listed: (1) the decedent's spouse and children, with a deceased child's share passing to his or her children; (2) the decedent's parents; and (3) the decedent's siblings, with a deceased sibling's share passing to his or her children. The allocation of the decedent's intestate estate between his surviving spouse and children differs from state to state. However, a common pattern is to allocate an amount equal to the greater of a specified sum or the value of a prescribed fraction of the estate to the surviving spouse and the balance to the children. For example, in some jurisdictions, a spouse is entitled to the first $100,000 and a percentage of the excess.

GIFTS IN TRUST AS A MEANS OF PROTECTING ASSETS AND PROMOTING VALUES

A gift may be made *outright* or *in trust*. An *outright gift* confers on the recipient full power to manage, consume, and dispose of the property given. A *gift in trust* subjects the recipient's enjoyment of the trust property to the conditions and restrictions embodied in the trust agreement. For example, concern about a child's spendthrift tendencies may be addressed by transferring the child's share of the estate to a trustee with instructions to apply it for the child's benefit during life and to distribute it to the child's children at death. The extraordinary flexibility of the trust device will accommodate a virtually infinite number of variations on that theme. The use of trusts as vehicles for protecting assets and promoting the best interests of successors is discussed in detail in chapter 11.

THE TRANSFER TAX FACTOR

Federal and state *estate, gift,* and *generation-skipping transfer taxes* loom as significant impediments to the transfer of substantial amounts of wealth to children and grandchildren. The imposition of such taxes not only makes Uncle Sam an uninvited heir; it also may require the sale of assets on unfavorable terms in order to raise the cash necessary to satisfy Uncle Sam's claim. Due to the availability of generous exemptions, less than one percent of the population is wealthy enough to be affected by such taxes. Moreover, even for those whose wealth exceeds their available exemptions, there are a number of proven strategies that can be employed to both reduce the taxes and ensure the availability of sufficient liquid assets to pay them. Several of these strategies are discussed in chapters 12 and 13. To provide context for that discussion the principal features of the federal transfer tax system are summarized below.

Federal Estate Tax

The federal estate tax is an excise tax levied on the privilege of transferring property at death. The tax is imposed on the *taxable estate*. The taxable estate is composed of the *gross estate*, less allowable *deductions*. The *gross estate* generally includes all of the decedent's beneficial interests in property, including insurance proceeds. *Deductions* are allowed for the decedent's debts, expenses of administering the estate, charitable contributions, and property passing to the decedent's surviving spouse.

The estate tax payable is the sum of the amounts determined by applying escalating rates to prescribed increments of value in the taxable estate and then subtracting certain *credits*. Taxable gifts made during the decedent's life are included in the tax base, but only for the purpose of determining the brackets applicable to the taxable estate. Of the available credits, the most important is the so-called *unified credit*. It is *unified* in the sense that the credit used against the gift tax reduces dollar-for-dollar the credit available to offset the estate tax. For example, an individual may use at death any credit not used during life.

For a decedent dying in 2003, the unified credit effectively exempts up to $1 million from the federal estate tax. The effective exemption is scheduled to increase in stages to $3.5 million by 2009. The increase in the effective exemption will be accompanied by a gradual decrease in the highest tax rate applicable to estates in excess of the exemption. Then, in a sleight of hand that allowed President Bush and members of Congress to claim credit for making good on a popular campaign promise without busting the budget, the estate tax will be "repealed" in 2010, only to be reinstated in 2011. With reinstatement, the effective exemption will revert to $1 million. This crazy quilt overlay on the federal estate tax is illustrated in the following table:

Year	Estate Tax Exemption	Marginal Estate Tax Rate
2003	$1 million	49 percent
2004	$1.5 million	48 percent
2005	$1.5 million	47 percent
2006	$2 million	46 percent
2007	$2 million	45 percent
2008	$2 million	45 percent
2009	$3.5 million	45 percent
2010	Estate tax repealed	N/A
2011	$1 million	55 percent

Whether Congress will permit these increases in the effective exemption and decreases in the top marginal rate to occur as scheduled remains uncertain. Even more uncertain is the prospect for total repeal of the estate tax. Ultimately, the fate of the transfer tax system depends on unpredictable economic, budgetary, and political developments.

Generally, the federal estate tax must be paid within nine months after the decedent dies. Failure to pay the tax on time results in the imposition of penalties and interest. To secure payment of the tax, a lien attaches to the decedent's property and follows it into the hands of the successors, who then become liable for payment of the tax.

Gift Tax

The gift tax is imposed on the aggregate value of all *taxable gifts* made during any calendar year. Generally, a *gift* is a transfer of money or property to another without the expectation of receiving money, property, or services of equivalent value in return. *Property*, for gift tax purposes, may include as little as the right to use or receive the income from property. For example, if you make an interest-free loan to your child, you will be deemed to have made a gift of the forgone interest.

A gift is *taxable* to the extent it exceeds available *exclusions* and *deductions*:

- The *annual exclusion* permits a donor to make a gift of $11,000 in each year to each of any number of donees without gift tax consequences. The amount of the annual exclusion is subject to periodic adjustment to reflect changes in the cost of living. To qualify for the annual exclusion, the gift must be of a *present interest* in property. Generally, a present interest is an interest that confers on the donee an immediate and legally enforceable economic benefit.
- A separate exclusion allows a donor to pay *tuition and medical expenses* on behalf of others, regardless of amount, without gift tax consequences. The exclusion is available only if the donor pays the tuition or medical expenses directly to the educational institution or health care provider.
- *Deductions* in unlimited amounts are allowed for gifts to the donor's spouse, political organizations, and charitable organizations.

The gift tax is determined by applying to the donor's aggregate taxable gifts for the year the same rate schedule that is used for purposes of determining the estate tax. Gifts made in prior years are included in the tax base, but only for the purpose of determining the brackets applicable to the current year's gifts. The tax thus determined is then reduced by the donor's unused unified credit. As noted, after 2003, the unified credit for estate tax purposes gradually increases until it peaks in 2009. For gift tax purposes, the credit remains at $1 million. Moreover, unlike the estate tax, the gift tax is not scheduled for repeal in 2010.

For planning purposes, it is significant that the gift tax base, unlike the estate tax base, does not include the tax itself. It is this *tax-exclusive* feature of the gift tax system that makes lifetime taxable gifts much more tax efficient than deathtime transfers. For example, suppose that you would like to transfer $1 million dollars to your child and that the applicable gift and estate tax rate is 50 percent. If you make the transfer during life, the gift tax would be $500,000. Thus, to get $1 million to your child by lifetime gift, you would have depleted your estate by $1.5 million. By contrast, if you were to wait to make the transfer until your death, you would have to pay $1 million in estate tax in order to pass $1 million to your child. The difference is attributable solely to the fact that for estate tax purposes, the tax itself is subject to tax.

Spouses can agree to treat gifts made by either as having been made one-half by each. Commonly referred to as *gift-splitting*, this technique allows spouses to take full advantage of the exclusions and credits available to each of them, without regard to which of them actually makes the gifts. For example, if you were to make a gift of $22,000 to your mother, your taxable gift would be $11,000. However, if you and your spouse were to agree to *split* your gifts, each of you would be deemed to have made a gift of $11,000 to your mother, with the result that the entire gift would be covered by annual exclusions. To be effective, a gift-splitting election must be made on a gift tax return for the year in which the gifts are made.

The gift tax return with respect to taxable gifts for any year is due on or before April 15 of the subsequent year. Any tax due must be paid with the return or penalties and interest will be imposed.

The Generation-Skipping Tax

The *generation-skipping transfer tax* (GSTT) is a federal transfer tax that applies independently of the federal estate and gift taxes. The event that triggers its application is a *generation-skipping transfer* (GST). Generally, a generation-skipping transfer is a transfer to a person who is more than one generation younger than the transferor. A generation-skipping transfer may or may not be a transfer that also is subject to estate or gift tax.

The generation-skipping transfer tax serves as a backstop to the federal estate tax by preventing the use of trusts to avoid exposing property to estate tax upon the death of the member of the *skipped* generation. To illustrate, assume that you transfer property to a trust and direct the trustee to distribute all of the trust income to your daughter during her life and the principal to her son, your grandson, upon her death. Because the trust principal is not subject to disposition by your daughter, it will not be included in her gross estate for federal estate tax purposes. However, because your daughter's death results in a transfer to a person more than one generation younger than you, it is an event that triggers the imposition of the generation-skipping transfer tax.

Generally, the exclusions available for gift tax purposes also apply for purposes of determining the base on which the generation-skipping transfer tax is applied. Thus, if you make an outright gift to your granddaughter of $11,000 and pay for her tuition and medical care, neither the gift tax nor the generation-skipping transfer tax is implicated.

Each person is entitled to an *exemption* that serves to hold the generation-skipping transfer tax in abeyance until the cumulative value of the person's generation-skipping transfers exceeds a prescribed amount. For 2003, the generation-skipping transfer exemption is $1,120,000. For transfers occurring in 2004 through 2009, the generation-skipping transfer exemption will be the same as the effective estate tax exemption. Like the federal estate tax, the generation-skipping transfer tax is scheduled for repeal in 2010, only to be reinstated in 2011.

CHAPTER NINE

Planning for an Abundant Life and a Dignified Death

Happiness, according to Thomas Hobbes, is "continual success in obtaining those things which a man from time to time desires, that is to say, continual prospering."[1] The philosopher's formula for a happy life has its roots in the proposition that joy is a consequence of the pursuit of meaningful ends. For most of us, the ends that are worthy of pursuit change over time. Early in life, our aim is to obtain the personal attributes that will enable us to compete successfully in a satisfying occupation. We then turn our attention to producing sufficient income and capital to provide for our current and anticipated needs and wants. Finally, with our finances secure, we turn to other personally satisfying pursuits. Success in each of those phases of life depends on our ability to look past the demands of the moment and lay plans for obtaining what beckons from our dreamscapes.

This chapter is concerned with principles and strategies that foster financial security. It describes proven approaches to the accumulation and protection of wealth and highlights circumstances that, absent foresight and proper planning, can lead to financial dependence and diminished well-being.

DETERMINING YOUR DESIRED STANDARD OF LIVING

In economic terms, your *standard of living* corresponds to the amount of goods and services you consume. Most of us strive for levels of consumption that will not only meet our basic needs for food, clothing, shelter, health care, and education, but also provide us with the comforts widely enjoyed by those in the mainstream of economic life.

Beyond the levels necessary to meet basic needs and provide modest comforts, differences in levels of consumption generally result from disparities in economic circumstances and differing views as to the importance of consumption to a happy and fulfilling life. The very rich are likely to consume more luxuries simply because they are able to do so without jeopardizing their long-term financial security. The "conspicuous consumer" derives personal satisfaction and self-esteem from the envy and attention such an apparently affluent lifestyle evokes in others. Your *desired* standard of living is largely a reflection of the importance you attach to comfort, pleasure, and social standing as contributors to your sense of personal fulfillment and well-being.

RESOURCES FOR MAINTAINING YOUR DESIRED STANDARD OF LIVING

Generally, the means necessary to achieve and maintain your desired standard of living comes from three sources: (1) earnings from personal services, (2) savings and investments, and (3) borrowing. Early in one's economic life cycle, earnings from personal services typically constitute the principal resource for funding consumption. Later in life, as physical and mental capacities wane, savings and investments supplement and eventually replace earnings from personal services as the primary means of maintaining a chosen lifestyle.

Maximizing Income from Personal Services

An estate plan formulated to enhance financial security necessarily includes strategies for developing, enhancing, and maintaining the capacity to generate income from personal services. Strategies commonly employed to those ends include the pursuit of general education, the acquisition of marketable skills, and the cultivation of personal attributes commonly associated with success in the workplace. As Ben Franklin observed: "If a man empties his purse into his head, no one can take it away from him. An investment of knowledge always pays the best interest."

The opportunity to enhance personal earning capacity continues for as long as we remain in the workforce. Yet, many waste their working lives stuck in low-paying occupations instead of acquiring the knowledge and skills necessary to qualify themselves for more lucrative endeavors. Often, even a modest "investment of knowledge" can make a significant difference in earning power. One middle-aged file clerk in a financial consulting firm, on her own time, became so proficient in the configuration of electronic spreadsheets that she was promoted to the position of technical assistant to the firm's managing partner and received a substantial increase in her compensation. She then went on to an even more ambitious program of self-study to become a financial analyst. What is remarkable about this woman's accomplishments and

IS THIS ALL THERE IS?

Craig, a successful tax lawyer at the peak of his career, is a case in point. Craig chose to study law because he believed that as a lawyer he could influence society to virtuous ends without foregoing the opportunity to make a good living. His exceptional performance in law school landed him a position at a prestigious law firm with a blue-chip clientele. For the next several years, he made the personal sacrifices required of those who aspire to partnership in a prominent law firm. He then claimed a place for himself in the leadership councils of both his firm and several prestigious professional organizations. Now, standing at the summit of his chosen career, he finds himself asking with countless others similarly situated: "Is this all there is?" His question betrays the feeling of emptiness that inevitably accompanies achievements pursued in response to others' expectations rather than one's own yearnings. It also reflects a profound sense of lost opportunity.

In his words: "For twenty years I've been making myself, my clients, and my partners richer; and what do I have to show for it? I have only fragmentary memories of my daughter's childhood; the only thing my wife and I have in common is that we were married on the same day; and I have nothing to look forward to but the waning of my professional prowess and prestige." Despite his despair, Craig is unwilling to take the steps that would take him back to the path of public service he envisioned as a law student. He readily admits that his unwillingness to make a change stems from his dependence on the wealth and status that attend his present station in life. His attachment to the trappings of success, so common a pitfall in our culture, prevents him from moderating his needs and desires, and traps him in a career that brings him only transitory satisfaction. Tragically, he will find his grief over lost opportunity increasingly difficult to bear as the prestige that now sustains him dissipates with age and diminished capacity. Neither prestige nor wealth can ever fully compensate for abandoned dreams that were once within easy reach.

aspirations is that her formal education ended with her graduation from middle school.

Regardless of the fact that a particular occupation has the potential to produce income sufficient to support your desired standard of living, you should pursue that occupation only if it is well-suited to your interests, aptitudes, and values. Do not risk damaging your sense of fulfillment and well-being by engaging in meaningless or unsatisfying work. High pay does not necessarily equate to job satisfaction. To the contrary, the devotion, compromises, and sacrifices demanded of those in the most remunerative occupations often leave them burned out and disillusioned.

Optimizing Saving and Investment

Unless you are the recipient of a substantial inheritance or other financial windfall, you have no alternative but to rely on savings and investments to replace diminishing income from personal services. That means that you may have to curtail your desired level of consumption until sufficient replacement capital is accumulated. An alternative to consuming less would be to work more; but that may prevent you from pursing other worthwhile individual and social endeavors, including spending more time with family and friends. Neglect of important relationships may be a price you are unwilling to pay to maintain a higher standard of living.

In formulating a savings and investment strategy, prudence should be the guiding principle. A prudent investor

- Chooses among alternative investments with a view toward preservation rather than speculation;
- Understands the relationship between risk and return;
- Appreciates the importance of diversification in managing risk;
- When presented with the prospect of high returns, does not let greed blind him to the associated risk or induce him to invest more than is warranted; and
- Understands that there are too many imponderables and too much randomness in the financial markets to presume that past performance is necessarily an accurate predictor of future performance.

In configuring an investment portfolio, keep in mind that choices have consequences that transcend the immediate goal of enhancing personal financial security. To understand those consequences is to appreciate the power of money as an instrument for fostering positive values in our communities and the larger society. In a society founded on the principles of democratic capitalism, a socially conscious investment strategy often has a greater influence on the formulation of public policy, the allocation of resources, and the development and maintenance of public morality than does the exercise of the right to vote. Consider, for example, the tremendous influence lobbyists for major corporations and trade groups have on the outcomes of elections, legislative debates, and administrative deliberations. The lobbyists' salaries are paid from the treasuries of corporations whose stock finds place in the investment portfolios of countless individuals and institutions. If you refuse to purchase the stock of a corporation whose activities are at odds with your values, you not only discourage the offensive activities, but you also diminish the corporation's economic clout and concomitant influence over the formulation of public policy.

The Imprudence of Debt-Financed Consumption

Rarely is it advisable to fund day-to-day consumption through borrowing. Debt must be repaid *with interest*. It thus limits the capacity to fund consumption in the future. Moreover, the high rates of interest associated with *consumer debt* significantly increase the cost of current consumption.

Of course, not all debt is inappropriate. Generally, it is prudent to incur debt to finance your education and the development and maintenance of marketable skills. It also may be appropriate to finance the purchase of tools and equipment, a start-up or expansion of a business, a personal automobile, and a personal residence. Reasonable debt incurred for those purposes is justified because it likely will enhance rather than diminish your earning capacity.

INSURING YOUR PERSONAL CAPITAL AGAINST THE RISK OF LOSS

If your family is dependent on earnings from personal services to finance current consumption and implement a saving and investment program, you should consider the purchase of insurance to protect against the loss of those earnings as a result of disability or death. The primary purpose of insurance is to protect against a risk of loss that cannot be funded from personal financial resources. Unfortunately, many fail to appreciate the magnitude of that risk until it is too late, as evidenced by the following sobering statistics:

- One in eight people will become disabled before reaching age sixty-five; and yet fewer than 15 percent of all wage earners in the United States have disability income insurance.
- Failure to adequately insure against the risk of death of a working spouse accounts for two-thirds of poverty among surviving women and more than one-third of poverty among surviving men.[2]

Disability Insurance

Disability insurance may be the most important safeguard against the loss of earning capacity. The economic impact of a disability can be even greater than that of death. The family of a disabled wage-earner not only is deprived of his earnings, but also must bear the financial burden of his support, medical care, and rehabilitation.

In selecting a disability policy, you should pay particular attention to the definition of "disability." Under standard low-cost policies, the insured is considered disabled only if he is unable to perform the duties, not just of his own occupation, but of *any* occupation for which he is prepared by training and experience. Thus, a commercial artist who loses a hand may nevertheless be denied benefits on the ground that she still is able to make a living marketing the services of a graphic design firm.

Other factors you should consider in evaluating a disability policy include the following:

- Eligibility for benefits in the event of partial disability
- The amount of time that must elapse before benefits are payable
- Provision for automatic increases in coverage to account for inflation and higher earnings
- The maximum period during which benefits are payable
- The conditions under which the company may cancel the policy

Long-Term Care Insurance

Long-term care insurance is a form of disability insurance for aging retirees. Steady increases in life expectancies over the past several decades have greatly increased the risk that you will spend at least some time in an assisted-care facility during your "golden years." The wealthy have the means to pay for their own long-term care and the impoverished can look to Medicaid and other governmental assistance programs. Those in between have to either purchase long-term care insurance or face the specter of having to first exhaust their savings and then rely on government assistance.

Assuming you have the need and can afford to pay the premiums, you should consider purchasing long-term care insurance as early as age fifty. Early acquisition of the policy will reduce the premiums and avoid the risk that your health will deteriorate to the point that you no longer will be insurable. In determining the appropriate amount and period of coverage, you should take into account other available resources and the fact that a stay in a care facility is unlikely to exceed three years. Also consider purchasing an *inflation rider* to ensure that the policy benefits will keep pace with anticipated increases in the cost of care. Finally, be certain that the policy covers *any* assisted care facility, not just those that provide skilled nursing and medical care.

If you are unable or unwilling to pay the premium for a policy with adequate coverage, you should consider asking your children to contribute. They likely will be eager to assume all or part of the burden of maintaining the policy in lieu of running the risk that their anticipated inheritance will be diverted to pay the cost of your long-term care.

Life Insurance

Life insurance is packaged and marketed in the form of a bewildering array of financial products. Many insurance policies are in fact hybrid products that provide both insurance protection and an investment feature. Common types of hybrid policies include *whole-life*, *variable life*, and *universal life*. Generally, the investment component of a hybrid policy does not compare favorably with alternative investment vehicles. Moreover, the presence of the investment feature substantially increases the cost of the insurance as a percentage of coverage. For those reasons, hybrid policies generally are unsuited to the need for pure insurance protection.

The least costly form of life insurance is *annual renewable term*. Term insurance provides the required protection at a cost based on the probability that the insured will die prematurely. For other than the elderly, that probability is low. Therefore, the cost of the coverage usually is quite manageable. The fact that the policy is "renewable" means that the premium increases each year to reflect the increasing probability that the insured will die in that year. However, because the purpose of having the insurance is to meet an interim need while capital is being accumulated, the fact that premiums increase from year to year ordinarily does not pose a problem.

Amounts of Insurance

You should purchase no more disability and life insurance than is necessary to maintain your family's desired standard of living, taking into account current and anticipated levels of consumption and all available financial resources other than insurance. For that purpose, an illiquid asset, such as real estate or an interest in a family business, should not be considered *available* unless you are reasonably certain that it can be sold for its full market value within a reasonably short period of time.

Due to the difficulty of identifying and accounting for all of the factors relevant to a determination of the appropriate amount of insurance, you may want to enlist the assistance of a financial advisor. In that event, you should choose an advisor who has nothing to sell but advice and counsel and has no referral, fee-sharing, or other arrangements or obligations that might compromise his or her duty of loyalty to you. An alternative would be to purchase financial-planning software that is specifically designed to yield an unbiased estimate of your insurance needs. An inexpensive consumer version of one of the leading software packages, ES Planner, is available for download at the developer's Web site, *www.esplanner.com.*

PROTECTING YOUR ASSETS AGAINST LIABILITY FOR INJURY TO OTHERS

If through act or omission you injure another person, you likely will be liable for the economic equivalent of the injury. You almost certainly will be liable if you negligently or intentionally caused the injury. And you *may* be liable even if you are not to any degree at fault. *No-fault liability* is a legal principle that is based on the notion that liability should rest with the person who is in the best position to mitigate the risk. It is illustrated by the rule adopted in some states that a person who loans his automobile to another is "vicariously" liable for the borrower's negligent driving. Others to whom no-fault liability may be imputed include: (1) a homeowner for injuries to guests and even intruders, (2) an employer for the negligent or intentional acts of his or her employees, and (3) parents for the acts of their children. Considering how difficult it is to manage another's conduct, prudence dictates consideration of other means of protecting assets against liability for injuries to others.

Liability Insurance

Liability insurance is the first line of defense against liability for damage to another's person or property. You undoubtedly already have policies covering your home and automobile. But the amount of coverage commonly associated with homeowner's and automobile policies may not be adequate protection against the myriad risks to which you may be exposed. Accordingly, consider supplementing your existing asset-based policies with an *umbrella* policy. An umbrella policy typically offers a minimum of $1 million in coverage for a modest annual premium and covers all manner of risks.

Other Asset Protection Strategies

If you are concerned that you may incur liability in excess of the protection afforded by insurance, you should consider other asset-protection strategies, including: (1) the declaration of a *homestead exemption* with respect to your principal residence; (2) the transfer of assets to or in trust for your spouse or other family members; (3) the conduct of your activities through limited partnerships, corporations, or limited liability companies; and (4) the creation of an *asset protection trust* of which you and other members of your family are eligible beneficiaries.

The efficacy of any asset protection strategy depends in the first instance on applicable state and federal law. Only a few states provide for a meaningful homestead exemption, and still fewer recognize the effectiveness of an asset protection trust of which the settlor is a beneficiary. All states, however, recognize the limited liability afforded by limited partnerships, corporations, limited liability companies, and trusts established for the benefit of third-party beneficiaries.

No asset-protection strategy will be effective if its purpose is to defraud or impede a creditor whose claim exists at the time the strategy is implemented. And even if the creditor's claim arises after the strategy is in place, a judge or jury may permit the creditor to reach the protected assets if to do otherwise would confer an unconscionable benefit on one clearly in the wrong. For example, if a corporate executive declares a homestead exemption with respect to his multimillion-dollar residence and subsequently engages in fraudulent conduct that costs his company millions of dollars, a court may strain to find a legal or factual basis on which to permit the company to pierce the protection afforded by the homestead exemption. To do otherwise would be to permit the executive to shift the loss caused by his fraudulent acts to the company's innocent shareholders.

PROVIDING FOR MANAGEMENT OF YOUR ASSETS IN THE EVENT OF INCAPACITY

Competent and prudent management of your accumulated wealth is essential to its preservation and growth. If you become physically or mentally incapacitated, responsibility for managing your financial affairs will fall to a court-appointed guardian or conservator. The appointment of a guardian or conservator usually involves a judicial hearing to determine incapacity and continuing court supervision of the administration of your assets. Such proceedings can be embarrassing to you and your family, lead to the appointment of someone you would not have chosen to manage your affairs, and involve considerable legal and other expenses.

The court appointment of a guardian or conservator, with its attendant disadvantages, can be avoided through the execution of a *durable power of attorney*. A *power of attorney* is a legal instrument by which an individual, as *principal*, designates another, as *agent*, to act on the principal's behalf with respect to specified matters. A power of attorney is *durable* if it specifies that it will survive or come into being in the event of the principal's incapacity. A specimen form of durable power of attorney is included as appendix C.

In its broadest configuration, a durable power of attorney authorizes the designated agent to do everything the principal could do on his own behalf. That does not mean that the agent has the same latitude as the principal in managing and investing the assets. The principal is free to assume any degree of investment risk and can apply the assets to any purpose without having to account to anyone else. The agent, on the other hand, is a *fiduciary* and as such is legally bound to conserve assets and apply them solely for the principal's benefit. The agent is precluded from taking imprudent investment risks even if he or she believes the principal would approve. Furthermore, the agent is strictly prohibited from taking any action with respect to the principal's financial affairs that would serve the agent's interests to the principal's detriment.

The fact that an agent is legally accountable will be scant comfort if his or her improper conduct leads to the dissipation of the principal's assets and he or she lacks the resources necessary to make the principal whole. Accordingly, it is important to choose as agent someone who is both trustworthy and competent to manage financial affairs. Spouses often name each other as agent with little thought as to whether one or the other is qualified to perform the necessary tasks. It may be preferable to name a trusted advisor or business associate with experience in financial matters. However, before choosing a business associate as agent, you should be certain that the appointment will not create conflicts of interest that may preclude him or her from acting or threaten the safety of your assets. To discourage your agent from dealing with your assets in a manner that is contrary to your best interests, you should require your agent to give periodic accountings to selected members of your family or trusted advisors and to obtain their prior consent to any transaction involving your assets to which your agent is a party.

One of the disadvantages associated with the use of a durable power of attorney as a safeguard against incapacity is that your designated agent may not be willing and able to act when the need arises. To protect against that eventuality, you should confirm your agent's willingness to act before making the appointment and designate a willing alternate to serve in the event your agent is unable to do so. You may also want to give your agent added incentive to act by specifying in the power of attorney that he or she is entitled to reasonable compensation for services rendered on your behalf.

Flexibility in the management of your assets can be enhanced if you use a power of attorney in tandem with a *revocable living trust.* Commonly associated with the avoidance of probate, a revocable living trust also serves as an effective means of empowering someone to manage your assets for your benefit. To create a revocable living trust, you or your agent must transfer your assets to a trustee for administration in accordance with your instructions as embodied in a written trust agreement. The trustee's acceptance of the property signifies his or her willingness to act in accordance with the terms of the trust agreement. Prior to your incapacity or death, you have a continuing right to revoke the trust or alter its terms in any way you see fit. Following your incapacity, the trustee manages and distributes the trust property as specified in the trust agreement. Typically, the trust agreement authorizes the trustee to distribute the income and principal of the trust to you in amounts sufficient to maintain you in your accustomed standard of living. It also designates the persons entitled to receive any property remaining in the trust at the time of death. It thus serves as a substitute for a will as the primary vehicle for disposing of your assets at death. The advantages and disadvantages of a revocable living trust as a will substitute are discussed in chapter 8.

PLANNING FOR A DIGNIFIED YET PRUDENT DEATH

For most of us, advances in health care promise to prolong and enhance the quality of our lives, thus giving us greater control over the timing and processes of our deaths. The responsible exercise of that control, through rational, timely, and careful planning, can preserve personal dignity, ease the burden borne by loved ones, and reduce the expenses associated with a final illness and funeral.

Most of us would prefer not to be kept alive by artificial means when there no longer is any realistic hope of recovery. Many of us worry that our survivors, burdened with grief and guilt, will purchase needless and expensive burial services and accessories. As rational stewards, we prefer to see precious family resources preserved for the needs of the living rather than consumed in a grandiose farewell gesture to the deceased.

One woman's terminally ill husband lingered for several weeks while she agonized over whether to consent to the termination of extraordinary life-sustaining measures. Then, after she had finally mustered the courage to let him go, she was so plagued with guilt over having "pulled the plug" that she spent lavishly to ensure that he had a "fitting" funeral and burial. Sadly, much of the emotional and financial cost of her ordeal could have been avoided if her husband had executed an *advance directive to health care providers* (often called a *living will*) and informed her of his wishes concerning his funeral and burial.

ADVANCE HEALTH CARE DIRECTIVE

An *advance directive to health care providers* (also known as a *living will*) communicates your wishes regarding the employment of artificial means to prolong your life when there is no longer any reasonable prospect for survival. Of course, it is operative for that purpose only if you are unable personally to make known your desires with respect to the initiation, continuance, or termination of a particular course of treatment.

Your advance directive should *clearly* and *unequivocally* express your desires with respect to the administration of *specific* categories of life-sustaining treatments. If you are unfamiliar with the circumstances in which the need for an advance directive may arise, you should consult with your physician. The more you know about the medical protocols pertaining to terminal conditions, the more specific you can be in formulating and expressing your desires. For example, if you are aware that the possibility of regaining consciousness following a severe stroke diminishes with the passage of time, you can prescribe a time limit for the administration of artificial measures based on your own perception of what constitutes a reasonable prospect of recovery. Or, if you are familiar with the types of treatments that are commonly administered, you may choose to authorize some but not others. For example, you may decide that tubular nutrition and intravenous hydration are acceptable, but that antibiotics, surgery, and artificial respiration are not. A specimen form of an advance directive is included as appendix D.

Despite your best efforts to become informed and craft an advance directive that clearly expresses your desires, there always is a chance that you will face a health care crisis that you failed adequately to anticipate. For that reason, it is important that you discuss your desires with members of your family. If they are familiar with your general preferences and intent, they can assist your physician in resolving the ambiguities in your advance directive. Your family's awareness of your wishes also will increase the likelihood that these wishes will be honored, as well as decrease the family's anguish and guilt that often accompany a decision that has a life-or-death consequence.

ADVANCE FUNERAL ARRANGEMENTS

Funerals are for the living, not the dead. And you can make yours a much more meaningful experience for your survivors if you have the foresight to leave a letter of instruction to your loved ones expressing your wishes with respect to your funeral and burial. The death of a loved one is difficult enough to bear without having to make on-the-spot decisions regarding the disposition of remains, a suitable memorial service, the content of an obituary, the location of interment, and a reception for sympathizers. When those decisions are influenced by guilt over real or imagined offenses toward the deceased, or just the natural desire to honor him or her, there is a significant risk for excess.

In preparing your letter, you should not disregard your family's need to give you a "proper send off" in the interest of being frugal. It may be *your* funeral, but it is *their* memorial. Through thoughtful planning, you can give full expression to the spirit and purpose of the occasion without lavishly spending on unnecessary accoutrements. Following are some of the specific matters you may want to address in your letter of instruction:

- The disposition of your remains—burial, cremation, or donation for medical study
- The content of your obituary
- The charitable recipient of memorial donations
- The services the funeral home will provide
- The type of casket
- The location and proceedings of any memorial service

CHAPTER TEN

The Power of Lifetime Gifts

Lifetime gifts constitute an effective means of achieving a variety of estate planning objectives. They permit spouses to order the ownership of their marital assets to optimum personal and tax advantage. They enable parents to assess and enhance the financial maturity, alleviate the financial burdens, and underwrite the worthy endeavors of their children. And they achieve income and transfer tax savings that are not available through transfers at death. This chapter highlights the advantages of lifetime gifts and describes the considerations involved in determining how much and to whom to give.

INTERSPOUSAL TRANSFERS

Gifts between spouses may serve as the means to right inequities inherent in state property law and to ensure that each spouse has sufficient assets to take advantage of the *unified credit* available for federal transfer tax purposes. Significantly, due to the availability of the gift tax *marital deduction*, gifts between spouses can be made in unlimited amounts without adverse gift tax consequences.

Transfers in Recognition of Relative Contributions

Most couples would readily acknowledge that the accumulation of marital property is due to their joint efforts in earning income, managing the home, and caring for the children. Yet, under the law of most states, a spouse who provides only domestic services acquires no direct ownership in property acquired with the other spouse's earnings.[1] The law's refusal to credit a homemaker with an ownership interest in the marital property based on the value of his or her domestic services is a vestige of *coverture*, the common law doctrine that ascribed ownership of family property to the husband and denied any economic entitlement to the wife. Although the doctrine's modern embodiment is gender-neutral, it continues to devalue work performed in the home by apportioning ownership of family property based solely on the spouses' relative *monetary* contributions to its acquisition. The obvious inequity in the doctrine is ameliorated to some extent by the mutual obligation of support that attends the marital relationship. That obligation finds expression in laws that give each spouse an interest in the other's property in the event of divorce, separation, or death. Even though such remedial measures may deter a spouse who otherwise would exploit the other's uncompensated endeavors on the family's behalf, they fall short of ascribing economic value to those endeavors in the form of a direct-ownership interest in marital property. Thus, it is up to you and your spouse to order the ownership of your marital property in a way that reflects your mutual view of the true worth of your respective contributions.

Preserving Your Spouse's Exemption

As noted in chapter 8, each individual has available a *unified credit* that effectively *exempts* from gift and estate tax cumulative transfers of up to a specified threshold amount. The effective exemption for 2003 is $1 million and it is scheduled to increase in stages to $3.5 million by 2009.

To the extent the effective exemption exceeds the net value of the assets in an individual's estate it will produce no tax benefit. Of course, that is a concern only if the combined value of the assets owned by the individual and his or her spouse can be expected to exceed the effective exemption available to the survivor's estate. Assume, for example, that Husband dies in 2003 with an estate of $200,000, which he leaves to his children, and that Wife dies in 2004 with an estate of $1.5 million. Each estate is fully sheltered by the available effective exemption and, therefore, the fact that the value of Husband's estate is less than his effective exemption is of no import. In contrast, if the value of Wife's estate were $2.5 million at the time of her death in 2004, the failure to fully utilize Husband's exemption would result in an unnecessary increase of nearly $400,000 in the tax imposed on Wife's estate.

As the foregoing example implies, you and your spouse can substantially reduce the tax imposed on your combined estate simply by making certain that each of you has an estate of sufficient size to fully utilize the available exemption. That easily can be accomplished through interspousal tax-free gifts. Thus, in the foregoing example, if Wife had made a lifetime gift to Husband of $800,000, no gift tax would have been imposed and the resulting increase in the value of Husband's estate would have prevented the waste of his effective exemption and saved nearly $400,000 in gift tax.

Even if you and your spouse have sufficient assets in your respective estates to fully use the available exemptions, the desired tax savings will not be realized if the survivor succeeds to *outright* ownership of the property that would otherwise be sheltered by the decedent's exemption. Thus, in the preceding example, if under the terms of Husband's will he had left the $1 million outright to Wife, the entire amount would have been subject to tax in Wife's estate and the reordering of the ownership of the marital assets would have produced no benefit. However, if Husband had left the $1 million in a *shelter trust* and limited Wife's access to the trust assets to amounts necessary for her health, support, and maintenance, the trust assets would not have been included in Wife's estate and the desired tax benefit would have been realized. For further discussion of the uses and features of a shelter trust, see chapter 12.

Reallocating Ownership

To be accorded legal recognition, a spouse's ownership interest in marital property must be *documented*. Generally, that means that the spouse's name must appear on the deed, certificate, registration, agreement, or other documentary evidence of ownership. Spouses may take title to marital property in *fee simple, tenancy in common,* or *joint tenancy.* Ownership in *fee simple* is exclusive and absolute. If you are listed as the sole grantee on the deed to your family home, then you alone have the right to occupy and sell it. To include your spouse as an owner of the home, you must execute and record a new deed listing both of you as grantees, either as *joint tenants* or *tenants in common.* Each form of *tenancy* denotes equal entitlement to the use, enjoyment, and any proceeds from the rental or sale of the property. However, the forms differ in one important respect. Upon the death of one of you, survived by the other, the deceased spouse's share of property held in *joint tenancy* automatically passes to the survivor. By contrast, the deceased spouse's interest in property held in *tenancy in common* passes pursuant to the terms of his or her will or revocable living trust. Thus, unless you and your spouse intend to leave your respective shares of the marital property outright to each other, *tenancy in common* is the preferred form of ownership.

Spouses who decide to arrange their affairs so that the survivor succeeds to *outright* ownership of a portion or all of the marital estate often do so based on the assumption that the survivor will leave his or her estate to the children. However, it is not uncommon for a surviving spouse to deplete the marital estate through imprudent management, extravagant consumption, or diversion to creditors, a second spouse, or others. Accordingly, if you desire assurance that your share of the marital property will be preserved for your children or others of your choosing, you should consider limiting your spouse's access to and control over the disposition of your share of the marital estate through the use of a trust. A trust facilitates the separation of the management and beneficial entitlements associated with the ownership of property. Through the use of a trust, you can give your spouse access to your share of the martial estate to the extent necessary to provide for his or her financial security and preserve the balance for ultimate distribution to your children or others. A gift in trust for a spouse's benefit generally does not qualify for the federal gift tax marital deduction. However, an exception applies for a trust that elects to be treated as a *qualified terminable interest property* (QTIP) *trust*. A trust qualifies for this election if, during the spouse's life: (1) all of the trust income must be paid to the spouse, and (2) no part of the trust principal may be applied for the benefit of anyone other than the spouse. Upon the spouse's death, the assets remaining in the trust pass as provided in the trust agreement.

LIFETIME INTERGENERATIONAL TRANSFERS

If your estate plan contemplates the transfer of your residual wealth to your children and grandchildren, and you have more than enough to provide for your own financial security, you should consider the personal and tax benefits associated with making lifetime gifts.

Nontax Benefits of Lifetime Gifts

The nontax advantages of lifetime gifts include the following:

- Lifetime gifts enable you to experience the personal satisfaction that comes from acting on your generous impulses.

- Modest lifetime gifts can relieve the pressure on your children to abandon their own educational and career goals in order to pursue more lucrative but possibly unsatisfying endeavors.
- Through lifetime gifts or low-interest loans, you can make available to a child the capital he or she needs to pursue a promising business venture.
- Lifetime gifts of securities, real estate, or other investment property help your children to understand and appreciate the difference between consumption and investment and give them valuable experience in wealth management. For further discussion on the topic of teaching children the principles of financial management, see chapter 6.
- Lifetime gifts to your children will provide you with the opportunity to observe and assess their level of maturity and expertise with respect to financial matters. For ideas on planning for children who may be financially immature or incapable, see chapter 16.
- Lifetime gifts made with the stated expectation that your children will devote some or all of the donated property to charitable causes will instill in them a sense of community responsibility and enable them to experience the satisfaction that comes from making financial sacrifices for the benefit of the less fortunate.

Tax Benefits of Lifetime Gifts

Lifetime gifts are considerably more tax efficient than transfers at death. The principal transfer and income tax benefits associated with lifetime gifts are summarized below.

- As of 2003, you may give up to $11,000 annually to each of any number of donees without the imposition of a gift tax. This *annual exclusion* increases to $22,000 if your spouse joins in the gift. All property that is the subject of annual exclusion gifts, including any income and appreciation in value, will be excluded from your estate for federal estate tax purposes.
- You may pay your children's and grandchildren's tuition and medical expenses with no gift tax consequences. There is no dollar limit on the amount that can be given in this manner.

- While the estate tax base is *tax-inclusive*, the gift tax base is *tax-exclusive*. In other words, while the estate tax is itself subject to transfer tax, the gift tax is not.
- The use of your effective exemption during your life will effect a tax-free shift to the donees of the post-transfer income and appreciation attributable to the transferred property. Assume, for example, that in 2003 you use your entire gift tax exemption by making a gift of $1 million in trust for your children. If you die in 2005, when the value of the property given has increased to $1.5 million, your effective exemption for estate tax purposes will be $1 million less, but the $500,000 in post-gift appreciation will have passed to your children completely transfer-tax free.
- Income tax savings can be achieved within the family unit by shifting income or gain from a taxpayer subject to a high marginal income tax rate to taxpayers with lower marginal rates.

OVERCOMING RELUCTANCE TO MAKE LIFETIME GIFTS

Despite their advantages, you may hesitate to make lifetime gifts for fear of jeopardizing your financial security or dampening your children's motivation to pursue their educational and occupational goals. Those concerns often can be allayed through: (1) a careful evaluation of your resources and anticipated needs and wants, (2) an appreciation for the tangible and intangible benefits that are associated with the ownership and control of wealth, and (3) the employment of techniques that permit you to retain management control of transferred wealth.

As noted previously, the functional essence of wealth is the power to *consume* and *control* financial resources. The power to *consume* financial resources enables you to establish and maintain your desired standard of living. Your *standard of living* corresponds to the amount of goods and services you consume. As your wealth increases, the portion that is devoted to maintaining your desired standard of living diminishes. The effect is the creation of *surplus*. Your surplus represents the portion of your wealth you can transfer during your life and still maintain your desired standard of living. For the sake of your peace of mind and financial security, you should be conservative in assessing your resources and liberal in assessing your needs; and you should steadfastly refuse to give more than your surplus.

The power to *control* financial resources confers on the holder a variety of intangible benefits, including status in the community, political and social influence, opportunities for service on boards of directors, and deference from bankers, corporate executives, and community leaders. In the words of one observer: "[People] may begin to acquire property to safeguard their lives from want, but they continue to acquire it because of the distinction that comes from its possession."[2]

If your sense of security and well-being derives from the intangible benefits associated with your wealth, you likely will be unwilling to transfer even your surplus unless you can do so and still maintain control. Fortunately, there are proven techniques that will enable you to maintain the power to control your surplus and still realize the tax and nontax benefits of lifetime gifts. Chief among those techniques is the use of a limited partnership or limited liability company as the repository of your surplus and the vehicle for implementing your gift program. If you name yourself as the general partner or manager and make your gifts in the form of interests in the entity, you are able to retain the power to manage the entity's assets and still to obtain the benefits of making lifetime gifts. For further discussion of the use of family limited entities, see chapter 12.

Selecting Assets to Give Away

In evaluating an asset's suitability as the subject of a lifetime gift, you should take into account the following considerations:

- If you paid more for the asset than it is now worth, it is not a good choice. Generally, your *tax basis* in an asset is the price you paid for it. If you were to sell the asset for less than your tax basis, you would generate a *loss* that you would be able to take as a deduction on your federal income tax return. If instead you were to make a gift of the asset, the donee's tax basis would *step down* to the asset's fair market value. Thus, the effect of making a gift of property that has depreciated in value would be to forfeit the deduction associated with the loss. The better alternative would be to sell the asset, deduct the loss, and make a gift of the sale proceeds.
- If you paid less for the asset than it is now worth, it may or may not be a good choice, depending on whether it will be sold or retained in the family. If you were to make a lifetime gift of an

asset that has appreciated in value, the donee's tax basis would be the same as yours. By contrast, if you were to retain the asset until your death, your successor's tax basis would *step up* to the asset's fair market value. Thus, if it is likely that the asset will not be sold prior to your death, you should retain it in order to take advantage of the *step-up* in tax basis. On the other hand, if it is anticipated that the asset will be sold, and if the donee's income tax bracket is lower than yours, a gift prior to sale will shift the gain to the donee and thereby subject it to a lower income tax rate.

- A gift of an income-producing asset to a donee whose income tax bracket is lower than yours will yield continuing income tax savings.
- A gift of property likely to appreciate in value will remove the appreciation from your estate without any gift or estate tax consequences.
- A gift of an asset that is subject to a mortgage or trust deed securing a liability in excess of the asset's income tax basis will be treated as a sale, with the result that gain will be recognized to the extent of such excess.

CHAPTER ELEVEN

The Use of Trusts to Protect Assets and Promote Values

"**M**oney is always on its way somewhere."[1] Unless you have the foresight and timing to die broke,[2] someone else inevitably will enjoy the fruits of your labor and frugality. The thought of undeserving heirs squandering their hard-earned bounty causes some to shrink from the task of formulating and implementing a succession plan. Like Solomon of old, they fear that fools "will have control over all the work into which [they] have poured [their] effort and skill."[3] Fortunately, the law recognizes your right to have a say in how your wealth is managed and consumed, even after your death. Thus, you need not assume the risk that undeserving "fools" will squander your hard-earned treasure. Instead, through carefully tailored restrictions and incentives embodied in a well-drawn trust agreement, you can preserve your wealth as the medium through which your values will find expression long after you are gone.

THE SALIENT FEATURES OF TRUSTS

Lord Maitland, an esteemed legal scholar, has called the trust idea "the greatest and most distinctive achievement performed by Englishmen in the field of jurisprudence."[4] Such lavish praise is due in no small part to the trust's extraordinary flexibility as a device for protecting and disposing of property. Through the use of a trust, it is possible to:

- Separate the benefits from the burdens of ownership
- Create successive interests in property

- Make the extent of the beneficiaries' interests dependent upon the trustee's discretion
- Prescribe the standards and norms that will guide the trustee in the exercise of its discretion
- Establish the acceptable range of investment risk the trustee is authorized to take
- Protect the beneficiaries' interests from their possibly imprudent spending habits, inappropriate influence from others, and the claims of their creditors

ADVANTAGES OF GIFTS IN TRUST

Gifts in trust offer several significant advantages over gifts made outright and without restriction:

- Outright gifts result in the fragmentation of ownership, which in turn can foster family disharmony and undermine management efficiency. If the assets are held in trust, asset management can be centralized in the hands of those best qualified to handle it.
- Whereas a recipient of an outright gift is free to dispose of it in an imprudent manner, a beneficiary of a trust is subject to the restrictions and limitations contained in the trust agreement.
- A trust can serve as a vehicle for teaching the beneficiaries the principles of financial responsibility and management.
- A gift in trust for a legally disabled beneficiary avoids the necessity of expensive proceedings involving the appointment and supervision of a conservator or other personal representative.
- Assets held in a discretionary trust for a physically or mentally disabled beneficiary are not considered resources for purposes of determining the beneficiary's eligibility for Medicaid, Supplemental Security Income, and other needs-based government entitlements.
- Property given in trust can be insulated from the claims and rights of the beneficiary's creditors, spouse, and survivors.
- The terms of a trust can be sufficiently flexible to accommodate virtually any change in the beneficiary's circumstances.

SELECTING THE TRUSTEE

You may appoint as trustee any individual who has the legal capacity to enter into contracts or any corporation that is authorized by law to administer trusts. Your first impulse may be to name yourself as trustee. However, you should not act on that impulse if your objective is to remove the trust assets from your estate for federal estate tax purposes. Your retention of any discretionary power to distribute or accumulate the trust's income or principal, even if exercisable solely in your capacity as trustee, will frustrate that objective. Your next impulse may be to name a close family member. That may be appropriate in some circumstances, but it is not without drawbacks. A family member may have the requisite integrity to serve as trustee, but lack the necessary skill and experience to manage the trust effectively. Moreover, a family trustee may find it difficult to resist the beneficiary's entreaties for distributions out of concern for preserving family harmony. If the trust has multiple beneficiaries, the family trustee may be put in the position of having to make decisions that favor one beneficiary over another, thus fostering hard feelings between beneficiaries. For all of those reasons, it often is desirable to name someone other than a family member as trustee.

The trustee should be someone who has the necessary integrity, knowledge, skill, temperament, and independence to manage the trust assets in accordance with your directions as set forth in the trust agreement. Selection of a trustee who lacks those attributes can thwart your purposes and leave the beneficiaries without adequate means to meet their needs. One settlor named his business associate as the trustee of a testamentary trust for his wife. Included among the assets of the trust was the settlor's stock in a corporation he owned with the trustee. The trustee took advantage of his position as trustee and caused the corporation to redeem the stock owned by the trust, thus depriving the settlor's family of any interest in the corporation. The trustee's action led to costly litigation and a settlement that was very unfavorable to the settlor's family. If the settlor had recognized the inherent conflict of interest he created by naming his associate as trustee, perhaps his family's interest in the business he had worked so hard to develop could have been preserved.

In addition to being impartial and trustworthy, a trustee must also be competent. The management of a trust is a complex endeavor that requires knowledge and experience in the fields of law, finance, accounting, and economics. An individual trustee often must rely on others to compensate for his lack of expertise in one or more of those disciplines. That diffusion of responsibility may result in added expense, inefficient management, and increased risk of loss. The risk of those adverse outcomes can be mitigated if you choose an individual with sufficient legal and financial savvy to be able to choose, oversee, and hold accountable the experts on whom he must rely. Individuals whose training and expertise may qualify them to serve as trustees include estate planning attorneys, financial planners, accountants, and investment managers.

A viable and often preferable alternative to an individual trustee is a corporate trustee. A corporate trustee is a bank or trust company licensed to engage in the business of administering trusts. A corporate trustee's principal advantage over an individual trustee is that it combines in one institution expertise in all aspects of trust management. A corporate trustee generally charges a fee based on a descending percentage of the value of the trust principal. The percentage actually charged often is negotiable, especially in the case of a trust of significant value. Taking into account the expenses that would otherwise have to be paid separately to investment managers, attorneys, and accountants, the fee a corporate trustee charges generally is not unreasonable. An added advantage of naming a corporate trustee is continuity. A corporation does not have a mid-life crisis, become senile, or die. If the trust officer responsible for your account leaves, another immediately takes his or her place; and well-established procedures usually ensure a smooth transition. Yet another advantage of a corporate trustee is that a regulated financial institution is required to maintain certain levels of capitalization and liability insurance. That means that if it is negligent in managing your trust, you are more likely to be able to recover your loss than you would be had you selected an individual trustee.

Weighed against the advantages of using a corporate trustee is the disadvantage of having to deal with an impersonal institution. A corporate trustee may be hampered in its ability to respond to a beneficiary's needs by burdensome decision-making procedures, sometimes involving committees that have no direct knowledge of the beneficiary's personal and financial circumstances. The beneficiary may be uncomfortable counseling with a trust officer with whom he does not have a personal relationship. And the trustee's investment policy may prevent the configuration of the trust's investment portfolio to meet the unique objectives of the trust. Finally, a corporate trustee is not well suited to the management of business and other assets that require continuous management and oversight. To protect against those eventualities and to provide leverage in persuading an inattentive trustee to respond to the beneficiary's needs, the beneficiary or other family member should be given the power to remove the trustee and appoint a successor. With that protection, a corporate trustee may be a suitable choice in appropriate circumstances despite its disadvantages.

INFLUENCING THE TRUSTEE'S DECISIONS

The trustee has the legal title to the property and has the power to deal with it as an owner. However, all of the trustee's actions are subject to the express directions contained in the trust agreement. Accordingly, if you use a trust as the vehicle for making transfers to your spouse or children, you must clearly and unambiguously state the purposes of the trust and the standards and guidelines that are to govern the trustee in furthering those purposes. As an extreme case, consider one notorious trust agreement that directed the trustee to distribute $250,000 to the settlor's child "upon marrying." This child took advantage of the precise wording and married multiple times to collect his "bounty" each time. The settlor easily could have prevented that misuse of the trust by being more precise in his direction to the trustee.

Discretionary Trust with Advisory Standards

The greatest degree of flexibility is achieved if the trustee has discretionary authority to make distributions to the beneficiaries. To guide the trustee in the exercise of that authority, the trust agreement should contain *advisory* (also called *precatory*) *standards* specifying the circumstances and conditions under which distributions should be made to, or withheld from, the beneficiaries. The inclusion of advisory standards gives the trustee a framework for exercising discretionary power without relinquishing the latitude to accommodate the beneficiary's changing needs and circumstances. Following are a few examples of advisory guidelines that are commonly included in discretionary trusts established for the benefit of the settlor's children. For a more comprehensive set of examples, see the specimen trust agreement in appendix B.

In determining whether to make discretionary distributions to a beneficiary of a trust governed by this agreement, the trustee should observe, but shall not be constrained or compelled by, the following guidelines:

- Generally, the trustee should not make distributions to a beneficiary if in the trustee's judgment such distribution would negatively affect the beneficiary's motivation to become productive and self-reliant
- Generally, the trustee should make distributions in support of a beneficiary who is (a) so physically or mentally disabled as to be unable to provide for his or her own support, (b) pursuing a career that is socially productive but not substantially remunerative, or (c) caring for one or more family members, including minor children or aging parents
- The trustee may make distributions to pay for any medical procedure, test, or treatment, including, without limitation, surgery, organ transplants, psychiatric care, physical therapy, hospitalization, convalescent care, and home care, as the trustee considers appropriate to preserve and promote the beneficiary's physical, mental, and emotional well-being
- The trustee may make distributions to enable a beneficiary to pursue technical, vocational, undergraduate, or graduate education at or under the auspices of any accredited institution, public or private
- If a beneficiary does not have sufficient financial resources to purchase a home of adequate size to accommodate his or her family, the trustee may distribute or loan trust income and principal to the beneficiary to partially or wholly fund such a purchase

Incentive Trusts

In addition to or in lieu of giving the trustee discretion with respect to distributions to the beneficiaries, it may be advisable to limit the trustee's authority to make distributions in certain circumstances or require the trustee to make distributions upon the occurrence of specified events. The purpose served by such limitations and requirements is to encourage the beneficiary to act in harmony with the settlor's values and expectations. For example, the trust might direct the trustee to make specified distributions to the beneficiary when he or she: (1) graduates from college, (2) earns a post-graduate degree, (3) achieves prescribed financial milestones, (4) overcomes drug or alcohol dependency, or (5) performs volunteer community service. Following are examples of provisions imposing such limitations and requirements on the beneficial interest of the settlor's child:

- "While my child is under the age of eighteen, the trustee shall distribute the net income and principal of the trust estate to or for the benefit of my child, at such times and in such amounts and shares as the trustee determines to be necessary to provide for my child's health, support, education, and maintenance."
- "After my child attains age eighteen, the trustee shall distribute the income and principal of the trust estate to my child on the following terms and conditions:
    - If my child is a full-time student at an accredited college, university, vocational school, or similar institution and is maintaining a grade point average of _____ or better on a scale on which 4.0 is an A grade, the trustee shall pay my child's reasonable educational expenses, including tuition, books, fees, supplies, travel, and living expenses (*educational costs*). Distributions in payment of educational costs for undergraduate education shall not extend beyond _____ years, and distributions in payment of educational costs for post-graduate education shall not extend beyond _____ years.
    - If my child is employed in a remunerative occupation or career to which the child devotes at least _____ hours of work per week, the trustee shall pay to my child in each calendar year an amount equal to my child's gross income from employment during such calendar year. For purposes of the foregoing, the term *gross income* includes both earnings from employment and earnings from self-employment, but does not include passive income, such as interest, dividends, or rent, if my child received the capital producing such passive income as a gift or inheritance.
- "When my child reaches the age of _____, the trustee shall distribute to my child one-third of all property then comprising the trust. When my child reaches the age of _____, the trustee shall distribute to my child one-half of all property then comprising the trust. When my child reaches the age of _____, the trustee shall distribute to my child all of the property then comprising the trust."

Some trust provisions that are calculated to constrain or induce certain types of behavior are contrary to public policy and therefore unenforceable. Examples of restrictions and conditions that courts have refused to enforce include those intended to (1) restrain the beneficiary's right to marry, (2) induce the beneficiary to divorce his or her spouse, (3) limit the beneficiary's freedom of religion, and (4) foster family or marital discord. In declining to enforce such restrictions and conditions, the courts have determined that society's interest in preserving fundamental freedoms and institutions is more important than a person's right to dispose of wealth as he or she sees fit.

Other restrictions or inducements, although legally enforceable, might do more harm than good. A case in point is Jay's ill-considered use of an incentive trust to induce his daughter Diane to abandon her career as an accountant to become a full-time homemaker. Jay was proud of Diane's professional success, but worried that her reliance on nannies would have a detrimental effect on her children's development. Motivated by that concern and with little thought of what was in Diane's best interest, he left her share of his estate in trust and directed the trustee to make no distributions to her while she remained in practice but to "compensate her generously" for her services as a full-time homemaker. Not surprisingly, Diane perceived the arrangement as a shameless and unjustified attempt by Jay to impose his will contrary to her best interests. Nevertheless, under pressure from her husband and other members of her family, she opted for the financial incentive and became a homemaker. Now, more than five years later, she regrets her decision to abandon her satisfying professional career and deeply resents her father and husband for depriving her of any meaningful choice in the matter. She also is convinced that her lack of enthusiasm for her role as a full-time mother has been detrimental to her relationship with her children. Clearly, Jay should have paid heed to Kahlil Gibran's timeless observation: "Your children are not your children. They are the sons and daughters of Life's longing for itself. You may house their bodies but not their souls, for their souls dwell in the house of tomorrow, which you cannot visit, not even in your dreams."[5]

CHAPTER TWELVE

Advanced Strategies for Saving Taxes and Enhancing Liquidity

Due to recent and anticipated increases in the exemptions, not to mention the possibility of repeal, an increasing number of people can look forward to the day when keeping the taxman at bay is no longer a primary planning concern. Meanwhile, if you are among those who have managed to accumulate wealth in excess of the currently available exemptions, there are proven strategies that can be employed to reduce or even eliminate the transfer tax burden. This chapter briefly describes the most popular of those strategies. Whether any of the enumerated strategies is suitable for inclusion in your personal estate plan depends on your unique circumstances and objectives. Accordingly, you should not attempt to implement any of them without the assistance of a trained estate planning professional.

USE OF A SHELTER TRUST TO AVOID WASTING UNIFIED CREDIT

Gifts you make under the terms of your will or revocable living trust to your spouse are fully deductible for federal estate tax purposes. However, if you leave your entire estate to your spouse, only your spouse's unified credit will be available to shelter the property passing to your descendants from federal estate tax. The waste of your unified credit may increase substantially the amount of estate tax payable upon your spouse's subsequent death. To illustrate, assume that the amount effectively exempted by the unified credit is $1.5 million, that you and your spouse each have an estate equal to that amount, and that your deaths occur in 2004 and 2005, respectively. If you were to leave your entire estate outright to your spouse, your estate would qualify for a marital deduction equal to the value of your estate and would pay no estate tax. However, upon your spouse's death the next year, his unified credit would shelter only half of the value of his estate, exposing the other half to needless estate tax of approximately $700,000. To avoid that result, you should consider leaving the amount effectively exempted by your unified credit to a *shelter trust*.

The amount you leave to a shelter trust will not qualify for the marital deduction and, therefore, will fully utilize your unified credit. Moreover, the property remaining in the shelter trust at the time of your spouse's death will not be included in his or her estate for federal estate tax purposes. The effect will be to make both unified credits available to shelter the amounts passing to your descendants upon the death of the survivor of you and your spouse. In the foregoing example, the use of both credits would reduce the estate tax payable on your spouse's death to zero.

Without jeopardizing the tax benefits associated with the use of a shelter trust, the surviving spouse can be given the substantial equivalent of outright ownership of the trust property. Among the rights and powers the spouse can have without causing the trust property to be included in his or her gross estate are the following:

- The spouse may have the right to withdraw principal to the extent necessary to provide for his health, support, education, and maintenance
- The spouse may have the right to withdraw from the trust each year the greater of $5,000 or 5 percent of the value of the trust property
- The spouse may have an unlimited right to appoint trust income and principal to any person other than himself, his creditors, his estate, or the creditors of his estate
- A person other than the spouse may have an unlimited right to distribute trust income and principal to the spouse and others
- The spouse may have the right as trustee or otherwise to direct the investments of the trust

DEFERRAL OF ESTATE TAX

If the value of your estate exceeds the amount allocated to the shelter trust, the excess will be subject to tax unless it passes to your spouse and therefore qualifies for the marital deduction. Assets qualifying for the marital deduction necessarily will be included in your spouse's estate, and may be subject to tax at a higher rate. Nevertheless, for the following reasons, it generally is advisable to take advantage of the marital deduction to defer any estate tax until the death of the surviving spouse:

- Deferral maximizes assets during the life of the surviving spouse, giving him or her greater financial security and the opportunity for increased spending and giving
- Deferral avoids tax-related liquidity problems at the death of the first spouse
- Deferral provides the opportunity for a step-up in basis upon the death of the surviving spouse
- Deferral protects the combined estates against the possibility that the estate tax will be reduced or even repealed between the death of the first spouse and that of the surviving spouse

If you are disinclined to make substantial gifts to your spouse out of fear that he or she might mismanage the assets or divert them to persons outside the family, you should consider the alternative of making the gifts in trust. Generally, a gift in trust does not qualify for the marital deduction. However, an exception applies with respect to two types of trusts: (1) a general power of appointment (GPA) trust, and (2) a qualified terminable interest property (QTIP) trust. In the case of either type of trust, the trustee must be required to distribute all of the income to your spouse. The significant difference between the two trusts pertains to the spouse's power to direct the disposition of the trust assets upon his or her subsequent death. In the case of a general power of appointment trust, the spouse must be given the power to appoint the trust assets to his or her estate. Of course, the spouse's power to appoint to his or her estate is equivalent to the power to give the property to anyone of the spouse's choosing. With a qualified terminable interest property trust, on the other hand, the assets remaining in the trust upon your spouse's death pass as provided in the trust agreement. Thus, if you are concerned that your spouse might divert the assets to someone outside the family, a qualified terminable interest property trust is the vehicle of choice.

STATE-SPONSORED COLLEGE SAVINGS PLAN

You may make tax-free gifts to your children, grandchildren, and other beneficiaries through the medium of a *state-sponsored college savings plan* (CSP). Congress authorized states to adopt college savings plans in 1996, as a tax-advantaged means of assisting families in meeting the rising costs of higher education. Recent changes in the law governing the tax incidents of college savings plans have enhanced their appeal as vehicles for making annual exclusion gifts.

To make a gift through a college savings plan, you deposit cash to an account established in your name for the benefit of a named beneficiary. You retain the right to specify the amount and the timing of any distribution from the account and need not inform the beneficiary of the account's existence. You also retain the right to direct the investment of the account and can choose among a variety of mutual funds managed by professional investment managers. Thus, ongoing maintenance is minimal and the account benefits from the investment manager's resources and economies of scale. The maximum cumulative deposit you can make to the account is limited, but in some states it can exceed $250,000.

Your contribution to a college savings plan qualifies for the annual exclusion for federal gift tax purposes. Moreover, an amount up to five times the annual exclusion may be prorated against the annual exclusions available over five years. Thus, in the current year you can deposit up to $55,000 to the account and prorate the gift over the next four years for purposes of the annual gift tax exclusion. Of course, the annual exclusions you telescope into the current year cannot be used again in the years to which they relate. Except for annual exclusion amounts prorated to periods beginning after your death, the account will not be included in your estate for federal estate tax purposes.

Investment income and gain accruing to the account are exempt from federal and state income tax. Moreover, distributions from the account are not taxable to your child provided they are used for his or her tuition, fees, books, room, and board. The earnings portion of distributions that are not used for qualified expenses is taxable to your child, but at the child's marginal rate, which likely will be lower than yours. It will also attract a penalty, unless the distribution: (1) is made following your child's death or incapacity; or (2) corresponds in amount to any tax-free scholarship or other educational benefits awarded to your child. However, a nonqualifying distribution will not be subject to tax or a penalty if it is rolled over within sixty days to a college savings plan account for another member of your family.

The college savings plans offered by the various states differ in important respects, including the aggregate amount that an individual can contribute, the options available for investment, the amount on deposit in the account, the extent, if any, to which the contribution is deductible for state income tax purposes, and whether withdrawals from the account are subject to state income tax. If the college savings plan sponsored by your home state does not compare favorably to that of another state, you are free to choose the latter over the former. However, before opting for an out-of-state plan, you should make sure your own state does not tax the earnings and withdrawals merely because the college savings plan is sponsored by another state. Some states discriminate against out-of-state college savings plans in that way in order to enhance the attractiveness of their own plans. Following are considerations that may be relevant for purposes of evaluating and comparing the college savings plans offered by the various states:

- The limitation on aggregate contributions
- The amount of the penalty for nonqualifying withdrawals
- The start-up and recurring management fees
- The reputation, stability, and past performance of the investment manager
- The transferability of the account
- Any residence or age restrictions
- Any time limit within which the funds must be withdrawn
- The imposition of state income tax

IRREVOCABLE LIFE INSURANCE TRUST

Contrary to popular belief, the proceeds of an insurance policy owned by the insured are subject to tax in the insured's estate even though they are paid directly to the designated beneficiary. Thus, if you purchase an insurance policy on your life and name your child as the beneficiary, the proceeds will be paid directly to your child but will be taxable as if they were part of your estate. A simple way to avoid that result would be for you to transfer the policy to your child during your life. If you live for at least three years following the transfer, the policy will not be taxable in your estate. However, because the proceeds will be paid directly to your child, they will not be available to meet the liquidity needs of your estate or to provide for the support of your spouse or other beneficiaries. Fortunately, you can exclude the proceeds from the reach of the estate tax and still make them available to satisfy liquidity and support needs through the use of an *irrevocable life insurance trust* (ILIT).

To create an irrevocable life insurance trust, the insured irrevocably transfers the policy to a trustee other than himself or herself. If the insured then lives for at least three more years, the proceeds will not be taxable in this estate. Of course, the insured's assignment of the policy to the irrevocable life insurance trust and the subsequent payment of premiums with respect to the policy are considered gifts for gift tax purposes. However, for that purpose, the value of the policy is not its face amount, but an amount roughly equal to its cash surrender value, plus any portion of the last premium that pertains to the period following the transfer.

A gift in trust generally is regarded as a gift of a *future interest* in property and, therefore, does not qualify for the annual gift tax exclusion. However, if the beneficiaries are given an immediate right to withdraw additions to the trust, the gift will be treated as if it were made directly to the beneficiaries and, therefore, will qualify for the annual exclusion. To be effective for that purpose, a beneficiary must be given notice of his withdrawal right. A right of which the holder is unaware is no right at all.

There is always the risk that a beneficiary might exercise his withdrawal right. However, if the beneficiary is advised of the purposes of the trust, he or she likely will be reluctant to do anything that would frustrate those purposes. To minimize the risk that a beneficiary might initially decide to refrain from exercising the withdrawal right and subsequently change his or her mind, the period during which the right may be exercised should be limited to the thirty-day period after the beneficiary is given notice of the right's existence.

The trustee of an irrevocable life insurance trust makes the proceeds available to meet the liquidity needs of the insured's estate by either making loans to, or purchasing assets from, the insured's estate. Provided the terms of those transactions are comparable to those of similar transactions between unrelated parties, the trustee's dealings with the insured's estate will not cause the proceeds to be subject to estate tax.

Typically, the beneficiaries of an irrevocable life insurance trust include the insured's spouse and children. The trustee distributes to the spouse such amounts of income and principal as may be necessary for his or her comfortable support. If the trustee determines that the insured's spouse is otherwise adequately provided for, it may distribute the income and principal to the insured's children or other beneficiaries. Upon the spouse's death, the trustee distributes the remaining trust assets to the children free of estate tax in the spouse's estate.

CHARITABLE REMAINDER TRUST

If you are inclined to make substantial charitable contributions, but are reluctant to do so out of concern for your financial security, a *charitable remainder trust* (CRT) may be the answer. A charitable remainder trust is an irrevocable trust to which you transfer assets in exchange for the right to receive periodic payments for your life or for a fixed period of no more than twenty years. The payment can be in the form of (1) a specified dollar amount, (2) a fixed percentage of the value of the trust estate determined annually (a *unitrust amount*), or (3) the lesser of a unitrust amount or the trust's net income. Upon your death or the expiration of the specified term, the property remaining in the trust is distributed to a designated charitable organization.

The tax benefits associated with a charitable remainder trust enhance its appeal as a vehicle for making charitable contributions. Following is a summary of those benefits:

- You will be entitled to an income tax deduction for the present value of the charitable organization's right to receive the trust property upon the expiration of your retained interest.
- Because a charitable remainder trust is tax exempt, the trustee can sell any appreciated property you may contribute to it without the immediate imposition of income tax. It is only as and when the sale proceeds are distributed to you as a component of your periodic payment that the gain will be subject to income tax.
- Provided the periodic payment can be made only to you or your spouse, no gift or estate tax will be imposed on the assets of the trust.
- If the payment to which you are entitled is expressed in terms of the lesser of a unitrust amount or the trust's net income,

the trustee can configure the trust's investment portfolio so as to defer the receipt of income until the optimum time for making distributions to you and your spouse. The tax-free enhancement of the trust's assets likely will result in a larger base on which your future payments will be computed. The charitable remainder trust can thus serve as a supplemental source of retirement income for you and your spouse.

CHARITABLE LEAD TRUST

If you are already making substantial charitable gifts on an annual basis, you should consider the potential transfer-tax benefits of a *charitable lead trust* (CLT). A charitable lead trust is an irrevocable trust that accommodates the division of property into a *lead interest* and a *remainder interest*. The lead interest goes to a charitable organization and the remainder interest typically goes to the settlor's descendants (or a trust for their benefit). The lead interest confers on the charitable organization the right to receive an annual payment expressed as either a specific dollar amount or a fixed percentage of the value of the trust's assets determined annually. The remainder interest embodies the right to receive whatever is left in the trust upon the expiration of the lead interest.

The transfer-tax benefit associated with the use of a charitable lead trust is based on the deductibility of the present value of the lead interest for gift and estate tax purposes. The longer the duration of the lead interest the more of the value of the trust property it attracts and the larger the deduction. Indeed, with the right mix of duration and payment rate, the entire value of the property transferred to a charitable lead annuity trust will be deductible for gift and estate tax purposes. If the trust generates income and appreciation in excess of the discount rate used in valuing the lead and remainder interests, it will accumulate value that will pass to the settlor's descendants free of gift or estate tax.

QUALIFIED PERSONAL RESIDENCE TRUST

A *qualified personal residence trust* (QPRT) is an irrevocable trust to which you transfer a primary or secondary residence. You retain the exclusive and unlimited right to use and occupy the residence for a specified period of years. While your right of occupancy continues, you are responsible for paying all expenses relating to the residence. Upon the expiration of your right of occupancy, the residence passes to your children or other designated beneficiaries. However, you can retain the right to lease the residence from the beneficiaries provided that the terms of the lease are comparable to those of a similar lease between unrelated parties. If you die prior to the expiration of your right of occupancy, the trust terminates and the residence is disposed of as you direct in your will.

The use of a qualified personal residence trust can substantially reduce the tax cost of transferring your residence to your children. The transfer is subject to gift tax and will consume your gift and estate tax exemption, but only to the extent of the present value of your children's right to receive the residence upon expiration of your right of occupancy. Obviously, that value will be less than the value of the residence itself. Assume, for example, that you are fifty-five years old, your residence is worth $500,000, your right of occupancy continues for twenty years, and the applicable discount rate is 5 percent. Based on those assumptions, your taxable gift would be approximately $127,000.

If you survive until the expiration of your right of occupancy, the full value of the residence, including any appreciation accruing after the date the qualified personal residence trust was established, will be excluded from your gross estate for federal estate tax purposes. If during the term of the trust the residence increases in value at a modest annual rate of 3 percent, its value at the end of the term will be about $900,000. That is the amount you will have effectively removed from your estate by making a present taxable gift of about $127,000.

FAMILY LIMITED COMPANY

A *family limited company* (FLC) is a flexible and sophisticated vehicle for managing, protecting, and transferring family wealth. It commonly is organized as either a limited partnership or a limited liability company. These two organizational forms have many features in common, and whether one is better than the other depends largely on the nuances of state law.

A family limited company is organized by filing a *certificate* or *articles of organization* with the appropriate state depository. The family limited company's management and financial affairs are governed by a written agreement to which all participants are parties. The participants receive their ownership interests in the family limited company in exchange for marketable securities, real estate, or other investment or business assets. That exchange alters the essential nature of what the participants own and in large part accounts for the tax and nontax advantages associated with the use of a family limited company as an estate planning tool.

Assume, for example, that you and your spouse organize a family limited company and capitalize it with cash and marketable securities having an aggregate value of $1 million. You and your spouse are elected as the family limited company's initial managers. As the family limited company's managing agents, you are bound under both state law and the family limited company's governing documents to act prudently and always in the family limited company's best interests. You are also required to distribute or accumulate the family limited company's income based on reasonably definite standards. Under applicable law and the family limited company's governing documents, a member may not withdraw or transfer his membership interest without the consent of the managers and all other members.

Following the family limited company's formation and capitalization, you and your spouse give a 10 percent interest in the family limited company to each of your five adult children. You have thus removed assets worth $500,000 from your and your spouse's estates. And yet, because the gifts were of minority interests in the family limited company, instead of fractional interests in the underlying investment portfolio, the aggregate value for gift tax purpose is substantially less than $500,000—say, $300,000. The justification for the discount is that the value for transfer-tax purposes is based on what a rational purchaser would pay for the transferred property. Obviously, a rational purchaser would not pay $100,000 for a 10 percent interest in the family limited company without some assurance that he could access his share of the underlying assets.

The change in the nature and value of the assets you and your spouse transfer to the family limited company also serves to insulate those assets from the claims of the participants' creditors. Instead of being able to attach the family limited company's assets directly, a participant's creditor must be content with a *charging order* against the participant's interest in the family limited company. A charging order confers on the creditor the right to the participant's distributions from the family limited company, but only *if and when made*. Obviously, a creditor who finds itself in such a position likely will be amenable to a reasonable settlement.

In recent years, due largely to its extraordinary flexibility in accommodating the often disparate objectives and interests of various family members, the family limited company has become increasingly popular as the vehicle of choice for family tax and succession planning. Enticed by that flexibility, aggressive advisors have devised strategies involving the use of family limited companies intended to produce tax consequences that the Internal Revenue Service (IRS) regards as abusive. In an effort to curb such abuses, the IRS has aggressively attacked family limited companies that it regards as mere alter egos of their founders. And while the few government victories in cases involving family limited companies bespeaks a judicial hesitance to assume responsibility for distinguishing between the abusive and nonabusive uses of a family limited company, it behooves anyone who organizes a family limited company for estate planning purposes to carefully observe all of the formalities, duties, and constraints required of one charged with responsibility for management of another's property and affairs.

DESIGNATING THE BENEFICIARIES OF IRA AND RETIREMENT PLAN PROCEEDS

Generally, the income tax basis of property included in your estate will be equal to the property's fair market value on the date of your death. That means, of course, that any unrealized gain inherent in the property at the time of your death will never be subject to federal income tax. Unfortunately, certain assets, including the balance in your individual retirement account (IRA) and your interest in a qualified retirement plan, do not qualify for that step-up in basis. Such assets thus may be subjected not only to estate tax but also to income tax. The combination of those two exactions can be so onerous as to leave your beneficiaries with little more than dashed hopes.

One of the only ways you can ameliorate the double-tax whammy on the proceeds from IRAs and qualified retirement plans is by deferring the taxes as long as possible. If you name your spouse as your beneficiary, you can postpone the payment of the estate tax until the survivor's death. By then perhaps the estate tax will have been repealed. But if not, the IRS will seek its due.

Fortunately, you have greater latitude in deferring the day of reckoning with respect to the income tax. The key to optimizing the income tax deferral opportunities is to name primary and successive contingent beneficiaries. To illustrate, assume that you name your spouse as your primary beneficiary. If your spouse survives you, he or she can roll the proceeds over into his or her own IRA and postpone the imposition of any income tax until he or she is required to commence withdrawals during the year after attaining age seventy and a half. If your spouse fails to survive you, then, unless you have named a contingent beneficiary, the proceeds will have to be fully distributed within five years after your death. If, however, you have named a contingent beneficiary—say, a child—then the proceeds can be paid out over your child's life expectancy. If your child is forty-five years old at the time of your death, the maximum distribution period will be about thirty-eight years, which is plenty of time to accumulate sufficient additional wealth on a tax-deferred basis to take some of the sting out of the IRS's second bite out of the apple. But what if your child dies before the end of his or her life expectancy? If you have planned properly, you will have named yet a second contingent beneficiary, who can then continue to receive the proceeds over the balance of your child's life expectancy.

Another technique for deferring the income tax on IRA and retirement plan proceeds is to name a charitable remainder trust as the beneficiary. Not only will that accommodate the deferral of the income tax, it will also give rise to an estate tax deduction equal to the value of the charity's right to receive the proceeds upon expiration of the lead beneficiary's payment right.

CHAPTER THIRTEEN

The Philanthropic Legacy

Despite misgivings about the negative effects of unearned wealth and concerns over burdensome transfer taxes, most people still are inclined to leave their estates to or in trust for their descendants. It is not surprising, then, that few are willing to divert resources away from their descendents to charitable causes. Indeed, an examination of federal estate tax returns filed in 2001 revealed that less than 18 percent of decedents with estates in excess of $600,000 made charitable bequests.[1]

If you are like most parents who prefer their descendents over charity as the recipients of their wealth, you likely view financial security in one-dimensional terms. You mistakenly believe that it is the wealth itself, rather than the power it confers, that is the source of financial security. Once you understand that financial security largely derives from the ability to *control* wealth, as well as to *consume* it, you will envision the *philanthropic legacy*—a legacy that at once benefits your children as well as your favorite charitable causes.

THE FEATURES OF A PHILANTHROPIC LEGACY

The philanthropic legacy is a lifetime or testamentary gift to a charitable organization controlled by members of the donor's family. The organization may take the form of a tax-exempt nonprofit corporation or a trust. The gift consists of the portion of the donor's wealth that exceeds the amount necessary to maintain the members of his or her family in their desired standard of living. As wealth that likely never will be accessed for consumption, it can be devoted to charitable causes without diminishing the family's standard of living. And yet the family's retention of control over its management and disposition, through their control of the charitable organization, enables them to enjoy indefinitely the intangible benefits associated with its ownership, including status in the community, political and social influence, and, most importantly, the satisfaction that comes from knowing that redundant family wealth is being used to virtuous ends.

The portion of the donor's estate that is the subject of a philanthropic legacy passes to the charitable donee undiminished by income or transfer taxes. To the extent of the taxes that otherwise would have been imposed, the philanthropic legacy effects a diversion of capital from the government to social causes of the donor's choosing. Assume, for example, that you have a portfolio of stocks and bonds worth $1 million that you know will never be needed to maintain your family's standard of living. If you were to retain the portfolio, its income and gain would continue to be subject to federal and state income tax and, upon your death, its value would be substantially diminished by the estate tax. If instead of retaining the portfolio you were to transfer it to a charitable organization controlled by you and your children, you would be entitled to immediate income and gift tax deductions, the portfolio's future income and gain would largely be exempt from income tax, the portfolio would attract no estate tax upon your death, and you and your family would still have management control over the portfolio and the right to apply its earnings in furtherance of your favorite charitable causes. Significantly, the amount subject to your control would include the amount that otherwise would have been paid in income and estate taxes. Thus, by placing the portfolio out of the taxman's reach, you would enhance the intangible element of your family's wealth in exchange for the relinquishment of the power to consume an asset that your family otherwise would not have consumed.

Benefits to Participants

Participation in managing and directing the disposition of a philanthropic legacy will provide the members of your family with valuable insights and experience regarding the power of wealth as an instrument for good. Specifically:

- They will derive the intangible benefits associated with the family's control of the fund's endowment and distributions
- They will experience firsthand the power of private philanthropy as an instrument for addressing challenging social problems
- Through their participation in the grant-making process, they will learn the importance of *due diligence, analysis, prioritization,* and *accountability*
- Through their involvement in the investment of the endowment, they will learn the principles of prudent money management, including the importance of diversification and the relationship between risk and reward
- They will learn to measure success with reference to the good they do rather than the amount of money they accumulate
- They will be more likely to embrace your philanthropic vision and other positive values as they unselfishly serve the causes to which the work of the foundation is devoted
- They will have the opportunity to make common cause with other members of the family in a satisfying and meaningful endeavor that is devoid of any personal financial interests and aspirations

The last-mentioned benefit deserves special note. As children attain adulthood, they move to other locations and begin families of their own. Over time it becomes increasingly difficult to persuade children to travel long distances to attend family gatherings when the only purpose of those gatherings is social. On the other hand, if the children were called upon to assist in the selection of grantees of the family's philanthropic fund, they likely would be more willing to participate in reunions for that purpose. For example, one family's members travel from five different states and one foreign country to attend the quarterly grant meetings of the family's charitable foundation. Not only does the foundation's business provide them with an expense-paid trip home, it also gives them the opportunity to associate with their parents and siblings in an endeavor that is purely altruistic. The goodwill that is engendered on those occasions strengthens the bond between the children and makes it much less likely that they will fight over matters pertaining to the use and allocation of family wealth.

THE CHARITABLE VEHICLE

The vehicle best suited to serve the purposes of the philanthropic legacy is a *family foundation*. A family foundation is a family-controlled trust or nonprofit corporation that is exempt from federal and state income taxes. The foundation's charitable purpose is to make grants to publicly supported organizations that address the needs of the community that are of most concern to its board of trustees.

Because of its potential for abuse, a family foundation is subject to strict and extensive reporting requirements. It also is subject to rigid constraints on its ability to divert its assets to the use of private individuals, including the founder and the members of his family. Accordingly, it is a suitable vehicle only for those who are committed to its charitable purposes and are willing to assume additional administrative burdens in order to give their families the opportunity to experience the many benefits associated with service as a steward over resources dedicated to the betterment of the community.

If the capital that will be the subject of your philanthropic legacy is not of sufficient magnitude to warrant the use of a family foundation, a *donor-advised fund* may be a suitable alternative. To establish a donor-advised fund, the donor makes a gift to a public charitable organization, such as United Way or your local community foundation, and earmarks it for administration as a separate fund under a name of his choosing— for example, "The Rodney J. Generous Foundation." As the fund's owner, the sponsoring charitable organization is legally responsible for investing it and applying its earnings to appropriate charitable ends. However, it will almost always defer to the "advice" of the donor and his family with respect to those matters. Thus, the donor and his family are able to enjoy many of the benefits of a family foundation without the expense and hassle of operating their own charitable organization.

PART

Facing Dangers and Seeking Fairness

CHAPTER FOURTEEN

Divorce and Financial Disharmony

Despite its archaic nature, local law will govern the financial aspects of a divorce unless the couple enters into a prenuptial or postnuptial agreement that reflects their shared values and unique family circumstances. A well-drafted and comprehensive agreement can promote family harmony, avoid unnecessary litigation expenses, effectuate an equitable division of marital assets, and assure a comfortable lifestyle for the children and future generations. A specimen prenuptial agreement is included as appendix E.

Even though marriages start with hope and optimism, almost half do not survive.[1] Sadly, in today's society, when a marriage fails, money and possessions all too often become the symbolic payment for emotional loss and failed dreams.

In the absence of an enforceable prenuptial or postnuptial agreement, applicable local law governs the division of property upon divorce. Laws vary widely, ranging from jurisdictions with community property laws, where assets will be divided equally, to those with equitable property laws, which means a judge will decide what is a fair and equitable settlement. In a community property jurisdiction, assets acquired during the marriage generally are divided equally. By contrast, in an equitable division jurisdiction, a judge or other official will take into account many factors, including the manner in which money was shared in the marriage, the number of years of marriage, and the earning potential of each spouse.

If the division of marital property cannot be settled amicably, a sizeable portion of the family savings may be consumed in paying attorney fees and other costs associated with legal actions. The longer such litigation lasts, the greater the depletion of the family assets. When there is substantial family wealth, property division can be complicated. The involvement of attorneys for the parties and others with a financial stake in the outcome can make it unnecessarily complicated and time-consuming. Additionally, in the divorce arena, one spouse can impose the burden of his or her legal fees on the wealthier spouse, which may cause an exponential increase in acrimony.

COLLABORATIVE FAMILY LAW/MEDIATION

Collaborative Family Law, a new model, is being gradually introduced to curtail these high costs and allow parents to reach joint resolutions, while using their respective attorneys as facilitators rather than combatants. All participants agree not to litigate the case. The attorneys work together to present viable settlement options based on the expressed needs of the clients. Mediation is another noncombative settlement option in divorce. Some jurisdictions mandate or allow for mediation or other methods of dispute resolution, including mediation with resort to binding arbitration, parent coordination, special mastering, and special advocacy.

Divorce is traumatic enough without substantial family assets being unnecessarily consumed in the process. As unromantic as it may sound, it is wise to contemplate the possibility of divorce and to gain an understanding of the laws governing the division of property before heading into a marriage. Forethought and planning with respect to your estate plan is advised before entering into a subsequent marriage.

WEALTH INEQUITY

Regardless of the wealth in a family, divorce can create profoundly different lifestyles and standards of living. This can be confusing to young children who lived with wealth. When divorce proceedings are initiated, one spouse moves out of the family home often to more modest accommodations, pending final settlement of the couple's financial affairs. This may take years in some instances, during which time there is a pronounced difference in the two homes between which the children move.

Whereas children are likely to be the prime focus of intense divorce battles, money takes a close second. Just because one spouse earned, won, or inherited the wealth, that spouse cannot assume he or she will leave the marriage preserving that wealth. Even in states that exclude "separate property" from the mix of assets subject to division, the gain in value of this separate property is not excluded and remains subject to division. A judge will often consider the nature and value of each spouse's separate property in ruling on an equitable division of the marital property.

WHAT IS A SPOUSE'S CONTRIBUTION TO THE MARRIAGE?

Reese, the chief executive officer of a large publishing company, tried to settle his divorce with his wife, Elyse, by offering $10 million out of a $100 million marital estate. She protested, arguing that her contribution behind the scenes enabled his earning power. Elyse had been throughout most of the parties' marriage a mother and homemaker; but she had also actively participated with Reese in the entertainment of authors, literary agents, advertising executives, and other business associates in various social and business settings. While Reese's entertainment of his business associates might or might not have been successful without Elyse's participation, certainly the emotional nurturing of the children by a dedicated and loyal parent represented a priceless contribution to the family's well-being. Without this contribution, Reese may not have performed professionally at the level necessary either to amass the family's fortune or to develop his extraordinary skills as a corporate executive.

In settling the couple's property rights, the court acknowledged that Elyse had made a contribution to the accumulation of the marital property in her role as a "corporate wife." The court felt Elyse was adequately compensated at 20 percent, raising the settlement by another $10 million, but refused to recognize her value at the 50 percent level. Taking a case of this nature to court yields no preassured outcomes. In reality, cases such as this often go on and on through the appeals process. Couples are well advised to negotiate these issues through collaboration or mediation to arrive at a mutually beneficial and less hurtful or random outcome.

Reese accumulated his wealth during the marriage, making it part of the marital estate and subject to division upon divorce. Wealth a spouse earns or inherits following divorce, however, is not in the marital estate and therefore belongs exclusively to that spouse. Once divorced, it generally is not possible to later claim assets earned by one spouse other than through petitioning the court for an adjustment of maintenance or a reassessment of child support. If the children are grown and legally emancipated, then there is no redress at all with respect to child support; nor is there any if one spouse later marries into wealth. The children, of course, might then live with tremendous wealth inequity between their two homes.

While the assets at the time of divorce may be divided equitably, future earning capacity may be overlooked in the division. For example, a young professional may spend as much as eighty hours a week committed to a promising career; this would not be possible without the spouse who stayed home and cared for the children. Yet, the spouse's economic contribution may not be realized in the divorce settlement.

Christopher, a middle-aged father, was distressed when his former wife married a very wealthy man. Christopher, who had too strongly defined his identity as family provider, now seriously questioned his value to his children at all; he doubted he had anything to contribute to his children now that they lived with such riches. He eventually came to realize that his contribution to his children's lives mattered in a way beyond what money could buy. At first comparing himself to their stepfather, he felt woefully inadequate. Gradually, Christopher came to realize that his contribution to his older son's character and motivation was uniquely his, as he proudly watched his son's great athletic and academic strengths grow as his son matured. His younger son, however, struggled with self-esteem issues. Christopher took responsibility for this as well, unable to accept reassurances that self-esteem issues are attributable to many variables. Christopher, like many parents, initially measured his self-worth by his financial well-being; he undervalued the importance of his parenting and overvalued the importance of his money in his children's development.

One divorced mother was furious when her ex-husband purchased an expensive car for their daughter. She felt he was buying her love with his financial advantage. Furthermore, she had expected their daughter to learn the valuable lessons that come with responsibility for the ownership, maintenance, and operation of a car. But her expectation was frustrated when her husband, acting in direct opposition to her values, indulged their daughter in this manner. Eventually, with some professional intervention, the mother was able to put her anger aside and realize that she did not have to compete with her ex-husband on these terms. She could still cultivate a loving and trusting relationship with her daughter and, in the context of that relationship, model and impart the values she embraced.

Typically, the wealth inequities are between the ex-spouses, but occasionally this results in children emerging as wealthier than one or both of their parents. In one instance, many years after a divorce, one father could barely manage his bills, whereas the mother had the means to live in luxury if she wished. Like many wealthy parents, this mom had gifted funds to her children each year to alleviate the burden of estate taxes. One of her children, without her knowledge, was passing a sizeable share of the gifts to the father who had so much less. The child's motivation in sharing the gifts with his father seemed to stem partly from his magnanimous spirit and partly out of subtle pressure from his father to do so, appealing to his son's sense of fairness and equity. Once a parent makes an outright gift to a child, the parent no longer has control over the disposition of the property that is the subject of the gift. Creating a trust for her child would have been one way this mother could not only have protected against the above scenario but also could have allowed her child to save face and resist if his father asked for money. Only the trustee would be able to disperse the funds and then only in accordance with the purposes specified in the trust agreement.

In using a trust to control the disposition of property that is the subject of a gift, a divorced parent faces an inherent dilemma. The child may view the restrictions on access to the funds as inconsistent with the notion of a "gift" and become resentful of the parent's evident lack of confidence in the child's ability to manage his or her own financial affairs. In contrast, use of a trust takes the child out of divorce conflict and provides additional protection from the claims and influence of others, both within and outside the family. A discussion with an attorney with expertise in the trust area could help the parent resolve these competing values.

If the parent decides to use a trust, the parent should discuss with the child the intention and the values the parent hopes to impart by doing so. Such a discussion could strengthen that parent's relationship with the child and diminish the risk that the child would interpret the arrangement as reflecting a lack of confidence in that child's abilities and money maturity. Without a discussion, the child may never understand the rationale for the parent's choice of a trust over an outright gift. Of course, it is also possible that the child would see such a discussion as the parent's veiled attempt to manipulate and control the child's choices. At the very least, discussing the matter with the child would highlight the pros and cons of a trust arrangement, thus enabling the child to formulate his or her own judgment as to the merits of the arrangement. Many children, as they mature in financial matters, will come to an understanding of the complexity of sharing wealth and learn to appreciate rather than resent the protection a trust affords against creditors, divorce settlements, and outside pressures.

Divorce laws were formulated when the majority of families were nuclear and stable, and usually only the father worked and contributed income. Gradually these laws are shifting, but not as quickly as the nature of the family is changing. In fact, today's average family is the product of at least one marriage, one divorce, and one remarriage.[2] The children may be biological to one or both parents, adopted or in foster care.

If the couple enters into an agreement governing their financial affairs while their relationship is full of love, hope, and optimism and the probability of divorce is low, they are more likely to agree to terms that are fair and equitable. At the beginning of a relationship, each person is likely to think of his or her partner with generosity and thoughtfulness. Later, in the midst of a possible divorce, all thought of such feelings may well have vanished.

Realizing that no relationship is immune to deterioration, the prudent couple will have entered into an agreement defining their financial rights before getting married. The prenuptial agreement displaces the antiquated divorce and estate succession laws that would otherwise apply and thus enables the couple to control the financial consequences of separation, divorce, or death. (The nature and purposes of prenuptial agreements are more fully discussed in chapter 7.) If a couple failed to enter into a prenuptial agreement, they can still define the financial aspects of their relationship through a postnuptial agreement (also discussed more fully in chapter 7). Similar to a prenuptial agreement, the objective is to settle in advance the difficult financial issues that commonly flow from remaining together, divorce, separation, or death. The couple enters into a postnuptial agreement after having gained the wisdom that comes from experiencing the marriage, both financially and emotionally.

A postnuptial agreement was very helpful for Paul and his wife, Jill, in preserving their marriage during a time of personal crisis. Over the years, Paul and Jill produced income through their individual careers, inherited family money on one side, and possessed investments in stocks and real estate to the point where they became reasonably wealthy by most standards. The only problem was that as their money grew, Jill's self-indulgent spending habits escalated out of control. She was pursuing a professional career and became enamored with designer-label suits and clothes, but most of all designer shoes. Her cravings to acquire approached obsessive proportions as her wardrobe outgrew the bedroom closet space and created budget problems for the family. The two continued to have a high level of emotional investment in each other, but Paul feared losing the painstakingly acquired assets they had agreed were to be preserved for the children's college educations and the couple's retirement. Constantly bickering, but not wanting to divorce, Paul and Jill turned to legal counsel to draft a postnuptial agreement that divided their assets and indebtedness. This alleviated the tension.

STEPFAMILIES

Stepchildren pose yet another set of considerations for a family. Emotionally, many individuals view stepchildren differently from biological or adopted children. There are no laws that bind a stepparent to provide financial support or assistance to a stepchild. Any wealth that a stepparent chooses to pass to a stepchild reflects the nature of the individual's unique relationship to that child.

If parenting a stepchild results in psychological attachment and parental bonding, the parent may feel comfortable in treating the stepchild as an heir in his estate. Otherwise, he may come to view his relationship with the stepchild as merely incidental to his relationship with the child's mother and give no thought to including the child within the circle of his generosity.

The biggest pitfall for stepfamilies is when one parent expects instantaneous complete acceptance of his or her children by the new spouse. This simply does not happen emotionally. It can happen over time, and usually does. Frequently, a stepparent will treat the children of the other spouse as his or her own after a bond of affection develops. The relationship needs to evolve naturally. Parents and stepchildren need time to know each other and to develop attachment. Financial considerations will be easier to resolve if they are not demanded but allowed to follow in kind.

CONTROL OR OVERCONTROL

All of the events, mishaps, marriages, and remarriages that might happen within an individual's lifetime sometimes engender an unfortunate lack of trust between parents and children. This may lead to a parent attempting to control "from the grave." A parent who needs to maintain this degree of control may be heard, while still alive, by making the statement, "If you don't do what I say, you are out of the will." Obviously, the recipient of this statement is made to feel dependent, incompetent, and infantilized, if not terrorized.

Of course, if a child is truly incapacitated due to a mental, physical, or legal disability, then planning through the use of a protective trust is indicated (see chapter 16). Otherwise, parents generally need to reaffirm the mature judgments and capacities of their adult children by not "attaching strings" to an individual's dreams and preferences concerning career path, marriage (if, when, and with whom), religious beliefs, and political views and affiliations. Ironically, attempting to constrain a child's freedom of choice on such intensely personal matters fosters gamesmanship and immaturity that may lead to the realization of the very things the parent most fears. Values-based trusts need to emphasize inducement, not constraint.

Jim, a very wealthy man, had three children from two different marriages. The two elder children were from Jim's first marriage. The eldest was in college and the other two were being raised by Jim and his second spouse. He had liberally supported his eldest child throughout college. When summer vacation arrived, Jim announced that his eldest would have to fend for himself during the summer months. Outraged, his son said, "This must be your new wife's idea. I'm going to mother and she will take you to court," to which father retorted, "Then you are out of my will." This literal contest of will continued to escalate. Ultimately, the father failed to see the monster he himself was creating. He had always financially supported his son, who had come to rely on him. With no explicitly stated warning that summer funds would at some point be terminated, with no plan to gradually wean the son from his financial dependence, the father suddenly and inexplicably withdrew the son's support. Cutting off this child was bound to create parent-child discord as well as sibling resentment and disharmony, which it did for many of the ensuing years of these three children's lives.

If money is not talked about in a family and placed in a perspective that represents family values, profound disharmony can result, eventually playing a part in the deterioration of a marriage or, even more likely, a remarriage. When divorce is then mixed with money, a truly explosive situation may result. In post-divorce conflict, money can be used in a very destructive manner, which harms children. There is danger in translating love into compliance and units of currency. Once that process begins, it can grow exponentially, creating family disharmony. Love flows with openness, communication, understanding, and acknowledgment. If you can flow with that stream, then you can move with your family toward harmony.

CHAPTER FIFTEEN

The Dangers of Wealth for Siblings

Many people carry an image of a will being read to a family. The scenario is perpetually portrayed in movies and novels. Most picture a family seated around a large mahogany table in the conference room of a luxurious law office or in the family's sitting room. The family attorney who prepared the estate plan has a stack of papers in front of him as the grieving family members sit anxiously around the table. Finally, the moment arrives and the disposition of the estate is revealed. Shock, dismay, happiness, and anger are the range of emotions that emerge. Is this how it really happens, or is this an image preserved from movies and books?

One attorney in estate planning was asked whether he truly had to undergo this ordeal over and over again in his business, and if so, how did he cope with such strong emotional content? Surprisingly, he said that only once in his entire career had a will been revealed in such a manner. He, of course, was aware of the contents of the will, but the family was not. In this instance, the mother who died had gone against his best advice, and he dreaded the moment of revealing what was in her will. Her husband had died many years previously and she had inherited his estate completely. They were parents to two grown daughters. The mother applauded the virtues of one daughter and strongly disapproved of the other daughter's life choices. The rejected daughter had followed a countercultural lifestyle and married someone the mother mistrusted, even despised. The mother elected to leave her "favored" daughter her share of the estate outright and to put the "rejected" daughter's share into a trust to be administered by— who else?—the favored daughter. The attorney had strongly advised the mother against this plan, explaining that resentment and dissension between the two sisters would be triggered and might never be mended. Perhaps sensing that something was amiss, each daughter arrived at the "unveiling of the will" with her husband and respective attorney. Six people, therefore, sat around the table. No sooner had the attorney explained the terms, than the "rejected" daughter stood up and angrily said that she would not tolerate her sister controlling her life. Her husband was the next to stand, stating that the two of them had planned for the money, made financial commitments, and expected it immediately. Finally, their attorney took to center stage and explained that he would be challenging the estate. Years of litigation, expenditure of estate assets, and family disharmony ensued.

SIBLINGS AS RIVALS

It is inherent in the very nature of sibling relationships to be competitive, vying for advantage and squabbling with each other. In this way growing children learn skills for peer-level socialization. It is noteworthy as well that siblings often model their parents' style of problem solving.[1] In bringing up children, parents typically teach how to share; they also teach that children not only do not get all that they wish, but they also do not get what they wish immediately. If parents withhold love and approval, if it is doled out like a finite commodity along with parental availability and praise, then greed and competitiveness with an edge of hostility, anger, and resentment may well be created. Sadly, some wealthy families are liberal in sharing material assets but stingy with sharing parental involvement and praise. Children growing up in this way may define themselves by their possessions while remaining shallow in their relationships. The most intense sibling rivalry comes from children who grow up in such emotionally impoverished families.

Squabbling among siblings is predictable and can be playful. Life-and-death struggles between siblings, however, are not normal. It also is not normal to deny the feelings of one's siblings or to exploit one's siblings for one's own well-being. Children need to be taught that siblings are lifelong companions who can offer family support to the individual long after the parents have died. Healthy competition is normal. Extreme envy and cruel gloating are not.

Despite popular belief, the most bitter family squabbles happen not when the assets are great or the financial stakes are high, but when there are strong differences in the sense of how parents value the contributions of the siblings. In some families, a disproportionate share of the family's resources goes to the less-capable sibling, creating resentment on the part of other siblings. In other families, the high-achieving sibling may receive more recognition and praise from the parents. For many of these individuals growing up in these environments with a scarcity of praise and recognition, money often grows to have greater worth than good family relationships. One suggestion made by Martin Shankman, an estate planning attorney in New York, was to divide 80 percent of the parents' assets among the children and to place the remaining 20 percent in a separate trust for emergency needs of any of the children.[2]

Many stories can be told of family assets being depleted through devastating quarrels and endless litigation. Typically, these feuds involve siblings or cousins fighting over the assets earned by a parent or grandparent. In one case, in which two brothers were left equal shares of their mother's estate but one (deemed more responsible) was the trustee for the other son's inheritance, the more responsible brother ultimately decided to terminate the trust, which was within his authority, and give the entire inheritance to his brother. While he considered other options, such as changing trustees, he realized that his brother would view this as further effort to keep the money out of his reach and a lifelong betrayal. He felt that the sibling relationship outweighed the preservation of the income.

EQUALITY VERSUS FAIRNESS

As has been stated, an unfortunate rivalry occurs when money and wealth have served as proxies for love or when one child holds to that viewpoint. When an outright inheritance is withheld and love is measured quantitatively, what is seen as unequal treatment in the will inevitably fosters resentment. Succinctly, the money comes to be perceived as the measure of a parent's love.

In one family, the presentation of a grandmother's will exposed intense rivalry and resentment that had remained buried for generations within a family. When the grandmother's first daughter was born of a failed marriage, the grandmother resented her; the baby was the result of unwelcome and unhappy circumstances. Later, the grandmother remarried, and another daughter was born. The grandmother prized and favored this daughter, and an intense rivalry and enmity developed between the sisters. The two children grew up and each married and had children. When the grandmother died, she revealed great wealth, previously hidden, in the formal reading of her will. In her will, the grandmother left her entire estate to her favored child and her heirs. The offspring of the disfavored daughter were completely omitted from the will. In this way, a generations-old dispute was instantly rekindled in the grandchildren with an intensity that replicated the sibling rivalry that had poisoned their mothers' relationship. Sadly, the family issues that had begun two generations earlier continued to perpetuate hurt and resentment.

ESTATE PROPERTY

Attorneys report that the most contentious disputes may not be over the division of money, real estate, or investments, but over personal effects and household property that have sentimental rather than material value. Children grow attached to objects in the home. Furniture, pictures, even mementos from a favorite vacation, may embody a surprising amount of sentimental value. Even families who prepare an estate plan often neglect to specify the manner in which personal objects are to be divided among the children. Sometimes the will directs the executor to sell all of the personal property and divide the proceeds equally among the heirs. Such an approach is insensitive to the value children attach to particular items of personal property. Such items may represent concrete memories and opportunities to pass these memories on to their own children. If families can talk prior to death and list the objects that are of value to particular children, symbols of happy memories can be preserved and appropriately allocated, averting potential hurt and pain. In many families, however, parents are unwilling to promise specific objects to particular children. To add to the turmoil, two or more children may desire the same heirloom, sentimental object, or piece of furniture, and mom or dad must decide. If such decisions prior to death are not palatable, a number of strategies can preserve family harmony while still assuring that possessions are shared equitably.

A Personal Property Memorandum

Many states allow a person to dispose of personal effects and household property informally by identifying each item and its recipient on a statement or schedule that is kept separate from the person's will. Such an approach affords added flexibility, in that it allows the person to make changes without going through the formalities associated with amending a will. Not every jurisdiction allows disposition by separate statements, so it is important to check with an attorney who is familiar with the laws of your particular jurisdiction. Another valuable legacy parents can leave to children is a compilation of letters, written stories, photographs, videos, and messages to future generations. If there is a valued collection that none of the children desire, perhaps it can be donated to a local museum, university, or institution.

Rotating Selection

The children can identify all objects they would like to remain within the family. Each child, in turn, selects an object of his or her choice until all items are fairly distributed to the different family members. Deciding the child who selects first can be problematic. A parent can specify that this be the eldest or the youngest, or that the children simply draw random numbers. If there are very few items of value, or only one item of interest, this method clearly may not work.

Gentle Pressure

Some parents have a clause in their will stating that personal and household possessions are to go to the children as the children themselves agree. If they cannot agree, the personal representative is instructed to sell these items. While dramatic, this method often forces the children to find a compromise solution, or risk losing what they value most.

Siblings talking together with their parents prior to death can prevent family insecurities and rivalries from playing out during the grieving period following death. Yet children don't wish to appear greedy and, therefore, are often reluctant to approach their parents. If one child takes the liberty without consulting the others, he or she appears to be going behind the backs of his or her siblings, and resentment builds. Just caring about an elderly parent can trigger such feelings.

In one family, a daughter, after having been out of touch for more than twenty years, returned when her mother needed placement in a nursing care facility. Understandably, the siblings grew suspicious of the daughter's sudden interest in the mother's welfare at a time when it was apparent she would not live much longer.

In another family, the siblings, although spread out across the country, arranged blocks of time to be with their elderly mother once she was placed in a care facility. Wanting to assure her of family visits and feelings of support, the siblings communicated well, respected the responsibilities each of them had for careers and children of their own, and shared the task of being available to mom. Chances are high this family will not squabble over mom's estate, but will demonstrate the same restraint, respect, and mutuality that was evident during the mother's declining health.

Not all sibling groups are so fortunate. One child may wish for such an arrangement only to find his or her siblings uninterested, unmotivated, or even annoyed at being bothered. One sibling may simply be irresponsible and incapable of entering into such an arrangement, or exploitative and untrustworthy of such responsibility. Each family carries its own unique dynamics, and a sensitive attorney or other professional can guide an individual or individuals who are willing to look at the emotional issues through this quagmire. For instance, some traditional as well as innovative solutions families have used include:

- An estate auction is held. Children have the first option to bid on whatever objects they want. The highest bidder gets those objects and all proceeds are divided equally among the heirs. The remainder of the estate can go to public auction. The drawback to this is the inequity in bidding power if the children represent greatly unequal wealth.
- There is a random drawing of numbers, and the heirs select objects of meaning in any number of rounds.
- Remember that family photos are easily duplicated and family movies can be placed in new electronic formats and easily reproduced.
- Heirs can be polled as to what objects they would most desire or cherish. The benefactor can be guided by these stated choices. This strategy promotes a discussion and can result in positive memories being shared. Parents are cautioned to keep

in mind that often a possession they dearly prize may not be valued by their intended heirs.

- An individual always has the right to designate the recipient of specific gifts or objects. This may include extended family members or significant friends beyond children and grandchildren.
- Remember that some objects, even of great monetary value, may carry negative memories or feelings. It is probably best to sell these objects and distribute the proceeds.

The Yellow Pie Plate Web site of the University of Minnesota (*www.yellowpieplate.umn.edu*) offers further discussion and ideas in this area.

TALKING TO PARENTS ABOUT THEIR WEALTH AND ESTATE PLANNING

For most people, talking to parents, especially elderly parents, about estate planning is most difficult. Heirs may fear they will appear greedy and that just bringing up the topic somehow violates intergenerational protocol. Some parents indeed feel it is presumptuous of their children to ask or even broach the topic. Others resist talking about such matters because it involves contemplating their own deaths. Typically, when parents are ready, they will make comments a child can use as an entry point for discussion. For example, one elderly mom mailed her daughter nothing more than a small slip of paper with the combination to her safe. This mom had never discussed her estate planning or other needs. The daughter was able to use this as a starting point for a conversation. It was quickly apparent that her mother could not tolerate much conversation. A number of subtle ways to introduce this topic are discussed below.

Utilize Natural Entry Points As They Arise

Look for entry points as they occur throughout life, especially when major life events impact the older or younger generations. Events such as marriage, divorce, illness, or death can be opportunities to have a discussion with parents about inheritance and estate planning. Many parents feel that their assets are a gift to their children, and it is their right to bestow this gift when they are ready and in the manner they choose. Some parents may not want to share their estate plans because they prefer to reserve the option to make revisions from time to time.

Use Your Own Estate to Invite Discussion

Talking and working together as a family from early on is the best approach. If this has not been the case in your family, you might try to bring up issues or concerns regarding your own estate planning and see if your parents will participate in such a discussion. Seeking advice relative to your own estate planning might spark an opportunity to work together as a family. Talking together does not necessarily mean asking for specific information, such as "how much are you leaving to me?" Rather, it can represent an opportunity to share ideas and to discuss the legacy and history of family ideals. The emotional value of certain objects and heirlooms can be discussed in this context as well.

Approach Parents As a Sibling Group

To the extent that it is feasible, siblings should approach the parents as a group rather then individually. Frequently, when fewer than all of the children are involved in the process, the remaining children become suspicious of their motives and resentful of their close involvement with their parents on matters that affect the family as a whole.

In approaching their parents, children should make clear that their only objective is to assist them in formulating a plan that conforms to the parents' desires and values. That does not mean, however, that children should refrain from sharing their own perspectives and preferences with regard to the proper disposition of family property. Certainly, parents committed to the well-being of their children will want to account for their views and wishes in formulating their intentions.

Ask Parents to Resolve Anticipated Disputes

Requesting that parents leave guidelines for the sharing of a particular asset can prevent intense sibling squabbles. Family harmony itself is a valuable asset and should be acknowledged and included in this way in the estate plan with careful forethought.

UNUSUAL REQUESTS

Occasionally, a will is opened to find a bizarre or troubling request. One attorney described to his law students a case encountered long ago in which a man left a request to be buried in the cockpit of his racecar wearing his black beret and with his hands placed on the throttle. This was a written request and, therefore, treated as a directive to be honored by his heirs, as strange as it was. Another situation involved an elderly woman who verbally told her only daughter that she was to have her much-loved dog euthanatized and buried with her at her death. Because this was not a directive in her will, the daughter was left to make her own choice as to whether to honor this request. As repugnant as the request to euthanatize the dog was, the daughter had to decide whether that was more unpalatable to her than the guilt she would feel by electing not to follow her mother's wishes. Difficult choices such as this one can be eliminated and children protected from these dilemmas if a parent simply writes a directive that must be honored. Better still, hold a frank family discussion of such directives prior to the parent's illness or death.

FAMILY BUSINESSES

Some families have significant investment in a family business that can be efficiently operated by only one family member. This is especially true of farming and ranching families for which the business may be capable of supporting only one family member. In such situations, the way the family business is capitalized can present a solution. Siblings can own the property used in the family business and lease it to the sibling who operates the business. If it is ever sold, then everyone shares. For family-owned businesses, control can be concentrated through voting stock and each sibling be entitled to regular dividends. The children who run and operate the business are paid extra for their efforts. Although this can minimize the sibling issues, it may not completely prevent them from occurring.

One successful entrepreneur bought out his siblings with generous settlements and turned a faltering family business into a tremendously profitable one. When he sold it years later, he chose to disburse the profits to his loyal company employees and among his own children and grandchildren. Some in his extended family then expressed resentment. This confident man took it in stride saying, "There are some human emotions which surface regardless of what you do." A magnanimous and generous man throughout his life, he felt neither threatened nor guilty.

A family is far more than a repository of common genes; a family provides an emotional bond that most individuals dearly value. Members of families are well served when they endeavor to define commonly held values and to find compromises for difficult circumstances. Sadly, however, occasions occur in which family values differ, conflict is sustained and intense, and compromise is simply not possible. Some individuals are relieved to be free of burdensome family relationships and finances; they simply prefer not to remain bound to a group of people with whom their only affinity derives from a common gene pool. Especially in such a situation, strategies for dissolving a family's financial ties are best devised with the assistance of an objective independent attorney with experience in settling family financial disputes amicably and equitably.

CHAPTER SIXTEEN

Children Who Are Not Ready for Money—and May Never Be

Without proper planning, your estate will pass to your heirs outright. If any of your heirs is a minor, a conservator or guardian will be appointed to manage his or her share of your estate. However, when the heir attains the age of eighteen, the guardian or conservator will be required to distribute that heir's share of your estate to him or her outright. Needless to say, even the highest functioning eighteen-year-olds are seldom ready to manage a substantial inheritance. Readiness for inheritance may be determined by several indicators, such as good academic functioning, maturity of judgment, and self-sufficiency, but these are only part of the equation. A young adult might demonstrate all of these qualities yet lack financial maturity.

Financial maturity can be thought of along two continua. The first might be defined as ranging from *consumerism* to *preservation*. Many young adults have used money only to spend and consume. They have not learned to save, nor do they understand the principle of preserving assets to assure growth and future earning potential. For money to serve individuals in the long run, they must understand this notion and implement it. Yet, many young adults have never been taught, nor have even contemplated, this end of the continuum. Typically, parents function as preservers and providers, and children as consumers. Money has been solely a means to facilitate consumption.

Another dimension may also be of value in defining financial maturity. This might be expressed as awareness of the power of money and interest in and capacity for investment management.

Some young adults might have experience in managing credit cards, checking accounts, debit cards, and a monthly allowance, but they frequently lack the education and perspective for managing wealth over time. Even in this millennium, few young adults have knowledge of stocks, bonds, and mutual funds, or even know where to gain this information. Schools generally do not teach this material. Economics classes are rarely offered at the pre-college level. Some young adults may have overheard their parents interacting with stockbrokers or investment managers, but neglected to learn the principles involved or the nature of the relationship. This is typical in our consumer-driven society. When offered the opportunity to learn money-management principles, some will opt out, preferring to remain passive for any number of reasons: it might be boring, it might seem too complicated, or their lifestyle choice rejects consumerism and the luxuries money can afford. These are acceptable choices. Young people who elect such paths are not necessarily rejecting a productive lifestyle; they simply are expressing little interest or aptitude for wealth preservation.

In evaluating your own children, you would be well advised to think through whether an outright inheritance at age eighteen poses a risk you are willing to take. If not, preserving family wealth through the options offered in a values-based trust might be a wise decision. Values-based trusts are discussed more fully in chapter 14 and will be mentioned again in this chapter as a tool for shaping the distribution of inherited wealth. To aid in making this decision, parents might conduct their own evaluation of their children along these two dimensions of *consumerism* and *money-management tools/interest* by the criteria in the sidebar below titled "Evaluating Your Children As Money Managers."

EVALUATING YOUR CHILDREN AS MONEY MANAGERS

- Gather information about financial maturity from others who know your child as well as from your child's money history. This might involve talking with teachers, friends, adult mentors, or simply evaluating your child's money management based on your observations. Have luxuries been too enticing? Has a portion of money earned been saved? Have you had to come to the rescue with bills and credit cards? Has a monthly allowance or college/high school debit card been managed with responsibility? An examination of the answers to these questions will help you to know your child as he or she actually functions in the money world.

- Consider giving your child an investment fund. Observe whether there is an interest in learning preservation concepts and approaches and, if so, offer the means to gaining knowledge along with the money.
- Discuss offering your child a graduation or birthday gift that presents a choice between **assets to manage** versus **assets to consume**. For example, what might your child select if offered an expensive night on the town for a special event or the same amount of money in shares of stocks or other investment instruments? Discuss the pluses and minuses for these options and assess his or her attitude.
- Many parents of wealth take advantage of the tax savings of a yearly gift to their children. Offer this gift outright to your child at age eighteen along with the opportunity to gain some money-management tools. Do not insist that the money-management education accompany the gift; it is a choice. If your child refuses to learn, it is best that you note it for now. Watch, over the course of the next few years, to see what choices your son or daughter makes with those funds.
- Offer the opportunity to learn money management through courses, seminars, meetings with trusted friends, professionals, and relatives. Note whether this holds any interest.
- Examine your son's or daughter's history of consumption. Is materialism appealing? Does he or she want the car, fancy clothes, stereo, or computer equipment that represents the finest? If so, has he or she offered to pitch in for some of the cost, or has the expectation been that you, as the parent, will absorb the cost? Is your son or daughter aware of the power of advertising? Can he or she decipher an ad and step back and not be completely persuaded by its message? Can he or she decipher a commercial message and identify it in a fad, movie trailer, or TV interview?
- Has your child participated in earning something he or she desired? For example, when it was time for the first car, did you discuss the cost of insurance, licensing, and the reality that tickets increase this cost? Did you expect some contribution from your son or daughter for insurance, gas, or maintenance?
- If your child ever worked, what happened to the earnings? Was any portion saved for something longed for or unspecified, or did the money "burn a hole in the child's pocket" and disappear before the next paycheck?
- How susceptible is your child to influences from peers? What are his or her social history and peer connections? Is it likely that a friend or acquaintance will ask for money as soon as your child has some? How has your child dealt with these issues in the past?
- Is there an addiction or history of addiction to substances, gambling, consumerism, or personal/business relationships with exploitative people?

You might explore your assessment of your child with your spouse, a trusted friend, a professional advisor, or a family member. Many parents underestimate their children's maturity and ability to handle money.

It is critically important that you examine whether your goal, if it is to place restrictions on your child's inheritance, is based on shaping values and choices, or whether it is based on your need to control. At times, this is not an easy question to self-evaluate. Most parents, in some form or another, wish to assure that their children wisely use money to foster family values. Watching your child stumble along the way triggers a surge of feelings. You may be prone to rescue, to become angry and rueful at the waste, to give the child less money in the future, to lecture, to threaten, or even to consider disinheritance. Money values, like other values, shape into character structure over time and then only with experience, mistakes, and important but possibly painful lessons learned. How much tolerance do you have for mistakes, wastefulness, consumption, or peer influence? Ask yourself if your desire to withhold money is based on a realistic appraisal of your son or daughter or more on your own intolerance for contrary decision-making, different yet not harmful values, or a need to maintain control.

Whatever your decision, a number of models exist that can help you to shape both responsible money management and estate planning options. These models all draw from the concepts of values-based estate planning. For example, assuring that inherited wealth flows into a trust rather than as an outright benefit to the inheritor provides protection at many levels. Not only will the wealth be managed and distributed in accordance with your values, as reflected in the restrictions and guidelines contained in the trust agreement, it also will be protected against your child's inexperience, imprudent behavior, and creditors' claims. Trusts can be shaped with as much or as little flexibility as you desire. The trustee might be likened to a surrogate parent who is guided by the principles written into the trust instrument. Obviously, the selection of a trustee is an important decision, and many families elect to name more than one trustee and to require that a consensus decision be reached for distributions from the trust. Although a family member may have the knowledge of family history and values, he or she may not have the financial sophistication you desire. As the heir develops and demonstrates financial maturity, he or she may become the trustee or the trust may be dissolved. Initially, requiring a consensus decision by both the family-member trustee and an outside financial trustee can assure financial sophistication and that family values are represented. If you are uncertain whether your child will grow in financial maturity, you can consider a *stepwise trust*, whereby funds are distributed outright at increasingly mature ages, or possibly two separate trusts that terminate at different ages.

One creative couple structured a small trust for each of their children that terminated outright at age twenty-one. This was supplemented by a much larger trust for each child that terminated at age thirty-five. Thus, the beneficiary came into some inheritance at the age of twenty-one, providing sufficient financial worth for a down payment on a home, to start a business, to fund an education, or even to indulge in a luxury. By postponing the major portion of the inheritance until mid-adulthood, full ownership of substantial wealth was averted until further maturity. These parents hoped to avoid the children feeling wealth had been withheld or controlled until a later age by disbursing money when beneficial at earlier stages of adulthood. This dual trust arrangement provided these children with the opportunity to gain financial knowledge, form relationships with money managers, and make their own decisions about whether to spend or preserve their wealth.

When the son was twenty-two, the parents became upset because he used his inheritance to assist a girlfriend with a legal problem. The parents would have been prepared for the purchase of a fancy car, boat, or airplane, but not payments to attorneys for a problem that was not even of his own making. The parents frantically called the attorney who drew up the trust, asking what could be done. "Not a thing," the attorney replied. "Remember that this is why you did this, so your son could learn. Consider this learning." By age thirty-five, when the son became entitled to his larger trust, he was a wiser manager, interested and actively involved with his investments, and, incidentally, happily married to this same former girlfriend. The opportunity to inherit early had benefited everyone.

A trust fund with "more strings than the philharmonic" characterized the trust that Kim Walker created for her two young daughters after a $27 million lottery win.[1] The trust provided for:

- Tuition at four-year colleges, if the girls took a prescribed number of hours each semester
- A dollar-for-dollar match of their salaries

- Matching funds up to $50,000 for a business start-up
- A "loser's clause" bestowing nothing to the children until age sixty-five if they failed to be productive in any of these areas

PLANNING FOR YOUR CHILD WITH AN INCAPACITY

Not being ready for money can take many forms. Some children may have a medical disability that will last a lifetime and require physical support equipment, special educational needs, and daily care. Others may have psychological impairments that cloud their judgment over the short term or long term. Or they may suffer from an addiction/dependency problem that may or may not abate over time. Each of these life conditions is best served by tailoring a flexible trust with carefully crafted stewardship provisions.

Addiction/Dependency

Children who fall into the addiction/dependency category might suffer with an addiction to substances such as alcohol or drugs, gambling, excessive spending, or involvement in a cult with a charismatic leader or others who are exploitative. Many have the potential to recover with treatment; some, sadly, do not recover. A trust may be tailored in a fashion that speaks to the possibility of recovery. Guidelines may be provided for the trustee to make distributions based on the values specified for the trust. In these cases, the guidelines need to be very specific, as there is a grave risk of relapse for many of the addiction/dependency disorders.

For example, a child who struggles with alcohol dependency may need to be sober for five years for the trustee gradually to entrust more funds to that individual's discretion. The trustee can be authorized to distribute what is needed for comfortable living but no more until sobriety has been demonstrated and maintained. Funds to seek treatment may be allowed for if the parent so desires. The trustee may be given the discretion to make distributions within the parameters of the guidelines set forth in the trust document.

Another possibility is to build incentives into the trust to reach a recovery goal. It is crucial that parents examine the use of incentives in terms of the guidelines outlined earlier in this chapter. Do the incentives intend to control or truly to protect? Do the incentives reflect the parents' value system or established standards of health and safety? For example, one wealthy mother found herself very troubled by her daughter's decision to join an order, renounce marriage, and follow an austere, ascetic life philosophy. This was not an exploitative cult or sect that demanded that the daughter turn over her assets, but merely one of ascetic, yet pro-social values, which called for personal sacrifice, isolation, and travel to work in trouble spots around the globe.

Unfortunately, many estate attorneys fail to examine psychological issues or such value-system questions with their clients when preparing an estate plan. With little or no training in psychological interviewing or processing, this is no surprise. Increasingly, attorneys and clients recognize this area as an important consideration in estate planning. Some attorneys will bring in psychologists or other family communication specialists to help parents process the family issues of control, values, and individuation. Chapter 13 explores some of the changing professional roles emerging in this field.

Psychological Impairments

Psychological disorders can impair judgment temporarily or permanently. Some of these disorders have their onsets during the adolescent or early adult years, so a parent may have created an estate plan with no indication that a child might later develop a difficulty that needs to be addressed, both with treatment as well as with estate planning. Disorders associated with psychotic thinking styles may make an individual prone to poor judgment, impaired thinking, or victimization. These need consideration in estate planning.

Other disorders can provoke grave concern about social and emotional functioning, including impulsiveness, control problems, and extreme moodiness, not infrequently associated with periods of excessive indulgence and spending. Some of these disorders can be contained and managed with regular and consistent medication. These include severe depression and bipolar disorder, schizo-affective disorder, and some types of schizophrenia. These individuals can function quite well as long as they adhere to a firm treatment plan and daily use of medication. Trust guidelines need to take this into account as well as guard against the eventuality that a child suffering from any of these conditions might voluntarily stop taking medication and revert to disrupted behavior or thinking patterns.

Finally, some disorders are associated with concrete thinking, which impairs an individual's sense of judgment, planning for the future, or ability to fully comprehend advice from a financial manager. A trustee would benefit from guidelines detailing the nature and specific treatment considerations for these disorders so as to more effectively assist with prudent financial planning in these instances.

Medical or Physical Disability

Provisions for appropriate care must be made for a child with mental or physical disability. A child who needs physical support or care may require a *supplemental needs trust*. A gift in trust shelters the assets and assures that they are not regarded as the child's resources when determining eligibility for Medicaid, Supplemental Security Income, or other needs-based government entitlements. This type of trust is discussed in greater detail in chapters 8, 11, and 12.

Equality among siblings in the estate plan may necessarily have to be sacrificed to assure that a child with extraordinary needs will have the required caretaking. Placing the inherited wealth into one trust for all siblings is one mechanism for assuring that the distribution does not have to be equal. Some, out of medical necessity, will tap into it; the healthier others will not. Another mechanism would be to establish an emergency trust from which funds can be drawn for such a child or if an injury or illness is sustained later in life.

Failure to mention a rightful heir in an estate plan may in some jurisdictions leave open the possibility of that heir contesting the will or creating considerable difficulties for his or her siblings. These siblings are then left carrying the burden of a parent's choice, which obviously can strain relationships. At least mentioning all of the rightful heirs and allocating funds with appropriate safeguards assures children are not left a troubling legacy.

CHAPTER SEVENTEEN

Changes of Fortune

Hard work, good fortune, inheritance, or the gradual progression of savings and investment can bring new or sudden wealth. In contrast, wealth can and does sometimes vanish quickly for reasons of personal mismanagement, missed opportunities, or economic downturns.

GAINING WEALTH

With the rapid development of technology in the nineties, some individuals found themselves millionaires at the beginning of their careers. Others found success with a business venture, investment, or invention. Lottery winners can be counted in this group; so can athletes, movie stars, pop musicians, and media personalities. Individuals with new-found wealth may gain a high profile from publicity or notoriety that accompanies their success or good fortune. One may also be a family member of such an individual. Those who come to the public eye through wealth frequently have difficulty maintaining anonymity, and their children may be affected by growing up in a media glare.

Sudden wealth, whatever the source, brings challenges for which many feel unprepared. The recipient has an array of choices he or she did not have previously. Although popular culture seems to perpetuate the myth that sudden wealth is both easily attainable and highly desirable, once that wealth is obtained, that same culture insinuates that newly wealthy individuals will be paralyzed with indecision, experience productivity crises, and lose their sense of values. During the late nineties, diagnostic labels such as "affluenza" or "sudden wealth syndrome" developed; these biomedical-sounding labels implied that invariably a wide array of woes would befall those "stricken" with such success.

In reality, newly attained wealth need not represent a crisis or pathology. Acquisition of new wealth will, however, bring new experiences and require choices as new opportunities and pathways open up, both positive and potentially hazardous. Sudden, unexpected wealth typically creates an initial elation, which is often followed by overwhelming feelings of fear and isolation. Expressing these feelings to old friends may engender a sarcastic "I would love to have your problems" rather than compassion. Realistically, sudden wealth disrupts even the most well-grounded individuals. Whereas some savvy individuals may know where to turn, others may lack resources, not knowing whom to trust.

Sudden wealth impacts every facet of an individual's life. The circle chart below defines the interpersonal connections that define a person's identity and sense of belonging. New wealth redefines all of them, much like moving to a foreign country where the new culture and its opportunities must be assessed, understood, and integrated if successful adaptation and acculturation is to take place.

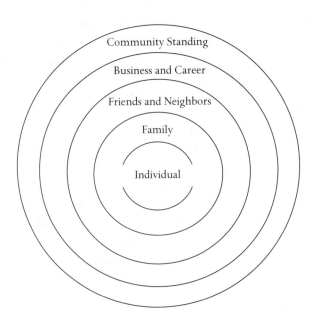

The circle chart illustrates the social spheres that each individual inhabits. Familiarity and accommodations need to occur within each stratum for adjustment ultimately to take place. This represents a struggle to greater or lesser extents within any one or more of the strata, and it is a normal, predictable progression for individual reacclimation to extreme environmental shifts.

As applied to new wealth, an individual may suddenly be able to afford luxuries far beyond those of co-workers and friends. Many assume such wealth will promote a spending spree, but surprisingly, often it does not. One young heir simply felt overwhelmed by the attention his new wealth brought. Feeling bewildered and unanchored, his choice was to give it away to charity and resume his previous life. In another family, one sister, fourth in a succession of five, who had always felt overlooked and undistinguished in her family, lavishly spent and flaunted her newly acquired money in a desperate attempt to establish an independent, distinctive identity. Although sudden wealth offers much to savor and enjoy, the experience in its entirety is so daunting and overwhelming for some that the joy may be short lived and the changed circumstances pointedly challenging to the individual's core identity and self-definition.

One area that all but certainly affects those who come into new wealth is whether to share this wealth with family, extended family, or friends. Some question whether their windfall will even be shared with a spouse. The new money may be placed in cotenancy if the individual is married, or kept in one name, creating financial inequity within the marriage. A husband's salary may now be minimal compared to the wife's resources, or vice versa. Grown children may expect the wealth to be shared or may see it as a family resource rather than as rightfully belonging to one individual. Aging parents may expect support or a nicer living environment. Should the money be kept or saved, shared with one's partner or kept for oneself, used to benefit the family, and, if so, which family members? The choices can strain family relationships and create disharmony. At these times the wealth may feel more like a burden than a blessing.

Issues with which those with newfound wealth must cope include the following:

- **Who to trust.** Those with newly acquired wealth fear alienation from family and friends. Some feel anxious about sharing news of their wealth and therefore hide it if they can. If, historically, family and friendships have been solid, they are likely to remain solid. Approach these relationships with trust and openness, and they will more than likely grow and transform to include new realms and greater depth.

- **Examining the meaningfulness of job and career; setting personal goals and standards.** It may no longer be necessary to remain at the same job or even to work at all. The meaning of a career, or a career aspired to, must be evaluated. A person might ask, "Why am I working at this job—or at any job? For the money or for other reasons?" Many individuals longingly consider what they might do if they had sufficient wealth to do whatever they pleased. One woman had always dreamed of going to full-time graduate school to obtain a Ph.D. in psychology and work with children. She had worked in a retail position because earlier in her life she could not afford to take the time off. Later in life, she did have that wealth and the freedom to fulfill her dream. She left her retail job but found herself delaying application to graduate school and becoming increasingly frustrated and self-deprecating. She finally announced that she was indeed making a contribution to the community as a grant writer and fundraiser for children's programs. Ultimately, she abandoned the plan to develop her own skills as a professional. She came to realize that her vision of herself as a professional had been arbitrary and was now both unrealistic and only creating a negative self-appraisal and sense of discontent. Indeed, she recognized that she had made a positive contribution to help children, but not as a mental health professional as she originally had envisioned and vowed to others.

Those who are self-made may feel the compulsion to repeat the success. A "Midas-touch self-image" drives them to try to strike gold a second or third time. This, of course, will be effective only some of the time. One determined businessman amassed an enormous fortune by good investments from inherited family wealth as well as the successful startup of a company, which he later sold for millions. After some years had passed, and a sizeable share of his resources had been depleted, he believed he could and should repeat this good fortune again. When he attempted to reenter the competitive business world, however, he found he had lost his edge. Fortunes can and do reverse. Rather than preserve the capital he had acquired, he tore through much of it, all the while confident that he could and would repeat his success.

- **How to identify and handle exploitative others.** Yes, others will approach the newly wealthy asking for loans, gifts, and contributions to risky business ventures. Those with new wealth have not had the social and parental modeling provided to those who grew up with family wealth, and may not know how to handle these uncomfortable encounters.

One young man, Jarred, inherited substantial wealth at a young age only to find one particular friend repeatedly asking for large loans. Not wanting to risk losing his friendship, he was troubled about how to handle these requests. Fortunately, Jarred had a wise counselor he could turn to who offered some advice. The advice was to make a one-time gift to his friend, explaining that it was a gift and not a "loan." There was no expectation of repayment and no contract between them. The money was gifted with the understanding that if his friend wished someday to repay it, that was fine. But the money also was gifted with the condition that his friend would never again ask for a loan. This gave control back to Jarred, who was able to be generous to his friend. It also took away the strain of the inequity of their financial circumstances, ended the discussion of loans forever, and preserved the friendship.

Kim Walker, the $27-million lottery winner mentioned earlier, still charges for her services as a dedicated children's ice-skating coach. "I might donate lesson time, but I try not to do that. If you give too much, people take advantage and don't appreciate it. You lose the [value]; there is no commitment."[1]

- **Will my children be ruined?** Many people express fear that their newfound wealth will spoil their children. The key here is how the wealth is regarded (see chapter 6 for a full discussion of developmentally instilling sound money values in children). Start to apply these measures with your children when you come into new wealth, no matter what age they are. Remember to stay involved, connected, and expressive with children at all ages. Some parents materially indulge their children without building values, and replace themselves with caretakers. This robs children of a solid framework of relationships upon which to build values, and thereby creates a disadvantage for them.

• **An embarrassment of riches.** With new wealth, more varied choices become available. Newly earned or inherited wealth can offer possibilities for new directions. Suddenly, decisions need to be made that were limited in the past by financial constraints. A bigger house or a second home may be a consideration. Private schooling for the children is an option. Even leaving a job can become a possibility. Financial necessity no longer dictates choices. There are varied and wonderful opportunities that each family and individual must sort out according to his or her own desires and values. A career path can now be defined solely by what a person loves, not by necessity. New wealth is an opportunity to examine one's identity, values, and what is held as meaningful in life's pursuits.

Recently, a young man with extraordinary wealth reported that his goal was to "own a house, a Jeep, and a Harley by the time he was twenty-five." Now twenty-eight, he owns all three, but, interestingly, he shifted his goals from material desires to relational ones: "My goals for reaching thirty are a lot less material. It's more about having solid relationships with my family and friends, giving back to the community, maintaining financial security, and being able to take care of myself."[2]

The issue of guilt for such good fortune prevents some from sharing their dilemmas and discussing their decisions with family and friends. Yet, allowing friends and family to be sounding boards ensures that their support will continue. It is often his or her own guilt, not rejection by others, that drives a wealthy person to isolation. Those with new wealth must challenge the capacity of established relationships to enter new realms of decision-making and friendship with them.

The dazzle of new wealth is intoxicating to some. Suddenly there are invitations to charitable balls and auctions, solicitations for social causes, and requests for contributions to organizations and causes far and wide. This newfound celebrity status can be engaging for a while, and enticing; gradually, however, this can start to feel invasive and exploitative. The resolution of this dilemma is to become proactive about giving rather than passive and reactive. To do this requires research into charities and causes as well as introspection and a personal definition of which causes to actively support and which to turn away. Children who grew up with wealth often had this modeled for them. Those without this background must forge their own pathways, which admittedly may be a daunting task at times. Organizations, family members, and trusted friends will no doubt be resources. Chapter 18 speaks to identifying professional resources that might assist in this process.

- **To share or not to share with family.** Wealth can be shared or not as the individual desires. When someone has earned or won rather than inherited a great deal, the chances are the rest of the family does not enjoy such wealth. An individual may suddenly be wealthy yet have parents or siblings who have minimal resources. Some family members may attempt to induce guilt or even try to exploit that person. Remember that there is no obligation to share personal wealth; nor, however, should one feel restriction in giving generously toward promoting the capacities of those who have been meaningful in one's life. Some feel enormously rewarded emotionally when they make gestures of generosity toward loved ones. One remarkable woman describes how she handled new wealth that came to her some years after she had faced a divorce, bankruptcy, and the loss of her home. Regarding a supportive brother who during those difficult times gave her a place to live, she says: "I married for love and got money in the bargain. As for the brother who took me in, I bought him a new home. . . . I did the same with my sister's house. And [I bought] my manicurist a car. . . . A limo driver told me about his dreams. . . . My dental hygienist worried about retirement . . . [She helped them all]."[3]

- **Where and how to find a good financial planner, estate planner, etc.** Unlike those who inherit family wealth, and the investment advisors, CPAs, and family offices along with it, the newly wealthy must educate themselves about money management. Chapter 18 speaks to this issue at length.

LOSING WEALTH

Poor planning, a lack of foresight, or an unwillingness to face the reality that previous cash flow no longer exists can leave individuals as well as families with a downturn of personal fortune. Whereas some individuals bring this fate upon themselves through denial that their financial reality is changing or that seemingly endless assets are being depleted, others face situations out of their control, such as an industry becoming obsolete, investment loss, a lawsuit, or unexpected medical expenses. Young entrepreneurs, especially, took many risks during the dot.com era when profits appeared to be a sure thing. Many then found themselves not only with no more innovations to peddle, but with lawsuits pending from others looking for a scapegoat for their own lost fortunes.

WHEN TRUSTING IS A MISTAKE

One older couple, for instance, received a huge windfall as beneficiaries of their daughter's life insurance following the death of their daughter and her husband in an accident. This tragedy also left them as legal guardians of their two school-age grandchildren. Wanting to preserve the assets for their grandchildren, they sought out an investment manager who was recommended as conservative, sensible, and trustworthy. Mistakenly thinking she could not miss the big gains, the manager invested in high-risk stocks, rather than slow, steady-growth stocks, and by the end of the nineties had lost the money this couple had hoped to preserve for their grandchildren's futures. They were combined victims of the market downturn and a less-than-prudent advisor.

One man in his avid quest to hold, preserve, and grow his assets, moved them to an offshore investment account, pursuing the triple-fold strategy that he would grow his assets, limit his liability to his creditors, and also find a tax haven. Unfortunately, the offshore investment itself turned out to be a scam, and he ultimately lost all of the assets he attempted to shelter in this way.

Other scenarios, some tragic, others self-imposed, can change a fortune overnight. Advertisers encourage high-risk investing and get-rich-quick schemes at every level in our society. Few sounded the alarm about the rapid shift in the economy at the end of the nineties, and some individuals lost through their own lack of acknowledgment of shifting economics, exuberance, greed, and lowering prudence. Other truly innocent victims, many of them employees of large corporations,

lost wealth and retirement assets due to corporate corruption, dishonesty, misjudgment, and even blatant violations of the law. Many
were left bewildered, struggling to understand the dynamics that
would drive a seemingly ethical business leader to blatantly violate
moral and legal standards, as well as long-established business relationships and friendships, all for personal gain.

There are many aspects of this bewilderment surrounding professional ethics. Some lie within the realm of interaction between an individual's personality and that individual's relationship with money. For
those who derive their self-esteem from wealth, the balance will be
tipped toward avarice over ethics, family relationships, and professional
commitments. For these individuals, the humiliation associated with a
loss of riches simply feels overwhelming. Others feel desperate and act
accordingly, never imagining that their questionable, illegal, or unethi-
cal behavior might be uncovered and exposed. Still others are driven by
an addiction to material acquisition or gambling, sometimes even to
drugs or alcohol; the fulfillment of an addiction so severe takes prece-
dence over all else.

Often underlying these troubling personal themes of sacrificing
almost everything in life for wealth is a childhood in which the value of
relationships, empathy, and connection to others failed to be instilled.
Materialism became the substitute for human connection and support.
Holding onto the wealth and what wealth can materially translate into
replaces not only family relationships, professional obligations, and
ethics, but goes so far as to supplant even personal dignity.

When an individual's sense of self is rooted in wealth and the social
standing associated with wealth, the loss of fortune is as aggrieving as
the loss of a family member or close friend might be for others. It, like
any other loss, can entirely change the course of one's life.

One woman was acutely and profoundly distraught following the
loss of her prized Caribbean home in a devastating hurricane. It had
been a showplace home in which she became well known for hosting
elaborate and spectacular parties. After her loss, when caring friends
and neighbors offered her basic necessities such as clothing and food,
she was utterly humiliated. Her self-esteem revolved around their
admiration of her and her finery; to be treated as destitute and in need
only angered and humiliated her. The only remedy in her eyes was to
quickly leave the island where her social standing had been so vio-
lated. The value of friends reaching out during her time of grief and

vulnerability completely escaped her notice as a precious intangible in her life. The stronger relationships, which might have grown from her acknowledging the reality of her own dire circumstances and her friends' concern, were not tolerated, let alone allowed to become treasures for her.

Coming into money or losing money affects an individual's sense of personal identity. If a lack of core values defines the person, then money and its purchasing power may come to define that individual's sense of self. This is tempting in our culture, which emphasizes individualism and autonomy. Certainly the loss of money creates profound insecurity and grief for most because money is the means through which basic personal and family needs are met. Those with core basic values connect to others in times of crisis; they draw strength from being part of a community. To them, vulnerability is not shameful, and accepting help from charitable, caring others builds meaningful mutuality. Gradually, these individuals rebound with resiliency and renewed optimism about life, richer for their relationships rather than poorer merely for their lack of financial resources.

CHAPTER EIGHTEEN

The Wise Use of
Professional Counselors

Estate planning is a complex and multifaceted endeavor that is best pursued with the assistance of professional advisors with training and experience in a variety of relevant disciplines. Depending on circumstances, a planning team comprised of one or more of the following may be necessary to formulate and implement a plan suited to the estate owner's unique circumstances and objectives: (1) an attorney, (2) an accountant, (3) an insurance agent, (4) a bank trust officer, (5) an investment counselor, (6) a financial planner, and (7) a mental health, communication, or family dynamics professional. The financial industry is gigantic. There are experts with all kinds of titles—money managers, stockbrokers, financial planners, investment consultants, estate planners, wealth consultants, family office managers, attorneys, accountants, and more. It seems newly defined and titled professionals are ever evolving. The task becomes to make sense of this array of possibilities.

SELECTING ADVISORS
In sorting out options, it is helpful to keep in mind that the very core of the notion of professionalism is dedication to client-centered practice. It is essential that professionals of all disciplines listen and reflect their understanding of the client's needs, issues, and values back to the client. The professional needs to tailor instruments and remedies—be they trusts, other legal agreements, or other financial or family plans—in

order to meet the unique needs identified by the client. Many professionals in the financial/legal arena have canned programs that reflect preconceived notions about who you are and what you need based on certain demographic indicators. A professional must listen to you and reflect in order to construct plans, remedies, and solutions suited to your unique circumstances. To find the right professional or team of professionals, try these steps:

1. Create a list of potential advisors from your own research, referrals from trusted friends, and referrals from reputable banks, law firms, and accounting firms.
2. Interview those on your list for a match in terms of expertise, investment philosophy, and values. Select a professional whom you can trust, and consult with that individual to work toward building a team by generating a network of possibilities.
3. Ask about a contract as well as how the financial professional is paid for his or her services (e.g., does he or she profit from selling certain securities or investment instruments, etc.?).
4. Ask for the names of other clients and contact them, with permission.
5. Select one or two advisors, but reevaluate in a set period of time based on both your overall financial picture as well as personal judgments and feelings.

Ordinarily, the planning process is initiated when the client engages a particular advisor to assist in formulating his objectives and selecting the appropriate techniques for achieving those objectives. Ideally, that advisor has nothing to sell but advice and counsel, and has no referral, fee-sharing, or other arrangements or obligations that might compromise loyalty to the client. An advisor who is unfettered by potential conflicts of interest is more likely to gain the client's trust and effectively assist in clarifying values and articulating objectives. The goal is finding an advisor in a unique position to assemble and coordinate the efforts of other members of the planning team.

Each professional advisor views the planning process through the prism of his or her own interests, expertise, and experience. Properly managed, differences in perspective enrich and invigorate the process and will generate an array of relevant and appropriate options. If a single perspective is permitted to dominate the process, both the analysis and the recommended course of action may well reflect a professional bias that may be contrary to the client's best interests.

High-quality professionalism strives to minimize the risk of such biases in the planning process. The attributes of such a professional are

- A willingness to place the client's interests ahead of all other considerations, including the advisor's own financial interests;
- Respect for the perspective and competence of other advisors; and
- A strong commitment to collaborative problem solving.

If each member of the planning team manifests these attributes, an outcome in harmony with the client's interests will be virtually assured.

An advisor should refrain from making assumptions concerning a client's objectives based solely on the client's family composition or financial profile or any other single or narrowly defined dimension. Each client is an individual with a unique mix of values, objectives, problems, and opportunities. Nothing more thoroughly destroys a client's enthusiasm for the process of estate planning than to feel that nothing more than an off-the-shelf plan is offered.

ADVISORS MUST NOT ABUSE THEIR POSITIONS OF TRUST

The advisor's role is to take the time to communicate effectively with the client and assist the client in clarifying, prioritizing, and articulating values and objectives. While the advisor's expertise makes him or her uniquely suited to that role, it also opens the door to the professional's entering into a role of power and influence over the less-informed client. Advisors must not abuse that position by seeking to impose their own values. This is not to say that it is inappropriate for the advisor to share principles, ideas, and options with the client. The advisor must remain aware that some individuals have given little thought to and are unable to articulate the core principles that govern their lives. The advisor's willingness to reveal his or her perspective on moral issues can help the client find a moral compass and the courage to abide by its dictates. The wise advisor listens, respects, and assists the client in telling his or her personal narrative. Through that narrative, the values an individual holds will emerge. These are the values that need to be molded into the final estate plan and comprise an individual's personal heritage and the true legacy to be passed on to the next generation.

Estate planning advisors are not peddlers, and estate planning techniques are not commodities. If the advisor views them as such, creative solutions will fail to be offered. Consider, for example, the advisor who shamelessly characterizes probate as "living hell" and promotes the revocable living trust as the only viable solution. Obviously, an advisor who engages in such hyperbole has little regard for the facts or for his client's best interests. The primary motivation is to sell wares whether the client needs them or not. Of course, in appropriate circumstances, the revocable trust may be the best vehicle for achieving the client's objectives, but its suitability should be based on the client's needs and circumstances and not the advisor's exaggerated claims concerning the evils of probate.

INDIVIDUAL VERSUS JOINT ESTATE PLANNING

Families have undergone enormous changes in the last few decades. Today, a married couple is comprised of two individuals who usually have distinct careers, income sources, interests, and personal finances. In the old cultural model, the male was typically the breadwinner and, in turn, the individual who contacted an attorney and executed the estate plan. It is more likely today that an attorney will be contacted by the couple together with each partner expecting equal dignity and joint representation. However, couples must realize that this model of joint representation requires full disclosure between the spouses. Unless there are overt signs of conflict within the marital relationship that would compromise the ability of the attorney to serve the interest of both individuals, the client is not the individual husband or wife; rather, the client becomes the marital relationship itself. An estate attorney must know how to move forward representing the interests of each individual when that may mean different perspectives, interests, and goals. The attorney must also know how to achieve full disclosure and make clear from the outset that there will be no secrets between the attorney and either partner in the relationship. Estate planning today is no longer simply an ordering of financial affairs. It is a process by which individuals come to terms with their relationships with family and community as well as money and view it as a vehicle for serving their values.

Communication skills are an essential part of this process. An inexperienced estate attorney can inadvertently walk into marital conflict. For example, a couple visited an attorney with the goal of creating an estate plan for their family. After they left, the attorney received a call from one spouse asking that an out-of-wedlock child be provided for but not revealed to the spouse. Bound by professional ethics, the attorney is obligated to disclose this secret. Joint representation from the first contact means there will be no secrets. If one partner tells the attorney something in confidence, it cannot be protected as privileged communication. Obviously, a long-held secret from a spouse such as an out-of-wedlock child could potentially disrupt a marriage. If the attorney has made abundantly clear the ground rules for joint representation, then this dilemma, if presented, can be avoided. The spouses are aware that family secrets will be exposed if revealed and can elect to either proceed with that process or find separate representation for constructing a separate estate plan. An attorney cannot construct a joint estate plan and keep information confidential from either spouse. An attorney aware of these issues will accordingly advise clients to plan individually or jointly.

There is abundant psychology literature on the burdensome nature of family secrets. It has been observed that family secrets that are revealed early in a relationship, or in childhood, can often be handled, integrated, and resolved. The longer a secret remains hidden, the more the relationship itself becomes built on deception. Marriages and other family relationships sometimes cannot survive the revelation of hurtful secrets. The foundation of trust is eroded, hurtful and negative feelings surface, and sometimes even the best of mental health counselors cannot repair the damage done. Sadly, some individuals have attained their very sense of themselves and their social acceptability based on innuendo, omission, or even outright lies. Some individuals opted for this to avoid feared stigma, harsh judgments of others, shame, and humiliation. Perhaps some will utilize the process of estate planning to unburden themselves and take the risks necessary to reintroduce honesty into the family relationships. Others may feel that the hurt of the truth will outweigh the benefits that truth-telling provides. Perhaps these individuals will be relegated to planning their estates individually rather than including the spouse or other family members in the process.

The process of estate planning involves discussing private matters involving not only one's history but also one's mortality. The process touches relationships between spouses as well as between parents and children. Many individuals start the process of estate planning and never complete it because there is such a high level of discomfort from disclosure or the threat of disclosure. Sometimes the process breaks down due to either disclosure issues or decision-making regarding guardianship of minor children. Some estate attorneys have sought training in helping a couple to resolve such tensions and have achieved a high level of skill and comfort. Others can sense when it is helpful to bring a communication specialist, therapist, or family dynamic professional into the process. The inability to approach and surmount such communication issues is one reason that some attorneys retreat and thrive instead on simply providing rote accounting regarding tax savings. Values-based estate planning is a very different process. It involves a caring and sensitive advisor who will not shy away from communicating and who will assist in constructing an outcome that is reflective of the family's relationships and interests.

CHAPTER NINETEEN

Can We Ever Be Fair?

The estate planning process often preoccupies itself with fairness. This largely arises from parents who hold the traditional and conventional belief that they must divide their estate equally among their children. Many believe this is the law and that if they fail to leave an equal share to each child, then their estate will be contested, causing family discord, and the probate court will apportion it equally anyway. This, however, is a myth. Only if a parent dies without a will is the estate divided equally. Interestingly, English law originally provided for only the eldest child to inherit the entire estate. Gradually, this changed to include only the male heirs. Female heirs received a dower share, the purpose of which was to tempt a suitor to marry them. Over time, these patriarchal principles were replaced by an egalitarian principle. This principle assumes that what works for one child will certainly work for each of the children; therefore, each of the children should inherit equally.

This fails to address the reality, however, which is that each family and each individual within each family is unique. There is no compelling reason for an equal division of assets other than a parent's fear that children will feel shortchanged, resentful, and, most importantly, less loved. One gentleman who planned his estate throughout his life was so preoccupied with this concept of equality that he built in an advancement factor. Throughout his lifetime, he carefully recorded the dates on which each child received any financial assistance. This included all gifts, loans, and payments advanced to or in favor of each child, including even school tuition and housing. He then factored in an interest rate to be added in to determine the precise amount advanced to each child during his lifetime. At his death, all of the children's accounts were tallied and balanced, and the remaining inheritance divided equally.

This gentleman denied the reality that life is not always fair or equitable. How good fortune, bad luck, or opportunity is doled out in life remains beyond the control of parents or parents' wealth. Fates shift; circumstances change over time. Some children seem to get all the good breaks and opportunities; others get none. Similarly, money may destroy some children, whereas it is beneficial for others. The question is how to distribute wealth in a fashion that embraces each child and brings out their best. Every decision a parent makes regarding the distribution of wealth conveys an emotional statement as well. We now know that the emotional meaning of money derives directly from family relationships and acquired values. If money is heavily weighted with symbolic meaning within a family, such as by a preoccupation with fairness and equality as if it could be translated into units of parental love, then the emotional consequences of an unequal division of wealth carry tremendous significance. In contrast, if wealth is viewed as an instrument for promoting values and opportunities such as personal development, education, community, or world concerns and service, then money takes on a different meaning. How parents think of money in the family, whether articulated or not, is significant for children. If parents use their wealth as a statement of a child's acceptance or acceptability, then the child who receives less may inherit a most destructive legacy of feeling unworthy and unloved. Similarly, parents who are secretive during their lifetimes about differential treatment of each child may well build resentment in the children.

Sadly, professionals are often not interested in working to define a family's values and explore its relationship to money, which will ultimately enhance opportunity for each child, by innovating unique and creative trusts. Rather, their interests often lie only in the efficiency of delivering services. The most efficient model remains generating an estate plan driven by tax savings. In this instance, the estate attorney is essentially driving the process with his or her values rather than opening the vista that wealth offers for furthering the family's values through a uniquely tailored estate planning process.

APPRAISING THE UNIQUE NEEDS
AND CIRCUMSTANCES OF EACH HEIR

Circumstances for each child are different. If a parent tries to hide that reality or obliterate it, they have started in motion an impossible treadmill. Families who are withholding with their expressions of love and praise may create the notion that love is finite, like money. Parents who view wealth as providing access to opportunity, however, often find that an equal amount to each child is not always in the child's best interest.

By conveying wealth into individual trusts for each child, parents can also convey their philosophical principles. Trusts with different amounts or different guiding principles cannot be challenged on the grounds that each child was entitled to an equal share. A trust offers flexibility in defining values as well as a vehicle for accommodating unforeseen or changing circumstances that a parent may not have anticipated. Furthermore, a trust protects the assets in that claims from creditors against an individual child cannot be made against the trust holdings. A trust, therefore, may not only preserve the family wealth by providing asset protection, but it can be shaped to enhance the development and opportunity for each child as a unique individual.

Some parents might consider establishing a philanthropic legacy for their children. If parents determine that they have ample resources for their own needs and ample resources for the needs of their children, the rest, the "redundant wealth," is not necessary for the family well-being. A family foundation established with such funds allows the children to enjoy the intangible benefits of this redundant wealth through managing or otherwise participating in the family foundation. If placed into a tax-exempt organization, no income tax or estate tax is paid, and the family benefits from association with philanthropic endeavors (see chapter 13).

Following the dazzle of easy money during the nineties, many families faced the realities of restriction and cutbacks. Many came to recognize the extraordinary treasure of enduring family values over material wealth. Creative estate planning can provide the means to preserve these values beyond the death of a parent without him or her controlling "from the grave." These chapters provide an array of options from which to choose, and hopefully challenge readers to dare to generate their own family plan. Experienced professionals know that one size does not fit all in defining a family's values and priorities, in assessing both an individual's potential and contribution, and in shaping and defining the individual's relationship with money and material wealth. Introspection, assessment, and ultimately family discussion, interaction, and participation are essential in arriving at a family's own wealth and legacy management strategies.

Specimen Last Will

DISCLAIMER: This specimen pourover will is for illustration only. There is no warranty, express or implied, that it is appropriate for use in any particular jurisdiction or circumstance.

LAST WILL
OF
PRUDENT PLANNER

I, Prudent Planner, of Orderly, Wyndiana, hereby make my last will and revoke all previous wills and codicils. I am married to Chary Planner. I have three living children: Marissa Planner, Lamont Planner, and Matthew Planner. All of my living children are adults. I have no deceased children.

ARTICLE 1: DISPOSITION OF ESTATE

1.1 Personal and Household Property.

(a) Gift By Written Statement. I give all personal and household property in my estate in accordance with a written statement signed by me or in my handwriting that I may leave at my death.

(b) Gift to Wife. I give all personal and household property not disposed of by written statement to my wife, if she survives me.

(c) Gift If Wife Fails to Survive. If my wife fails to survive me, I give all personal and household property not disposed of by written statement to my children who survive me. My children shall allocate such property among themselves as they may agree. If they are unable to agree with respect to the allocation of all of such property within three months after my death, they shall allocate such property among themselves by selecting one item of such property in turn until all items of such property have been selected. My children shall make their selections in ascending order of their ages. If any of my children is under a legal disability, such child's parent or legal guardian shall represent such child for all purposes of this Article 1.1(c).

(d) Payment of Costs. My personal representatives shall pay the costs of securing, storing, insuring, packing and shipping all personal and household property as an expense of administering my estate.

1.2 Residue.

(a) Devise to Living Trust. By trust agreement dated January 1, 2003 (the "trust agreement"), my wife and I established The Planner Family Trust. I give the residue of my estate to the trustees of The Planner Family Trust, for administration, division, and distribution in accordance with the trust agreement, as in effect on the date of my death.

(b) Discharge of Personal Representatives. Receipt by the trustees of The Planner Family Trust of the residue of my estate shall constitute a full discharge of my personal representatives' responsibility for such property.

(c) Confidentiality of Trust Records. Neither the trust agreement nor any inventory or other record relating to The Planner Family Trust shall be filed with the records of my probate estate, unless required by law.

ARTICLE 2: FIDUCIARIES

2.1 **Personal Representatives.** I nominate as my personal representatives the persons who are to act as trustees of The Planner Family Trust following my death.

2.2 **Guardian and Conservator.** I nominate as guardian of the person and conservator of the property of my legally disabled children the person I may designate in a statement signed by me or in my handwriting that I leave at my death.

2.3 **Powers of Alternate Fiduciary.** A duly appointed alternate fiduciary shall have all of the title, rights, powers, and duties of the original fiduciary without any act of transfer. No alternate fiduciary shall be obligated to examine the accounts, records, and acts of any previous fiduciary or to proceed against any previous fiduciary for any act or omission to act.

2.4 **Ancillary Fiduciaries.** If a representative of my estate is required to qualify as a fiduciary in a jurisdiction other than my domicile, I nominate the person (including my domiciliary personal representatives) my domiciliary personal representatives appoint. The ancillary fiduciary shall have in the other jurisdiction all of the rights, powers, and duties of my personal representatives under this will and under the laws of the other jurisdiction.

2.5 **Bonds Waived.** Each fiduciary shall be permitted to qualify without giving a bond or other undertaking in any jurisdiction for the performance of the fiduciary's duties, or, if bond is required by law, without the necessity of sureties.

2.6 **Compensation of Fiduciaries.** Each fiduciary is entitled to reasonable compensation commensurate with services actually performed and to reimbursement for expenses properly incurred.

2.7 **Exculpation.** A fiduciary shall not be liable for an act or omission done in good faith to promote the best interests of the beneficiaries, unless the act or omission constitutes gross negligence, intentional misconduct, or a knowing violation of law. A fiduciary's act or omission shall be presumed to be a proper exercise of the fiduciary's authority, in the absence of clear and convincing proof to the contrary.

ARTICLE 3: ADMINISTRATION OF ESTATE

3.1 **Payment of Taxes.** All estate, transfer, inheritance, and similar taxes payable by reason of my death shall be paid and apportioned by the trustees of The Planner Family Trust in accordance with the direction contained in the trust agreement.

3.2 **No Supervised Estate Administration.** My personal representatives shall administer my estate free from active court supervision unless changed circumstances that I could not have anticipated justify court supervision to protect the interests of my estate or its beneficiaries.

3.3 **Administrative Powers.** My personal representatives shall have full power, authority, and discretion to administer my estate, including, without limitation, the power, authority, and discretion granted under the Wyndiana Probate Code.

3.4 **Tax Elections.**

(a) General Grant of Authority. My personal representatives may make any elections and give any consents with respect to tax matters applicable to me or my estate.

(b) <u>Trustees' Decision Controls</u>. If both my personal representatives and the trustees of The Planner Family Trust are authorized to act with respect to any tax matter applicable to my estate, the trustees' decision shall control and my personal representatives shall sign and file such documents and take such other action as may be necessary to effectuate the trustees' decision.

3.5 Release of Powers. Any fiduciary at any time may release any authority, right, or power pertaining to the administration of my estate, temporarily or irrevocably, by signed notice filed in the records of my estate.

3.6 Third Party Reliance. For the purpose of verifying a fiduciary's authority to perform any act referred to in this Article 3, any person dealing with the fiduciary may rely on a copy of this will or selected excerpts from this will, certified as correct by a notary public, to the same extent as if the certified copy were the original. No person dealing with a fiduciary shall be under any obligation to see to the application of any payment made to the fiduciary or to inquire into the validity, expediency, or propriety of any of the fiduciary's acts or omissions.

ARTICLE 4: MISCELLANEOUS PROVISIONS

4.1 Persons under Legal Disability. The guardian or conservator of the estate of a person under legal disability or, if none, the person having the right of custody of the person, and any adult ancestor of an unborn person, may act for the disabled or unborn person for all purposes of this will, including, without limitation, receipt of notices and reports, approval of investments and accounts and consent to allocations and distributions.

4.2 Effect of Opposition to Will. If any beneficiary under this will, in any manner, contests or objects to the admission of this will to probate, disputes the validity or effect of any provision of this will or exercises any right to take a share of my estate contrary to the provisions of this will, such beneficiary and all of his or her descendants shall be deemed to have predeceased me for all purposes of this will.

4.3 Definitions. Unless the language or context clearly indicates that a different meaning is intended, the terms in quotations have the meanings specified in this Article 4.3.

(a) <u>Wife</u>. "My wife" means only Chary Planner.

(b) <u>Children</u>. "My children" means only Marissa Planner, Lamont Planner, and Matthew Planner.

(c) Personal and Household Property. "Personal and household property" means tangible personal property used for personal purposes, including personal automobiles, recreational vehicles and equipment, boats, household goods, furniture, furnishings, garden and lawn equipment, tools, books, china, crystal, jewelry, silverware, works of art, collections, clothing, personal effects, pets, and similar items of tangible personal property. A devise of my personal and household property includes any associated insurance policies, including pending claims, and is subject to all liens and encumbrances.

(d) Person. "Person" means a legal entity, including, without limitation, a natural person, a corporation, a partnership, a limited liability company, a trust, and an association.

(e) Fiduciaries. "Personal representatives" and any pronoun in reference to personal representatives always refer interchangeably to the male or female person or persons or to the institution or any combination of them then acting. "Fiduciary" refers to any person acting in a fiduciary capacity.

4.4 **Constructional Rules.** The following constructional rules shall govern the interpretation of this will.

(a) Court Decrees. Any decree of adoption or divorce at any time rendered by a court of record shall conclusively be deemed valid.

(b) Governing Law. Wyndiana law shall govern all questions as to the validity and construction of this will.

(c) Other Principles of Construction. Words in any gender include the other gender; the singular includes the plural and vice versa; and the headings and underlined paragraph titles are for guidance only and shall have no significance in the interpretation of this will.

IN WITNESS WHEREOF, I, Prudent Planner, the testator, sign my name to this instrument this 1st day of January, 2003, and, being first duly sworn, declare to the undersigned authority that I sign this instrument as my will and that I sign it willingly, that I sign it as my free and voluntary act for the purposes expressed in it, and that I am 18 years of age or older, of sound mind, and under no constraint or undue influence.

_____

Prudent Planner

We, Roenna True and Lavern Faithful, the witnesses, sign our names to this instrument, being first duly sworn, and declare to the undersigned authority that the testator signs and executes this instrument as his will and that he signs it willingly, and that each of us, in the presence and hearing of the testator and of each other, hereby signs this will as witness to the testator's signing, and that to the best of our knowledge the testator is 18 years of age or older, of sound mind, and under no constraint or undue influence.

Witness: _____
Address: 3521 North Willmont Drive
Orderville, WD 84602

Witness: _____
Address: 3521 North Willmont Drive
Orderville, WD 84602

STATE OF WYNDIANA   )
)ss.
COUNTY OF ORDERLY   )

Subscribed, sworn to, and acknowledged before me by Prudent Planner, the testator, and subscribed and sworn to before me by Roenna True and Lavern Faithful, witnesses, this 1st day of January, 2003.

Witness my hand and official seal.

[SEAL]   _____
                                 Notary Public

                                 My commission expires: _____

Specimen Revocable Living Trust

DISCLAIMER: This specimen revocable living trust agreement is for illustration only. There is no warranty, express or implied, that it is appropriate for use in any particular jurisdiction or circumstance.

THE PLANNER FAMILY TRUST

THIS AGREEMENT (this "agreement"), dated January 1, 2003, is between Prudent Planner and Chary Planner, as grantors (referred to in the first person plural), and Prudent Planner and Chary Planner, as trustees (referred to as the "trustees").

ARTICLE 1: CREATION OF TRUST

1.1   **Trust Estate.** With the execution of this agreement, we have transferred to the trustees, as the initial trust estate, the property described on Schedule A. The trustees shall administer and distribute the initial and any additions to the trust estate in accordance with the provisions of this agreement.

1.2   **Name of Trust.** The name of the trust created by this agreement is The Planner Family Trust.

1.3   **Additions to Trust.** At any time either of us may transfer additional property to the trustees for administration and distribution in accordance with this agreement.

1.4   **Purposes of Trust.** The purposes of The Planner Family Trust are (a) to provide for the convenient and efficient management of our commonly owned assets during our lives and (b) to facilitate the orderly transfer of our interests in such assets upon the death of the survivor of us.

ARTICLE 2: OWNERSHIP OF BENEFICIAL INTEREST

2.1   **Ownership of Trust Estate During Our Joint Lives.** The property comprising the initial trust estate and any additional property we may add to the trust estate during our joint lives shall be deemed to be owned by us in equal undivided shares.

2.2   **Allocation of Additions Made Upon Deceased Grantor's Death.** Property added to the trust estate by reason of the death of the first of us to die shall be allocated to the deceased grantor's separate share of the trust estate and administered and accounted for as the deceased grantor's separate property.

2.3   **Accounting for Rents, Profits, and Income.** All income and all proceeds from the sale, exchange, or other disposition of property in the trust estate shall have the same character as the property from which such income or proceeds were derived.

ARTICLE 3: ADMINISTRATION DURING OUR JOINT LIVES

3.1   **Reserved Powers.**
   (a)   Enumeration of Powers. We reserve the following powers:

      (1) Revocation. Either of us may revoke, in whole or in part, the trust governed by this agreement. Promptly upon receipt of an instrument of revocation, the trustees shall distribute to us in equal undivided shares the portion of the trust estate specified in such instrument.

      (2) Amendment. We may amend this agreement in any manner. However, no amendment shall increase the trustees' duties and responsibilities without their prior written consent.

      (3) Trustees. We may change the identity and number of the trustees. Our reserved power under this Article 3.1(a)(3) includes, without limitation, the power to (i) remove any trustee, with or without cause, (ii) appoint an alternate trustee to serve in the place of any trustee who ceases to act and (iii) appoint additional trustees for general or limited purposes and for specified or indefinite terms.

(4) Investments. We may direct the management, investment, and reinvestment of the trust estate. Our reserved power under this Article 3.1(a)(4) includes, without limitation, the power to direct the purchase, retention, sale, lease, exchange, mortgage, option, encumbrance, or abandonment of any item of property in the trust estate. Absent direction from us, the trustees shall manage, invest, and reinvest the trust estate pursuant to their power and authority under Article 9.

(b) Scope of Powers. Our reserved powers under this Article 3.1 are exercisable from time to time and in our absolute discretion. Except as provided in Article 3.3, neither the trustees nor any beneficiary shall have any right or power to enforce or object to the exercise of such powers.

(c) Exercise of Powers. Our reserved powers under this Article 3.1 are exercisable only by signed instrument delivered to the trustees while we are both still living.

3.2 **Distributions.**

(a) As Directed. The trustees shall distribute the net income and principal of the trust estate to such persons, at such times and in such amounts and shares as we may direct by written instrument signed by us and delivered to the trustees during our joint lives.

(b) Absence of Direction. Absent direction from us, the trustees shall distribute to us from time to time such amounts of income and principal as the trustees consider necessary to provide for our medical care, maintenance, support, and reasonable comfort in our accustomed manner of living.

3.3 **Incapacity.**

(a) Effect. If during our joint lives either of us becomes incapacitated (the "incapacitated grantor"), (1) the incapacitated grantor shall cease to be eligible to serve as a trustee; (2) an attempt by the incapacitated grantor to exercise any of his or her reserved powers shall be without force and effect; and (3) the trustees on the incapacitated grantor's behalf may revoke the trust, in whole or part, or transfer to themselves on the terms of this agreement any property the incapacitated grantor may own outright. The trustees' power to act on the incapacitated grantor's behalf during his or her incapacity shall be construed and interpreted as a durable power of attorney to act as the incapacitated grantor's attorneys in fact and agents and shall be in addition to all other powers bestowed upon the trustees by this agreement.

(b) Termination of Incapacity. Upon termination of the incapacitated grantor's incapacity, the provisions of Article 3.3(a) shall cease to apply. However, notwithstanding the termination of the incapacitated grantor's incapacity, he or she shall be reinstated as a trustee only through the express exercise of our reserved powers.

ARTICLE 4: DISPOSITION UPON DECEASED GRANTOR'S DEATH

4.1   **Trust Irrevocable.** Upon the death of the first of us to die (referred to as the "deceased grantor"), the trust governed by this agreement shall become irrevocable and the survivor of us (referred to as the "surviving grantor") shall thereafter have no power to amend the provisions of this agreement.

4.2   **Additions to Trust Estate.** Upon the deceased grantor's death, the trustees shall add to the trust estate any property received by reason of the deceased grantor's death, including any property devised under the deceased grantor's will and any insurance proceeds or other death benefits.

4.3   **Disposition of Trust Estate.** Upon the deceased grantor's death, the trustees shall distribute the trust estate, as augmented by the additions described in Article 4.2, in accordance with the following provisions of this Article 4.3.

(a) Expenses. The trustees may pay from the deceased grantor's share of the trust estate (1) the expenses of the deceased grantor's last illness, funeral, and burial, (2) the deceased grantor's unpaid income and gift taxes, and (3) the expenses of administering the deceased grantor's estate.

(b) Allocation to The Survivor's Trust. The trustees shall allocate to The Survivor's Trust, for administration and distribution in accordance with the provisions of Article 5:

(1) the surviving grantor's share of the trust estate;

(2) any property received by the trustees under the terms of the deceased grantor's will or any beneficiary designation that is specifically allocable to The Survivor's Trust; and

(3) an amount equal to the smallest amount of the deceased grantor's share of the trust estate that must be allowed as a marital deduction to eliminate the federal estate tax with respect to the deceased grantor's gross estate.

(c) <u>Allocation to The Family Trust</u>. The trustees shall allocate the rest of the trust estate, if any, to The Family Trust, for administration and distribution in accordance with the provisions of Article 6.

ARTICLE 5: THE SURVIVOR'S TRUST

5.1 **Distributions.**

(a) <u>As Directed</u>. The trustees shall distribute the net income and principal of The Survivor's Trust to such persons, including the surviving grantor, at such times and in such amounts and shares as the surviving grantor may direct by written instrument signed by the surviving grantor and delivered to the trustees during the surviving grantor's life.

(b) <u>Absence of Direction</u>. Absent direction from the surviving grantor, the trustees shall distribute to the surviving grantor from time to time such amounts of the income and principal of The Survivor's Trust as the trustees consider necessary to provide for the surviving grantor's medical care, maintenance, support, and reasonable comfort in the surviving grantor's accustomed manner of living.

5.2 **Termination.**

(a) <u>Terminating Events</u>. The Survivor's Trust shall terminate on the earlier of (1) the exhaustion of the trust estate or (2) the date of the surviving grantor's death.

(b) <u>Disposition upon Termination</u>. As soon as practical following termination of The Survivor's Trust, the trustees shall distribute any property remaining in the trust estate as follows:

(1) The trustees may pay from such property (i) the expenses of the surviving grantor's last illness, funeral, and burial, (ii) the surviving grantor's unpaid income and gift taxes, and (iii) the expenses of administering the surviving grantor's estate.

(2) The trustees shall pay from such property all inheritance and estate taxes payable by reason of the surviving grantor's death and attributable to the property comprising The Survivor's Trust.

(3) The trustees shall distribute any of such property that is not effectively disposed of under the foregoing provisions of this Article 5.2(b) to

such persons, including the surviving grantor's estate, in such amounts, shares, and interests as the surviving grantor may have appointed by his or her last will.

(4) The trustees shall allocate any of such property that is not effectively disposed of under the foregoing provisions of this Article 5.2(b) to The Family Trust, for administration and distribution in accordance with the provisions of Article 6.

ARTICLE 6: THE FAMILY TRUST

6.1   **Distributions.** The trustees may distribute the income and principal of The Family Trust to the surviving grantor, our descendants, and our descendants' spouses, at such times and in such amounts and shares as the trustees determine. If the trustees determine that the present and anticipated needs of the surviving grantor, our descendants, and our descendants' spouses are adequately provided for, the trustees may distribute the net income and principal of The Family Trust to qualified charities, at such times and in such amounts and shares as the trustees determine.

6.2   **Surviving Grantor's Power to Appoint Principal.** The surviving grantor may appoint the principal of The Family Trust to such of our descendants, our descendants' spouses, and qualified charities, at such times and in such amounts, shares, and interests as the surviving spouse determines.

6.3   **Termination.**

(a)   Terminating Events. The Family Trust shall terminate on the earlier of (1) the exhaustion of the trust estate or (2) the death of the surviving member of a class composed of the surviving spouse and our children.

(b)   Disposition of Trust Estate. Upon termination of The Family Trust, the trustees shall distribute any property remaining in the trust estate in the following order of priority:

(1) to our then living descendants, by representation; or

(2) if none of our descendants is then living, to Friends of Nature, Inc., of Northpark, Wyndiana, for its general purposes; or

(3) if Friends of Nature, Inc. is not then an existing qualified charity, to such qualified charities as the trustees in their discretion may designate.

ARTICLE 7: PROVISIONS GOVERNING DISTRIBUTIONS

7.1 **Advisory Standards.** In determining whether to make discretionary distributions from The Family Trust to our descendants and their spouses, the trustees should take into account, but shall not be compelled or constrained by, the following considerations and guidelines.

(a) Statement of Purpose. Our primary purpose in establishing The Family Trust is to ensure that the wealth we have accumulated during our lives is preserved and employed as a means of instilling in our descendants and their spouses the following values: (1) *stewardship*—recognition that all one owns is entrusted to him for the purpose of fostering the physical, emotional, and spiritual well-being of himself and the members of his family and community; (2) *enterprise*—creativity, initiative, and willingness to take prudent risks to foster self-reliance and add value to the larger economy; (3) *personal growth*—recognition and development of personal aptitude and abilities; (4) *integrity*—honesty, sincerity, and trustworthiness; and (5) *community*—interdependence that fosters security and aggregates strength. Our hope and expectation is that the trustees will be guided by those same values in exercising their discretionary powers with respect to The Family Trust.

(b) Specific Guidelines.

(1) Generally, the trustees should not make distributions to a beneficiary if in the trustees' judgment such distributions would negatively affect the beneficiary's motivation to become productive and self-sufficient.

(2) The trustees are encouraged to make distributions to a beneficiary who is (i) so physically or mentally disabled as to be unable to provide for his or her own support, (ii) pursuing a career that is socially productive but not substantially remunerative, (iii) caring for one or more family members, including minor children or aging parents, or (iv) engaging in other endeavors that impede the beneficiary's ability to become and remain financially self-sufficient but are nevertheless consistent with the values referred to in Article 7.1(a).

(3) The trustees may make distributions to pay for any medical procedure, test, or treatment, including, without limitation, surgery, organ transplants, psychiatric care, physical therapy, hospitalization, convalescent care, and home care, as the trustees consider appropriate to preserve and protect the beneficiary's physical, mental, and emotional well-being.

(4) The trustees may make distributions to enable a beneficiary to pursue technical, vocational, undergraduate, or graduate education at or under the auspices of any accredited institution, public or private.

(5) If a beneficiary does not have sufficient financial resources to purchase a home of adequate size to accommodate his or her family, the trustees may distribute or loan trust income and principal to the beneficiary to partially or wholly fund such purchase.

(6) If a beneficiary desires to engage in a business or profession, the trustees may distribute or loan trust income and principal or acquire assets for such purpose, if the trustees determine that to do so will not jeopardize the reasonably foreseeable needs of the other beneficiaries and that there is a reasonable chance that the enterprise will be successful.

(7) If a beneficiary desires to volunteer his or her time to activities intended to relieve the suffering, enhance the quality of life, and promote the self-sufficiency of the poor and needy, the trustees may make distributions to defray any portion or all of the reasonable expenses the beneficiary incurs in the pursuit of such activities.

(8) The trustees should consult with the surviving grantor before making distributions of income and principal to our descendants and their spouses and give serious consideration to his or her suggestions.

(9) The preservation of principal is not as important as accomplishment of the foregoing purposes.

7.2 Limitations on Discretionary Powers.

(a) Limitation Based on Ascertainable Standard. If a person is both a trustee and a beneficiary of The Family Trust, then, notwithstanding any other provision of this agreement, the extent of the trustee's duty to exercise and not to exercise any discretionary power to distribute income and principal of the trust to such person shall be determined based solely on such person's needs for health, education, support, and maintenance.

(b) Proscription against Discharge of Legal Obligation. The trustees' exercise of their discretionary power to distribute the income or principal of The Family Trust shall not discharge any trustee or any other person from any personal legal obligation, including any obligation to support or maintain any person.

(c) Insurance on Life of Trustees. If at any time the property comprising The Family Trust includes an insurance policy on the life of a trustee, the other trustee or trustees then serving or, if the trustee is serving alone, a special trustee appointed pursuant to the provisions of Article 8.1(a) shall have exclusive power and authority to exercise all rights, privileges, and incidents of ownership with respect to the policy and its proceeds.

7.3 **Method of Distribution.** The trustees may distribute any property distributable to a beneficiary: (a) directly to the beneficiary, even though the beneficiary is incapacitated or under a legal disability; (b) indirectly to the beneficiary through payment of the beneficiary's expenses, debts, and obligations; (c) to an incapacitated or disabled beneficiary's guardian, conservator, or agent acting under a durable general power of attorney; (d) to the custodian of a minor beneficiary's property, including a custodian acting under any statute governing transfers to minors; or (e) except with respect to distributions from The Survivor's Trust, to the trustee of any trust in which all of the present and future interests are vested in the beneficiary or the beneficiary's estate. The trustees shall have no responsibility for the proper application of any payment made pursuant to this Article 7.3.

7.4 **Class Distributions.** The trustees' discretionary power to distribute income and principal among the members of a class includes the power to make unequal distributions and the power to withhold all distributions of income or principal from any member of the class.

7.5 **Discretion of Trustees.** The trustees' power to determine the extent and nature of any distribution under this trust shall be exercisable in their discretion and no beneficiary or other interested person shall have standing to object to the reasonable exercise of such power.

ARTICLE 8: TRUSTEES

8.1 **Appointment, Resignation, and Succession.**

(a) Appointment of Additional Trustees. The trustees of a trust at any time may appoint one or more additional trustees of the trust by signed notice filed in the trust records and delivered to each appointed trustee and each beneficiary then eligible to receive the trust's income. The appointment may be for general or limited purposes and for a specified or indefinite term. The appointment shall be effective upon delivery of the notice of appointment to the appointed trustee or on such later date as may be specified in the notice.

(b) Resignation. A trustee at any time may resign by signed notice filed in the trust's records and delivered to each beneficiary then eligible to receive the trust's income. If the trustee is a co-trustee, the resignation shall be effective on the date the notice of resignation is filed in the trust's records or on such later date as may be specified in the notice of resignation. If the trustee is the sole trustee, the resignation shall be effective on acceptance by a properly appointed alternate trustee.

(c) Incapacity. A trustee who becomes incapacitated shall be considered to have resigned as of the date the physician's statement certifying the trustee's incapacity is filed in the trust's records.

(d) Removal.

(1) Power to Remove. The surviving grantor, during his or her life, and, after his or her death, our adult children at any time may remove any trustee of any trust governed by this agreement by signed notice filed in the trust's records and delivered to the removed trustee and each beneficiary then eligible to receive trust's income. The removal shall be effective on the date that is 15 days after the date the notice is delivered to the removed trustee.

(2) Limitation on Power to Remove. A power to remove a trustee may be exercised only in furtherance of trust purposes and not as a means of improperly influencing the trustee in the exercise of its discretionary powers with respect to the beneficial enjoyment of trust income or principal. If a removed trustee believes that a substantial purpose of the removal was to improperly influence the exercise of its discretionary powers, the removed trustee may stay the removal by delivering an affidavit substantiating the basis of its belief to the person or persons exercising the power of removal within 15 days after receiving notice of the removal. The removed trustee's delivery of the affidavit shall render the removal ineffective unless and until a court of competent jurisdiction determines that to improperly influence the exercise of the removed trustee's discretionary powers was not a substantial purpose of the removal.

(e) Alternates. Subject to the provisions of Article 3.1(a)(3):

(1) if either of us ceases to act as trustee, First Harvest Bank & Trust Company, a Wyndiana corporation, shall act as co-trustee with the survivor of us; and

(2) if both of us cease to act as trustee, First Harvest Bank & Trust Company shall act as sole trustee.

(f) Vacancy. If at any time a vacancy exists in the office of trustee, an alternate trustee shall be appointed pursuant to the following methods, applied in the order of priority listed:

(1) We or, after the deceased grantor's death, the surviving grantor may appoint an alternate trustee by signed notice filed in the trust's records and delivered to the alternate trustee and each beneficiary then eligible to receive the trust's income.

(2) Our adult children may appoint an alternate trustee by signed notice filed in the trust's records and delivered to the alternate trustee and each beneficiary then eligible to receive the trust's income.

(3) A trustee may appoint its own alternate by signed notice filed in the trust's records prior to the date on which the trustee ceases to serve. The trustee may change an appointment from time to time by substituting a later notice for a prior notice in the trust's records. If there are two or more notices in the trust's records at the time the trustee ceases to serve, the notice bearing the latest date shall control. Any notice filed by a trustee who is subsequently removed from office shall be ineffective.

(4) Any person interested in the trust may petition the court having jurisdiction over the administration of the trust for the appointment of an alternate trustee.

(g) <u>Appointment Interval</u>. A person's right to participate in the appointment of an alternate trustee under the provisions of Article 8.1(f) shall expire if not effectively exercised within 30 days after the person first receives notice of the vacancy.

(h) <u>Eligible Trustees</u>. Any person authorized by law to administer trusts is eligible to serve as an alternate or additional trustee. However, a beneficiary who is entitled to remove a trustee of The Family Trust may not appoint as alternate trustee a person who is related or subordinate to the beneficiary within the meaning of section 672 of the Internal Revenue Code.

(i) <u>Majority Decisions</u>. Except as may otherwise be provided in this agreement, if at any time there are more than two trustees acting with respect to any trust, the decision of a majority of the trustees shall control. Any trustee not included in the majority with respect to any decision or action may be absolved from personal liability by filing a signed notice of dissent in the trust records within ten days after receiving notice of the action or decision. A dissenting trustee shall act with the other trustees in any way necessary or appropriate to effectuate the decision of the majority.

8.2 **Powers of Alternate Trustee.** A duly appointed alternate trustee shall have all of the title, rights, powers, and duties of the original trustee without any act of transfer. No alternate trustee shall be obligated to examine the accounts, records, and acts of any previous trustee or to proceed against any previous trustee for any act or omission to act.

8.3 **Bonds Waived.** Each trustee shall be permitted to qualify without giving a bond or other undertaking in any jurisdiction for the performance of the trustee's duties, or, if bond is required by law, without the necessity of sureties.

8.4   **Compensation of Trustees.** Each trustee (other than either of us) is entitled to reasonable compensation commensurate with services actually performed and to reimbursement for expenses properly incurred. Generally, a fee based solely on a percentage of income or principal shall not be considered reasonable compensation. However, a fee determined with reference to a published fee schedule that compares favorably with the published fee schedules of other corporate fiduciaries having comparable capitalization and doing business in the same community may be considered reasonable compensation. Under no circumstances shall the trustee be entitled to a fee based on a percentage of principal for services rendered in connection with a change in fiduciaries or an interim or terminating distribution of principal.

8.5   **Exculpation.** A trustee shall not be liable for an act or omission done in good faith to promote the best interests of the beneficiaries, unless the act or omission constitutes gross negligence, intentional misconduct, or a knowing violation of law. A trustee's act or omission shall be presumed to be a proper exercise of the trustee's authority, in the absence of clear and convincing proof to the contrary.

ARTICLE 9: ADMINISTRATION OF TRUSTS

9.1   **Allocation of Death Taxes.**

(a) Sources of Payment.

(1) The trustees shall pay all estate and inheritance taxes payable with respect to the deceased grantor's share of the trust estate from the portion of the deceased grantor's share of the trust estate that does not qualify for the marital deduction.

(2) The trustees shall pay all estate and inheritance taxes payable with respect to the surviving grantor's share of the trust estate from The Survivor's Trust.

(b) Alternative Source. All estate and inheritance taxes payable by reason of either of our deaths with respect to property not passing under this agreement shall be apportioned against and paid out of such property based on the principle of equitable apportionment as prescribed by Wyndiana law.

(c) Trustees' Decision Final. The trustees' determination of the portion of each tax that must be paid out of and apportioned against any property includable in our respective gross estates shall be final and binding on all persons interested in the matter.

9.2 **No Supervised Administration.** The trustees shall administer each trust free from active court supervision unless changed circumstances that we could not have anticipated justify court supervision to protect the interests of the beneficiaries.

9.3 **Administrative Powers.** Subject to any limitations under other provisions of this agreement, the trustees shall have power and authority, without authorization or approval of any court, to perform every lawful act they consider advisable in the management of each trust, including, without limitation, the following powers:

(a) Tax Elections. To make all elections and allocations and to take all other appropriate actions with respect to taxation of every kind applying to either of us or any trust.

(b) Allocations. To determine whether items should be charged or credited to income or principal or allocated between income and principal, without regard to how the items are treated for federal and state tax purposes, including, without limitation, the power (1) to amortize or not amortize any part or all of any premium or discount, (2) to apportion any part or all of the profit resulting from the maturity or sale of any asset, whether purchased at a premium or a discount, between income or principal, and (3) to charge expenses, including expenses of administration, to income or principal.

(c) Retention of Assets. To retain any property for such period as the trustees shall determine, without liability for loss or diminution in value.

(d) Reserves. To establish reasonable reserves for depreciation, obsolescence, amortization, and depletion.

(e) Settlement of Claims. To settle, compromise, or abandon debts or claims due to or made against any trust.

(f) Investments. To acquire by purchase, lease or otherwise, and to retain, temporarily or permanently, all kinds of real and personal property, wherever located, including, without limitation, common and preferred stocks, puts, calls, and other instruments or contracts relating to the sale or purchase of securities, unsecured obligations, interests in common trust funds and in investment trusts or companies, life insurance policies and annuities, and interests of all kinds in real estate, water, mineral and oil and gas properties, partnerships, ventures and syndicates, all without diversification as to kind or amount.

(g) <u>Business Entities</u>. To participate in and transfer property to corporations, partnerships, limited liability companies, syndicates and other business associations; to exercise stock options, vote securities, and participate in voting trusts; to enter into partnership agreements, operating agreements, and shareholders' agreements; and to consent to exchanges, conversions, mergers, dissolutions, and reorganizations of all kinds.

(h) <u>Real Estate</u>. To lease all real property and all tangible personal property used in connection with real property for such periods, to such tenants and upon such terms as the trustees consider advisable, and to execute and deliver leases containing such covenants as the trustees consider appropriate to effect any leasing; to partition or divide in such manner as they consider appropriate any real property owned jointly or in common with others; to construct buildings and improvements of every kind and to carry on alterations and remodeling; to employ and pay real estate brokers and managing agents; to settle and determine any disputed real property boundaries; and otherwise to deal with real property in any manner customary in the real estate business.

(i) <u>Environmental Powers</u>. To take the steps necessary to protect the trustees and the property of any trust against liability for violation of any federal, state, or local law, regulation, or ordinance pertaining to protection of the environment or public health (an "environmental law"), including, without limitation, power (1) to determine compliance with any environmental law through inspection, review, testing, and analysis; (2) to refuse to accept property as an asset of any trust, if they consider that there is a substantial risk that the property is contaminated by a hazardous or toxic substance; (3) to take any action necessary to avoid, prevent, abate, or otherwise respond to any actual or threatened violation of any environmental law affecting estate or trust property; (4) to renounce or release any right or power under any document, statute, or rule of law that may result in personal liability under any environmental law; (5) to charge against property of any trust the cost of any inspection, testing, analysis, avoidance, prevention, abatement, response, compliance, or remedial action relating to any environmental law.

(j) <u>Sales and Disposition</u>. To sell, lease, exchange, mortgage, option, encumber, or otherwise dispose of any property, making sales publicly or privately and wholly or partly on credit.

(k) <u>Loans</u>. To loan money to or borrow money from any person, including any beneficiary or trustee, at any time and on any terms, and to secure any loan by encumbrance on any property. Without limiting the generality of the foregoing, the trustees shall have power to borrow on margin for the purpose of carrying or trading in securities of all kinds.

(l) <u>Nominees</u>. To hold property in the name of any nominee, including any trustee, with or without designation of fiduciary capacity.

(m) <u>Agents</u>. To employ and pay the fees and expenses of agents, consultants and advisors, including investment counsel, property managers, appraisers, custodians, accountants, and attorneys. Without limiting the generality of the foregoing, the trustees shall have power to delegate responsibility for the investment of the assets of any trust to investment advisors and shall incur no liability for losses resulting from investment decisions made by such investment advisors.

(n) <u>Division of Trusts</u>. To divide any trust into two or more separate trusts with terms identical to those of the original trust. With respect to the separate trusts: (1) the trustees may (i) make tax elections differently, (ii) exercise discretionary powers differently, and (iii) invest the property comprising the trusts differently; and (2) any beneficiary may disclaim or release interests or powers differently.

(o) <u>Consolidation of Trusts</u>. To combine the assets of separate trusts for the purpose of more convenient administration or investment for any period of time, preserving the separate character of the beneficiaries' proportionate shares, and to merge the assets of any trust with those of any other trust, by whomsoever created, maintained for the same beneficiaries upon substantially the same terms and having the same trustees.

(p) <u>Change Place of Administration</u>. To change the place of administration of any trust. Following a change in the place of administration of a trust, Wyndiana law shall continue to govern all questions as to the validity and construction of the trust, but the law of the new place of administration shall govern all questions pertaining to the administration of the trust.

(q) <u>Distribution in Cash or Kind</u>. Subject to the provisions of Article 10.3(c)(4), to distribute property in shares composed of any combination of cash or interests in property.

9.4 Delegation of Powers. Subject to the provisions of Article 7.2, a trustee at any time may (a) delegate to any co-trustee authority to exercise any of the trustee's rights or powers under this agreement and (b) revoke in whole or part a delegation previously made. The delegation or revocation shall be effected by an instrument signed by each trustee joining in the delegation or revocation and delivered to the delegate. While a delegation is in effect, the delegate may exercise the rights and the powers delegated with the same force and effect as if the delegating trustee had personally joined in the exercise of the delegated rights and powers. However, the delegating trustee shall not be liable for any action so taken.

9.5   **Release of Powers.** Any trustee at any time may release any authority, right, or power pertaining to the administration of each trust, temporarily or irrevocably, by signed notice filed in the records of the trust.

9.6   **Access to Records.** The trustees' records with respect to each trust shall be open at all reasonable times to inspection by the beneficiaries of the trust and their authorized representatives.

9.7   **Third Party Reliance.** For the purpose of verifying a trustee's authority to perform any act referred to in this Article 9, any person dealing with the trustees may rely on a copy of this agreement or selected excerpts from this agreement, certified as correct by a notary public, to the same extent as if the certified copy were the original. No person dealing with a trustee shall be under any obligation to see to the application of any payment made to the trustee or to inquire into the validity, expediency or propriety of any of the trustee's acts or omissions.

ARTICLE 10: MISCELLANEOUS PROVISIONS

10.1 **Persons under Legal Disability.** The guardian or conservator of the estate of a person under legal disability or, if none, the person having the right of custody of the person, and any adult ancestor of an unborn person, may act for the disabled or unborn person for all purposes of this agreement, including, without limitation, receipt of notices and reports, approval of investments and accounts, and consent to allocations and distributions.

10.2 **Definitions.** Unless the language or context clearly indicates that a different meaning is intended, the terms in quotations have the meanings specified in this Article 10.2.

(a) Children. "Our children" means only Marissa Planner, Lamont Planner, and Matthew Planner.

(b) Descendants. "Our descendants" means all of our lineal descendants, with the relationship of parent and child at each generation being determined by the definitions of those terms applicable for purposes of intestate succession under Wyndiana law. However, an adopted person shall be considered our lineal descendant only if the adopted person has been adopted while under the age of 18.

(c) Descendant's Spouse. Our descendant's "spouse" means a person who at the time the relationship is to be determined is lawfully married to our descendant or, if our descendant is not then living, was lawfully married to our descendant at the time of our descendant's death. If our descendant's spouse remarries after our descendant's death, our descendant's spouse shall cease to be our descendant's spouse for purposes of this agreement.

(d) Deceased Grantor. The "deceased grantor" means the first of us to die.

(e) Surviving Grantor. The "surviving grantor" means the last of us to die.

(f) Trust Estate. "Trust estate" in reference to a particular trust means all property comprising the trust at the time the term requires definition.

(g) Deceased Grantor's Share of Trust Estate. The "deceased grantor's share of the trust estate" means (1) the deceased grantor's undivided interest in the property added to the trust estate by us or either of us during our joint lives and (2) all property added to the trust estate by reason of the deceased grantor's death, including any property devised under the deceased grantor's will and any insurance proceeds or other death benefits.

(h) Qualified Charity. "Qualified charity" means a charitable, educational, scientific or religious entity, gifts to which are deductible for federal and state gift, estate, and income tax purposes.

(i) Incapacitated Person. A person is "incapacitated" if the person's personal physician states in writing that the person is impaired by reason of mental illness, mental deficiency, physical illness or disability, chronic use of drugs, chronic intoxication, or other cause to the extent of lacking sufficient understanding or capacity to make or communicate responsible decisions.

(j) Gross Estate. A person's "gross estate" means all property, real or personal, tangible or intangible, that is included in the person's gross estate for federal estate tax purposes.

(k) Marital Deduction. "Marital deduction" with reference to the deceased grantor's estate means the federal estate tax marital deduction allowed under Section 2056(a) of the Internal Revenue Code.

(l) Internal Revenue Code. "Internal Revenue Code" means the Internal Revenue Code of 1986, as amended, or the corresponding provisions of any subsequent federal tax law.

(m) Person. "Person" means a legal entity, including, without limitation, a natural person, a corporation, a partnership, a limited liability company, a trust, and an association.

(n) <u>Trustees</u>. "Trustee" or "trustees" and any pronoun in reference to trustee or trustees always refer interchangeably to the male or female person or persons or to the institution or any combination of them then acting.

10.3 **Constructional Rules.** The following constructional rules shall govern the interpretation of this agreement.

(a) <u>Distributions by Representation</u>. A distribution to "our descendants, by representation" shall be divided into as many equal shares as there are, at the time such distribution is required to be made, living descendants in the generation nearest to our generation that contains one or more living descendants and deceased descendants in the same generation who have living descendants. One share shall be distributed to each living descendant in the nearest generation to our generation and one share shall be divided among the descendants of each deceased descendant in the same manner.

(b) <u>Ascertainable Standard</u>. For purposes of determining the scope of a limitation on the trustees' power to determine the extent and nature of distributions based on a beneficiary's health, education, support, and maintenance: (1) distributions necessary for health include distributions to pay medical, dental, hospital, nursing, and invalidism expenses; (2) distributions necessary for education include distributions to pay the expenses of private schools and colleges and professional and postgraduate education; and (3) the terms "support" and "maintenance" are not limited to the bare necessities of life, but mean support and maintenance in reasonable comfort and in the distributee's accustomed manner of living.

(c) <u>Determination of Amount Allocable to Survivor's Trust</u>. For purposes of determining the amount allocable to The Survivor's Trust pursuant to Article 4.3(b)(3) (the "allocable amount"):

(1) All other deductions shall be taken into account, including the marital deduction with respect to all property and interests in property that are not part of the deceased grantor's share of the trust estate but qualify for the marital deduction. For that purpose, property that is not part of the deceased grantor's share of the trust estate shall be deemed to qualify for the marital deduction even though such property may in fact be the subject of a qualified disclaimer by or on behalf of the surviving grantor or is "qualified terminable interest property," within the meaning of section 2056(b)(7) of the Internal Revenue Code, but with respect to which an election is not in fact made by the deceased grantor's personal representative. In all other respects, the elections actually made by the deceased grantor's personal representative shall control.

(2) All credits shall be taken into account, except that the credit for state death taxes shall be taken into account only to the extent that the use of such credit would not result in an increase in the amount of state death tax payable.

(3) All values, deductions, and credits shall be those finally determined for federal estate tax purposes with respect to the deceased grantor's gross estate.

(4) The allocable amount shall be comprised of property and property interests that (i) are fairly representative of the net appreciation or depreciation, to the date of distribution, in the value of all assets comprising the deceased grantor's share of the trust estate and (ii) qualify for the marital deduction.

(5) No part of the allocable amount shall be liable for the payment of (i) any estate or inheritance taxes payable with respect to the deceased grantor's share of the trust estate or (ii) any debts or expenses payable from the deceased grantor's share of the trust estate that are not allowed as deductions for federal estate tax purposes.

(d) Qualification for Marital Deduction. All provisions of this agreement shall be so construed and applied that the portion of the deceased grantor's share of the trust estate that is allocated to The Survivor's Trust shall qualify for the marital deduction. The trustees shall not exercise any power in a manner inconsistent with that construction and application. Without limiting the generality of the foregoing and notwithstanding any other provision of this agreement:

(1) the trustees shall not allocate to The Survivor's Trust any property or property interests in the deceased grantor's share of the trust estate that would not qualify for the marital deduction; and

(2) the trustees' power to retain unproductive property in The Survivor's Trust shall be subject to the surviving grantor's right to require the trustees to make or convert the property into productive property within a reasonable time.

(e) Remainder Interests. The provisions of this agreement that create remainder interests upon termination of preceding estates shall not limit or otherwise affect the trustees' discretionary power to distribute principal, even though a discretionary distribution may have the effect of terminating a trust through exhaustion of the trust estate.

(f)   Powers of Appointment.

(1) In the exercise of the surviving grantor's powers of appointment with respect to The Survivor's Trust or The Family Trust, the surviving grantor may: (i) impose spendthrift restrictions and other lawful conditions; (ii) make appointments by deed or will; (iii) make appointments outright or in trust; (iv) create limited interests, including term and life estates and remainder interests; and (v) create a general or special power of appointment.

(2) Rule Against Perpetuities. The surviving grantor may not exercise any power of appointment in violation of applicable rules against perpetuities or similar rules. Any attempt to do so shall be ineffectual, and the gifts made in default of appointment shall take effect.

(3) Restrictions. The surviving grantor may not exercise his or her power of appointment with respect to The Family Trust (1) in the discharge of his or her legal obligation or the legal obligation of his or her estate; or (2) with respect to any interest in a policy of insurance on his or her life.

(4) Method of Exercise. The surviving grantor must exercise his or her power of appointment by a signed instrument that specifically refers to and clearly shows an intention to exercise the power. General exercises of powers of appointment shall not have that effect. In determining whether the surviving grantor has exercised his or her testamentary power of appointment, the trustees may rely on an instrument admitted to probate in any jurisdiction as his or her last will, or act on the assumption he or she died intestate if the trustees receive no knowledge of the existence of his or her last will within three months after his or her death.

(g)   Child in Gestation. A child in gestation who is later born alive shall be considered a living child throughout the period of gestation.

(h)   Court Decrees. Any decree of adoption or divorce at any time rendered by a court of record shall conclusively be deemed valid.

(i)   Governing Law. Wyndiana law shall govern all questions as to the validity and construction of this agreement.

(j)   Other Principles of Construction. Words in any gender include the other gender; the singular includes the plural and vice versa; "pay" and "distribute" also mean assign, convey and deliver; and the table of contents, headings, and underlined paragraph titles are for guidance only and shall have no significance in the interpretation of this agreement.

10.4 **Spendthrift Provision.** Income and principal payable to a beneficiary may not be assigned by the beneficiary or attached by or subjected to the interference or control of any creditor of the beneficiary, or reached by any legal or equitable process in satisfaction of any debt or liability of the beneficiary, prior to its actual receipt by the beneficiary.

IN WITNESS WHEREOF, we have signed this agreement on the date first above written.

_____
Prudent Planner, Grantor and Trustee

_____
Chary Planner, Grantor and Trustee

STATE OF WYNDIANA   )
)ss.
COUNTY OF ORDERLY   )

On this 1st day of January, 2003, personally appeared before me Prudent Planner, a signer of the foregoing instrument, who duly acknowledged having executed the same as grantor and trustee.

Witness my hand and official seal.

[SEAL]   _____
                Notary Public

STATE OF WYNDIANA   )
)ss.
COUNTY OF ORDERLY   )

On this 1st day of January, 2003, personally appeared before me Chary Planner, a signer of the foregoing instrument, who duly acknowledged having executed the same as grantor and trustee.

Witness my hand and official seal.

[SEAL]   _____

                               Notary Public

Specimen Durable Power of Attorney

DISCLAIMER: This specimen durable power of attorney is for illustration only. There is no warranty, express or implied, that it is appropriate for use in any particular jurisdiction or circumstance.

DURABLE POWER OF ATTORNEY

I, Prudent Planner, of Orderly County, Wyndiana, designate my son, Lamont Planner, as my agent and attorney-in-fact ("my agent") to act in my name and for my benefit in accordance with the provisions of this General Power of Attorney (this "power of attorney").

11. **General Grant of Power.** I grant to my agent the power to exercise or perform any act, power, duty, right, or obligation that I now have or in the future may acquire the legal right, power, or capacity to exercise or perform, including, without limitation, the powers enumerated in paragraph 2 below.

12. **Enumeration of Powers.** Without limiting the generality of my agent's power and authority, I grant to my agent the specific powers enumerated in this paragraph 2.

(a) Powers of Collection. To collect, receive and possess, by any lawful means, all cash and property, real or personal, intangible or tangible, that I now or in the future may own, and to sign and deliver in my name and on my behalf all receipts and releases for such cash and property.

(b) <u>Acquisition of Assets</u>. To acquire by purchase, exchange, distribution, lease, gift, or otherwise, and to retain, temporarily or permanently, any property, real or personal, tangible or intangible, on such terms and conditions as my agent deems appropriate.

(c) <u>Disposition of Assets</u>. To sell, exchange, option, or otherwise dispose of any property, real or personal, tangible or intangible, that I now or in the future may own, on such terms and conditions as my agent deems appropriate.

(d) <u>Loans</u>. To loan money to or borrow money from any person, including my agent, at any time and on such terms and conditions as my agent deems appropriate, and to secure any loan by encumbrance on any property, real or personal, tangible or intangible, that I now or in the future may own.

(e) <u>Management of Assets</u>. To manage, maintain, repair, improve, insure, lease, encumber, partition, and in any other manner deal with any property, real or personal, tangible or intangible, that I now or in the future may own, on such terms and conditions as my agent deems appropriate.

(f) <u>Banking Powers</u>. To make, receive, and endorse checks and drafts, deposit and withdraw funds and acquire and redeem certificates of deposit, in banks, brokerage companies, credit unions, savings and loan associations, and other financial institutions.

(g) <u>Motor Vehicles</u>. To apply for and receive, and to endorse and deliver, a certificate of title to any motor vehicle, and to represent that the title to such motor vehicle is free and clear of all liens and encumbrances, except those specifically enumerated.

(h) <u>Business Interests</u>. To participate in and transfer any property to corporations, partnerships, limited liability companies, syndicates, and other business associations; to exercise stock options, vote securities and participate in voting trusts; to enter into partnership agreements, operating agreements, and shareholders' agreements; to execute an election under Subchapter S or any other provision of the Internal Revenue Code; and to consent to exchanges, conversions, mergers, dissolutions, and reorganizations of all kinds.

(i) <u>Brokerage Accounts</u>. To open and maintain on my behalf a brokerage account at any financial institution; to deposit any or all cash and securities to such account; to execute powers of attorney authorizing transactions for such account; to sell, assign, endorse, and transfer securities on deposit in such account; to receive statements, summaries, notices, and tax forms pertaining to such account; to confirm and approve any or all transactions executed for such account; to receive any and all notices, calls for margin, or other demands with respect to such account; and to enter into any agreement with such financial institution with respect to such account.

(j) Safe Deposit Boxes. To enter, remove any or all of the contents from and surrender any safe deposit box rented by me at any institution.

(k) Vote Securities. To vote in person, or by general or limited proxy, with or without power of substitution, all securities that I now or in the future may own.

(l) Life Insurance and Annuities. To acquire, assign, sell, encumber, surrender, change the beneficiary under and exercise all other incidents of ownership with respect to any and all life insurance and annuity policies that I now or in the future may own.

(m) Social Security Administration and Other Agencies. To make application on my behalf for benefits administered by the Social Security Administration or any other federal, state, or local agency and to receive Social Security and other benefits on my behalf.

(n) To Receive Mail. To enter, maintain, and surrender any mail box that now or in the future may be in my name; to sign for any certified or registered mail directed to me; and to execute any order required to forward mail to any location my agent selects.

(o) Funding of Revocable Trust. To transfer any or all cash and property, real or personal, tangible or intangible, that I now or in the future may own to the trustee of any existing revocable trust of which I am a grantor, for administration and distribution in accordance with the terms of such trust.

(p) Creation of Revocable Trust. If to my agent's knowledge there is no existing revocable trust of which I am a grantor, my agent may create a revocable trust on my behalf and transfer to the trustee of such trust any or all cash and property, real or personal, tangible or intangible, that I now or in the future may own, for administration and distribution in accordance with the terms of such. The purposes of any revocable trust my agent creates on my behalf shall be to serve as a vehicle for the management of some or all of my cash and property and to provide for my health, support, maintenance, and comfort during my life. The provisions of the agreement governing such trust must be consistent with those purposes. My agent or any other person eligible to administer trusts may act as the trustee of such trust. My agent on my behalf may revoke such trust at any time by written notice delivered to the then acting trustee. If not previously revoked, such trust shall terminate as of the date of my death and, upon such termination, the trustee shall distribute all property then comprising the trust estate to my personal representative, for administration and distribution as part of my probate estate.

(q) <u>Tax Powers</u>. To prepare, sign, and file joint or separate income tax returns or declarations of estimated tax for any year or years; to prepare, sign, and file gift tax returns with respect to gifts made by me or my spouse for any year or years; to consent to any gift and to utilize any gift-splitting provision or other tax election; and to prepare, sign, and file any claims for refund of any tax.

(r) <u>Change My Domicile</u>. To do all things necessary to change my legal domicile to any jurisdiction my agent deems appropriate.

(s) <u>Resignation As a Member, Officer, or Fiduciary</u>. To effect my resignation as a member or officer of any organization or entity, or as a trustee, executor, conservator, custodian, personal representative, or other fiduciary of an estate or trust, however denominated.

(t) <u>Care of Principal</u>. To perform any act, power, duty, right, or obligation that I now or in the future may have relating to matters involving my health and medical care, including, without limitation, admission to a hospital or nursing home or other health or residential care facility.

(u) <u>Disclaimers</u>. To execute on my behalf "qualified disclaimers," within the meaning of Section 2518 of the Internal Revenue Code or any comparable section of any federal or state statute, notwithstanding that the exercise of such qualified disclaimer directly or indirectly may benefit my agent.

(v) <u>Gifts</u>. To make gifts of any and all property that I now or in the future may own to my wife, my descendants (including himself), and qualified charities, at such time and in such amounts, shares, and interests as my agent determines. However, my agent shall not make a gift to any donee in an amount that exceeds in any calendar year the annual gift tax exclusion allowed under Sections 2503(b) and 2503(e) of the Internal Revenue Code. If my agent determines to make gifts to minors, he may make such gifts directly to the minor, to the minor's parent, conservator, or guardian, or to a custodian under the Uniform Transfers To Minors Act.

(w) <u>Beneficiary Designation</u>. To designate any of my spouse, my descendants, qualified charities, and a revocable living trust of which I am a grantor as the beneficiary under any contract, trust, or other relationship pursuant to which I have the power to designate the person entitled a monetary benefit upon my death, including, without limitation, any annuity, insurance policy, retirement plan, individual retirement account, payable on death account, or transferable on death account.

13. **Revocability.** I may revoke this power of attorney at any time by written notice to my agent. However, with respect to any person who may rely on my agent's authority under this power of attorney, including, without limitation, any governmental agency, bank, depository, trust company, insurance company, transfer agent, or financial institution, any revocation shall not be effective until such person has received written notice of the revocation, signed by my agent or me.

14. **Passage of Time.** This power of attorney shall not be revoked or otherwise become ineffective in any way by the mere passage of time, but rather shall remain in full force and effect until revoked in the manner described in paragraph 3.

15. **Disability of Principal.** This power of attorney shall not be affected by my incapacity or disability.

16. **Third-Party Reliance.** Any person dealing with my agent may rely upon my agent's representations as to any matter within the scope of my agent's power and authority under this power of attorney. Any person who acts in reliance on my agent's representations or authority shall incur no liability to me or to my heirs, legal representatives, successors, or assigns. My agent may take legal action on my or my estate's behalf for any damages that may result from a person's refusal to accept or rely on my agent's representations or authority or to permit my agent to exercise the authority granted my agent by this power of attorney.

17. **Inducement.** For the purpose of inducing any persons, including, without limitation, any governmental agency, bank, depository, trust company, insurance company, transfer agent, or investment banking company, to act in accordance with the powers I have granted my agent in this power of attorney, I hereby represent, warrant, and agree, for myself and my heirs, legal representatives, successors, and assigns, that if this power of attorney is terminated for any reason, I and my heirs, legal representatives, successors,

and assigns shall hold such person harmless from any loss suffered or liability incurred by such person in acting in accordance with this power of attorney prior to such person's receipt of written notice of such termination.

18. **Exculpation.** Under no circumstances shall my agent incur any liability to me, or to my heirs, legal representatives, successors, or assigns, for acting or refraining from acting hereunder, except for my agent's own willful misconduct or gross negligence.

19. **Revocation of Prior Powers of Attorney.** I revoke any and all other powers of attorney that I previously may have executed, except those powers of attorney that pertain solely to signatory power over savings or checking accounts.

20. **Duty of Agent to Account.** My agent upon my request shall account to me or such other person as I shall direct in writing. If a conservator or guardian of my property is appointed my agent shall account to such conservator or guardian.

21. **Notice and Accounting to Interested Persons.**

(a) Incapacity. If I become incapacitated, my agent shall (1) within 30 days after learning that I am incapacitated, notify all interested persons of his status as my agent, (2) upon any interested person's request, promptly provide such interested person with a copy of this power of attorney and a schedule of all of my property and sources of income, and (3) upon any interested person's written request, provide such interested person with an annual accounting of his acts with respect to my income and property.

(b) Death. If I die while I am incapacitated, my agent shall (1) within 30 days after learning of my death, promptly notify all interested persons of my death and (2) upon any interested person's written request, promptly provide such interested person with an accounting of his acts with respect to my income and property during my incapacity.

22. **Appointment of Successor Attorney.** If at any time Lamont Planner, resigns or ceases to act as my agent under this power of attorney, I appoint my daughter, Marissa Planner, to serve as my successor agent. Any person to whom this power of attorney is presented may rely upon a certificate by my successor agent that my initial agent has resigned or ceased to act as my agent. If I am incapacitated or disabled at the time my successor agent

becomes my agent, then, within 10 days after my successor agent becomes my agent, she shall notify all interested persons of her status as my agent.

23. **Nomination of Guardian or Conservator.** If an action is commenced to have a guardian or conservator appointed due to my incapacity, I nominate my agent as such guardian and conservator.

24. **Fiduciary Powers.** Notwithstanding any other provision of this power of attorney, my agent shall have no rights or powers with respect to any act, power, duty, right, or obligation relating to any person, matter, transaction, or property owned by me, or in my custody, as a trustee, custodian, personal representative, or other fiduciary.

25. **Compensation.** My agent is entitled to reasonable compensation for services rendered as agent under this power of attorney.

26. **Governing Law.** Wyndiana law shall govern all questions as to the validity of this power of attorney and as to the construction of its provisions.

27. **Principles of Construction.** For purposes of interpreting this power of attorney:

(a) Incapacitated. I shall be deemed to be "incapacitated" if my personal physician states in writing that I am impaired by reason of mental illness, mental deficiency, physical illness or disability to the extent that I lack sufficient understanding or capacity to make or communicate responsible decisions.

(b) Interested Person. An "interested person" is a person who will succeed to an interest in my probate estate under the terms of my will or, if I have no will, a person who will be entitled to a portion of my probate estate under the applicable laws of intestate succession.

(c) Other Principles of Construction. "Person" means a legal entity, including, without limitation, a natural person, a corporation, a partnership, a limited liability company, a trust, and an association; words in any gender include the other gender; the singular includes the plural and vice versa; and the headings and underlined paragraph titles are for guidance only and shall have no significance in the interpretation of this power of attorney.

28. **Counterparts and Photographic Copies.** This power of attorney may be executed in counterparts. Each executed counterpart is an original and any photographic copy of this power of attorney shall have the force and effect of an original.

Signed this 1st day of January, 2003, to be effective immediately.

_____
Prudent Planner

STATE OF WYNDIANA   )
) ss.
COUNTY OF ORDERLY   )

On this 1st day of January, 2003, personally appeared before me Prudent Planner, the signer of the foregoing instrument, who duly acknowledged to me that he executed the same.

Witness my hand and official seal.

[SEAL]   _____
                    Notary Public

                    My Commission expires: _____

Specimen Directive to Providers of Medical Services

DISCLAIMER: This specimen directive to providers of medical services is for illustration only. There is no warranty, express or implied, that it is appropriate for use in any particular jurisdiction or circumstance.

DIRECTIVE TO PROVIDERS OF MEDICAL SERVICES

I, Prudent Planner, of Orderly County, Wyndiana, willfully and voluntarily make this Directive to Providers of Medical Services (this "Directive") for the purpose of exercising my right to decline life-sustaining procedures in the event I have a terminal condition or am in a persistent vegetative state.

1. **On Life and Death.** I value a full life more than a long life. What I value most in life is the opportunity to interact with others. If due to injury or illness I am permanently and irreversibly deprived of that opportunity, I have no desire to prolong my life through life-sustaining procedures. Accordingly, if I lack sufficient understanding and capacity to make and communicate responsible decisions concerning the use of life-sustaining procedures to unnaturally prolong my life, my physicians and other providers of medical services will abide by my desires and directions as expressed in this Directive.

2. **Directions.** If at any time I have a terminal condition or am in a persistent vegetative state, as determined by two physicians who have personally examined me, I direct that:

   a. all life-sustaining procedures be withheld or discontinued; and

b. all nutrition and hydration be discontinued, unless my attending physician determines that such discontinuance would increase my pain or discomfort.

3. **Definitions.** For all purposes of this Directive:

a. "Attending physician" means a licensed physician who has primary responsibility for my care and treatment.

b. "Life-sustaining procedure" means any medical procedure or intervention that, in the judgment of my attending physician, would serve only to prolong the dying process but not avert my death, including, without limitation, assistance in respiration, artificial maintenance of blood pressure and heart rate, blood transfusion, intravenous injection of antibiotics, kidney dialysis, and other similar procedures. However, "life-sustaining procedure" does not include (1) the provision of nutrition and hydration or (2) the administration of medication or the performance of any medical procedure that is intended to alleviate pain or discomfort.

c. "Nutrition and hydration" means food and fluids given through a nasogastric or intravenous tube and does not include nonintrusive methods such as spoon feeding or moistening of the lips and mouth.

d. "Persistent vegetative state" means a condition that according to reasonable medical judgment constitutes complete and irreversible loss of all of the functions of the cerebral cortex and results in a complete, chronic, and irreversible cessation of all cognitive functioning and consciousness and a complete lack of behavioral responses that indicate cognitive functioning, even though autonomic functions continue.

e. "Terminal condition" means an incurable condition caused by injury, disease, or illness that according to reasonable medical judgment will cause death within six months, even with the application of life-sustaining procedures in accordance with the prevailing standard of medical care.

4. **Declaration of Capacity.** I declare that I am emotionally and mentally competent to make this Directive and willingly and voluntarily accept its consequences as the final expression of my desire and direction concerning my medical care in the circumstances to which it pertains.

5. **Reservation of Right.** While I have sufficient understanding and capacity to make and communicate responsible decisions concerning my medical care, I may give contemporaneous directions to my physicians and other providers of medical services, even if such directions conflict with this Directive.

6. **Revocation.** I revoke any prior directives to providers of medical services.

7. **Miscellaneous.**

a. No physician or other provider of medical services who withholds or discontinues any medical or other procedure in reliance on and in accordance with this Directive will be liable to me or to my heirs, legal representatives, successors, or assigns.

b. I have signed this Directive in Wyndiana with the intent and expectation that it will be legally enforceable in any jurisdiction in which it is presented.

c. A copy of this Directive is intended to have the same effect as the original.

Signed on January 1, 2003, to be effective immediately.

_____

Prudent Planner

We, the undersigned witnesses, certify that each of us is at least 18 years old; that each of us personally witnessed Prudent Planner ("Planner"), sign or direct the signing of this Directive; that we are acquainted with Planner; that we believe Planner to be of sound mind; that we believe that Planner's desires and directions are as expressed in this Directive; that neither of us is a person who signed this Directive on Planner's behalf; that neither of us is related to Planner by blood or marriage; that neither of us is entitled to any portion of Planner's estate according to the laws of succession of any jurisdiction or under Planner's will, living trust or other dispositive instrument; that we are not directly financially responsible for Planner's medical care; and that we are not agents of any health care facility in which Planner may be a patient at the time this Directive is signed.

Witness: _____
Address: 3521 North Willmont Drive
          Orderville, WD 84602

Witness: _____
Address: 3521 North Willmont Drive
          Orderville, WD 84602

Specimen Prenuptial Agreement

DISCLAIMER: This specimen prenuptial agreement is for illustration only. There is no warranty, express or implied, that it is appropriate for use in any particular jurisdiction or circumstance.

PRENUPTIAL AGREEMENT

THIS AGREEMENT (this "Agreement"), dated January 1, 2003, is between Marissa Planner, of Orderly County, Wyndiana, and Stout Foresight, of Prescience County, Wyndiana.

Recitals and Acknowledgments

A. The parties expect to be married in the near future.

B. Each party owns certain property and expects to acquire additional property through investment, gift, inheritance, and other means.

C. The parties desire to (1) define their respective property interests and rights and (2) release their rights to the property of the other party in the event of divorce, separation, or death.

D. Each party (1) acknowledges that he or she has received from the other reasonable disclosure of the general nature and extent of the other's property and financial obligations in sufficient detail to make an informed decision to enter into this Agreement and (2) waives any right to disclosure of the property and financial obligations of the other beyond the disclosure already received.

E. The parties recognize that their separate property may appreciate or depreciate in value during their marriage.

F. The parties acknowledge that each has authorized the other to employ a professional adviser to review in detail his or her financial circumstances.

G. The parties acknowledge that they have entered into this Agreement after consultation with separate and independent attorneys licensed to practice law in Wyndiana.

H. The parties acknowledge that (1) they have been fully advised by their respective attorneys of the rights they would have in the absence of this Agreement and (2) they fully understand and accept all of the provisions of this Agreement.

Agreement

Therefore, in contemplation of their marriage and in consideration of the premises and the mutual promises contained in this Agreement, the parties agree as follows:

SECTION 1: MARITAL RIGHTS AS SURVIVING SPOUSE

1.1 **Waiver of Rights as Surviving Spouse.** Each party irrevocably and permanently waives and renounces all rights the party would otherwise have as the other party's surviving spouse and heir-at-law in and to the other party's Separate Property. The rights waived and renounced include, without limitation: (a) the right to an elective share, allowance, or exemption provided under the law of Wyndiana and every other jurisdiction; (b) the right to act as executor, administrator, or personal representative of the other party's estate; and (c) all rights as the other party's surviving spouse and heir-at-law under all other statutes, rules, regulations, decisions, and customs of Wyndiana and every other jurisdiction.

1.2 **Rights Unaffected by Waivers.** Notwithstanding the provisions of Section 1.1:

(a) Either party may designate any person, including the other party, as the beneficiary of any insurance policy on the party's life. Neither party has agreed or promised to name the other party as beneficiary of any insurance policy on the party's life or to assign any insurance policy to the other party.

(b) Either party may acquire property in, or transfer property to, the names of the parties as joint tenants with right of survivorship and, when so acquired or transferred, the property may pass to the survivor by operation of law. Neither party has agreed or promised to create any joint tenancies with respect to the party's property.

(c) Either party, during life or by will, may make gifts to the other party and the other party may receive and accept any such gifts. No such gift will constitute an amendment or waiver, in whole or in part, of this Agreement.

SECTION 2: MARITAL RIGHTS ON DIVORCE OR SEPARATION

2.1 **Release of Rights in Separate Property.** Each party irrevocably and permanently waives and renounces all right to or interest in the other party's Separate Property in the event of an action for divorce or separation. The rights waived and renounced include, without limitation: (a) the right to an equitable division of the other party's Separate Property under the laws of Wyndiana and every other jurisdiction; (b) the right to receive or possess the other party's Separate Property under the laws of Wyndiana and every other jurisdiction; and (c) any right to or interest in the other party's Separate Property under any other statute, rule, regulation, decision, or custom of Wyndiana and every other jurisdiction.

2.2 **Release of Rights to Support.** Each party irrevocably and permanently waives and renounces the right to alimony, support, or maintenance that a court of competent jurisdiction may otherwise award in the event of an action for divorce or separation under any statute, rule, regulation, decision, or custom of Wyndiana and every other jurisdiction.

SECTION 3: LIABILITIES

3.1 **Liabilities Incurred Prior to Marriage.** Each party will remain solely responsible for and will discharge all liabilities that party incurred prior to the contemplated marriage, and the other party's income and property will not be charged or otherwise burdened with the discharge of those liabilities.

3.2 **Liabilities Incurred During Marriage.** Each party will be responsible for and discharge all liabilities that party incurs during the contemplated marriage without the other party's consent and joinder, and the other party's income and property will not be charged or otherwise burdened with the discharge of those liabilities.

3.3 **Indemnification.** The party who is responsible for the discharge of a liability pursuant to this Section 3 will indemnify, defend, and hold harmless the other party with respect to the liability.

SECTION 4: LIVING EXPENSES

4.1 **Contribution.** The parties have not established a specific formula by which they will contribute to their mutual living expenses. However, they intend to contribute to such expenses in such shares as they consider equitable. It is contemplated that each party will contribute his or her share of such expenses to a joint checking account from which the mutual living expenses will be paid. All funds deposited by either party to such joint checking account, regardless of the source of such funds, and all property acquired with or derived from such funds, will be owned by the parties in equal undivided shares.

4.2 **No Right of Reimbursement.** Neither party is entitled to reimbursement for any contribution to the parties' mutual living expenses.

SECTION 5: MANAGEMENT OF SEPARATE PROPERTY

5.1 **Management and Control.** Each party retains the exclusive right to control and manage his or her Separate Property, including, without limitation, the right to encumber or dispose of such property, without the consent or joinder of the other party, as freely as though no marriage had taken place.

5.2 **Accommodation.** If either party desires to encumber or dispose of any of his or her Separate Property, the other party will sign, acknowledge, and deliver such documents as may be necessary to effectuate the transaction, but such participation will not create any personal liability or property interest in the other party.

5.3 **Bank Accounts and Credit Cards.** With respect to his or her Separate Property, each party will maintain his or her own savings and checking accounts and will obtain and use his or her own credit cards. Neither party will make any credit purchases using the credit cards of the other party.

SECTION 6: INVESTMENTS

6.1 **No Obligation to Present Investment Opportunities.** Neither party is obligated to present any investment opportunity to the other party and may elect, without incurring any liability to the other party, to make any investment for his or her separate account. If either party elects to make an investment for his or her separate account, it shall not constitute a violation of any existing fiduciary duty nor shall it be a basis for a claim that the other party is entitled to the first opportunity of investment.

6.2 **Joint Investments.** If the parties jointly invest in property, such investment shall be evidenced by a separate written agreement containing the specific terms and conditions relating to such investment and signed by both parties. Title to any property that is the subject of a joint investment will accurately reflect the parties' actual interests in the property.

SECTION 7: GENERAL PROVISIONS

7.1 **Definition of Separate Property.** For all purposes of this Agreement, a party's "Separate Property" includes:

(a) all personal and real property, tangible or intangible, of any nature and in any place owned, leased, held, or in which the party has any right, title, or interest of any kind whatsoever on the date of this Agreement or at the time of the parties' marriage, and all accumulations or increases in the value of any such property, whether attributable to market conditions or to the management, services, skills, effort, or work of either party;

(b) all distributions of income and principal received by the party during the marriage from any trust established at any time by one or more members of the party's family, and all accumulations or increases in the value of any such distribution, whether attributable to market conditions or to the management, services, skills, effort, or work of either party;

(c) all property received by the party during the marriage by gift, devise, bequest, or inheritance, or as a beneficiary of any insurance policy or retirement account, and all accumulations or increases in the value of any such property, whether attributable to market conditions or to the management, services, skills, effort, or work of either party; and

(d) all property acquired by the party during the parties' marriage that is derived from the proceeds, income, or appreciation in value of any item of the party's property described in the foregoing provisions of this Section 7.1 and all accumulations or increases in the value of any such property, whether attributable to market conditions or to the management, services, skills, effort, or work of either party.

7.2 **Income Tax Returns.** The parties may agree to file joint income tax returns. Neither the filing of such joint tax returns nor the payment of taxes shall create or be deemed to create any interest of one party in the Separate Property of the other party. If the parties file a joint tax return, each party shall pay the percentage of the joint tax that he or she would have paid of the total tax that would have been paid by both if each had filed a separate tax return and paid his or her own taxes on such returns. Neither party shall have a right to reimbursement for any alleged payment of the other's taxes on a joint tax return.

7.3 **Effective Date.** This Agreement will become effective upon the marriage of the parties and will have no effect unless and until the marriage takes place.

7.4 **Obligation of Support.** Nothing in this Agreement will absolve either party of the statutory obligations to support the other party during the marriage.

7.5 **Entire Agreement.** This Agreement contains all the terms of the parties' agreement with respect to the subject matter.

7.6 **Amendment and Termination.** This Agreement may not be amended, supplemented, or terminated except by an instrument in writing expressly referring to this Agreement and signed by the party sought to be charged with the amendment, supplement, or termination.

7.7 **Further Instruments.** Each party will execute, acknowledge, and deliver such instruments as may be advisable or necessary to effectuate or confirm the provisions of this Agreement including, without limitation, disclaimers, renunciations, and relinquishments of any rights or interests in the other party's property.

7.8 **Governing Law.** Wyndiana law governs this Agreement's validity and interpretation.

7.9 **Binding Effect.** This Agreement is binding on and inures to the benefit of the parties and their respective heirs, devisees, personal representatives, and assigns.

7.10 **Severability.** If any provision of this Agreement is for any reason invalid or unenforceable, the other portions of this Agreement nevertheless will continue in full force and effect.

Signed on the date first above written.

_____

Marissa Planner

_____

Stout Foresight

STATE OF ORDERLY   )
) ss.
COUNTY OF WYNDIANA   )

On this 1st day of January, 2003, personally appeared before me Marissa Planner and Stout Foresight, the signers of the foregoing instrument, who duly acknowledged that they executed the same.

Witness my hand and official seal.

(SEAL)

_____

Notary Public

Notes

FOREWORD
1. Nicomachean Ethics.
2. J. Gokhale and L. Kotlikoff, *The Baby Boomers' Mega-Inheritance—Myth or Reality?* Economic Commentary, Federal Reserve Bank of Cleveland, October 1, 2000.

CHAPTER 1
1. L. Robert Kohls, *Values Americans Live By,* (Washington, DC: Washington International Center, 1984). Available at *www.cs.utah.edu/~alee/extra/American_values.html.*
2. Scott C. Fithian, *Values-Based Estate Planning: A Step-by-Step Approach to Wealth Transfer for Professional Advisors.* (New York: Wiley, 2000). See Appendix C.

CHAPTER 2
1. A. J. Woodman, *Tacticus Reviewed* (London: Oxford University Press, 1998).
2. P. Brickman, D. Coates, and R. Janoff-Bulman, "Lottery Winners and Accident Victims: Is Happiness Relative?" *Journal of Personality and Social Psychology* 36 (1978): 917–927; Michael Argyle, *The Psychology of Happiness,* (London: Methuen, 1986).
3. D. Myers, "The Finds, Friends and Faith of Happy People." *American Psychologist* (January 2000): 56–67.
4. E. Diener, J. Horwitz, and R. A. Emmons, "Happiness of the Very Wealthy." *Social Indicators* 16 (1985): 263–274.

5. Abraham H. Maslow, *Motivation and Personality* (New York: Harper, 1954).
6. Myers, op. cit.
7. Nelson W. Aldrich, *Old Money: The Mythology of Wealth in America* (New York: Allworth Press, 1996), xiii. See Foreword by Tad Crawford.

CHAPTER 3

1. Robert E. Lane, *The Loss of Happiness in Market Democracies* (New Haven: Yale University Press, 2000).
2. Angus Campbell, *The Sense of Well-Being in America: Recent Patterns and Trends* (New York: McGraw-Hill, 1981).
3. Robert C. Bartlett and Susan Collins, eds., *Action and Contemplation: Studies in the Moral and Political Thought of Aristotle* (Buffalo: State University of New York Press, 1999).
4. Myers, op. cit.

CHAPTER 4

1. Jean Kilbourne, *Deadly Persuasion: Why Women and Girls Must Fight the Addictive Power of Advertising* (New York: Free Press, 2000).
2. Jonathan Dee, "But Is It Advertising?" *Harpers* (January 1999): 65–66, as cited in Kilbourne, 2000.
3. S. Gonzales, "No Safety Net for Future Kids." *Denver Rocky Mountain News,* (January 1, 2000): 13D.
4. Gary Ruskin, "Why They Whine: How Corporations Prey on Our Children." *Mothering* (November/December 1999): 41–50.
5. Margery Williams, *The Velveteen Rabbit* (New York: Henry Holt, 1983).
6. Jacob Needleman, *Money and the Meaning of Life* (New York: Doubleday, 1991).
7. Ibid., pp. 20–21.
8. Jessie H. O'Neill, *The Golden Ghetto: The Psychology of Affluence* (Center City, MN: Hazelden Publishing, 1997).

CHAPTER 5

1. Stan Davis and Christopher Meyer, *Blur* (New York: Warner Books, 1998).
2. K. Gibson, B. Blouin, and M. Kiersted, *The Inheritor's Inner Landscape: How Heirs Feel* (Blacksburg, VA: Trio Press, 1994).

CHAPTER 6

1. John Levy, "Coping with Inherited Wealth," unpublished paper, 1990.

2. John Levy, "Trust vs. Trust," unpublished paper, 1991.

3. "Credit Card Usage Continues among College Students." Available at *www.nelliemae.com/library/cc_use.html*.

CHAPTER 7

1. Howard J. Markman, Scott M. Stanley, and Susan L. Blumberg, *Fighting for Your Marriage* (San Francisco: Jossey-Bass, 1994).

2. J. Pouliot, "Don't Let Money Trouble Ruin Your Marriage." *Parade*, (April 16, 2000): 24–25.

3. Natalie H. Jenkins, Scott M. Stanley, William C. Bailey, and Howard J. Markman, *You Paid* How *Much for That?! How to Win at Money without Losing at Love* (San Francisco: Jossey-Bass, 2002).

4. John Levy, "For Richer, for Poorer," unpublished paper.

CHAPTER 9

1. Thomas Hobbes, Richard Tuck, ed., *Leviathan* (Cambridge: Cambridge University Press, 1991).

2. B. D. Bernheim, K. G. Carman, J. Gokhale, and L. J. Kotlikoff, "The Mismatch between Life Insurance Holdings and Financial Vulnerabilities: Evidence from the Survey of Consumer Finances," *Working Paper 02–01*, The Federal Reserve Bank of Cleveland, 2002.

CHAPTER 10

1. In a few states, property acquired during marriage is characterized as *community property*. Spouses are deemed to own community property in equal undivided shares, regardless of the source of the consideration or the form of title. States that have adopted the community property regime include Arizona, California, Idaho, Louisiana, Nevada, New Mexico, Texas, and Washington.

2. Ernest Beaglehole, *Property: A Study in Social Psychology* (New York: Macmillan, 1974), 309.

CHAPTER 11

1. This observation often is attributed to motivational speaker and author, Gary Ryan Blair, but without reference to a specific source.

2. Some financial advisors assert that "dying broke" is the ideal estate planning strategy. They argue that to do otherwise is to "put the quality of your death before the quality of your life." See Stephen Pollen, *Die Broke: A Radical, Four-Part Financial Plan* (New York: HarperCollins, 1998).

3. *Ecclesiastes* 2: 19–20.

4. Herbert Fisher, ed., *The Collected Papers of Frederic William Maitland* (Buffalo, William S. Hein & Company, 1981), 271.

5. Kahlil Gibran, *The Prophet* (New York: Alfred A. Knopf, 1923).

CHAPTER 13

1. "Federal Estate Tax Returns Filed in 2001," *IRS Statistics of Income, Unpublished Data*, April 2001.

CHAPTER 14

1. Elizabeth M. Ellis, *Divorce Wars* (Washington, DC: American Psychological Association Press, 2000), 34.

2. Ibid.

CHAPTER 15

1. Stephen P. Bank and Michael D. Kahn, *The Sibling Bond* (New York: Basic Books, 1982).

2. Kelly Greene, "Pass It On." *Wall Street Journal* (March 25, 2002), R5.

CHAPTER 16

1. Kevin Simpson, "Secrets to Surviving Success." *Sunday Denver Post*, (October 6, 2002).

CHAPTER 17

1. Simpson, op. cit.

2. D. J. Weinstein, "Success Comes Early for Young Marketer." *Denver Rocky Mountain News* (June 18, 2000): 34A.

3. R. A. Harnisch, "The Bank of Larry." *More Than Money* 25, (2000): 9.

Selected Bibliography and Web Sites

ESTATE AND FINANCIAL PLANNING

Books

Akright, Carol, CFP. *Funding Your Dreams Generation to Generation.* Chicago: Dearborn Trade Publishing, 2001.

American Bar Association. *The American Bar Association Guide to Wills and Estates: Everything You Need to Know about Wills, Trusts, Estates and Taxes.* New York: Times Books, 1995.

Barney, Colleen, and Victoria Collins. *Best Intentions: Ensuring Your Estate Plan Delivers Both Wealth and Wisdom.* Chicago: Dearborn Trade Publishers, 2002.

Briles, Judith. *Money Phases: The Six Financial Stages of a Woman's Life.* New York: Simon and Schuster, 1985.

Condon, Gerald, and Jeffrey Condon. *Beyond the Grave: The Right Way and the Wrong Way of Leaving Money to Your Children (and Others).* New York: HarpersBusiness, 2001.

D'Souza, Dinesh. *The Virtue of Prosperity: Finding Values in an Age of Techno-Affluence.* New York: The Free Press, 2000.

Edelman, Ric. *The Truth about Money.* New York: HarperCollins Publishers, Inc., 1996.

Fish, Barry, and Les Kotzer. *The Family Fight: Planning to Avoid It.* Continental Atlantic Publications Inc., 2002.

Fithian, Scott C. *Values-Based Estate Planning: A Step-by-Step Approach to Wealth Transfer for Professional Advisors.* New York: John Wiley & Sons, Inc., 2000.

Gomes, Peter J. *The Good Life: Truths That Last in Times of Need.* New York: HarperCollins Publishers, Inc., 2002.

Greenway, Nancy, and Barbara Shotwell. *Pass It On: A Practical Approach to the Fears and Facts of Planning Your Estate.* New York: Hyperion Press, 2000.

Kinnard, Melly. *Get Organized! Life Planner.* Dubuque, Iowa: Kendall/Hunt Publishing Co., 2002.

Klegerg, Sally S. *The Stewardship of Private Wealth: Managing Personal and Family Financial Assets.* New York: McGraw-Hill, 1997.

Link, E. G. "Jay." *Family Wealth Counseling: Getting to the Heart of the Matter.* Franklin, Indiana: Professional Mentoring Program,1999.

Phillips, David T., and Bill S. Wolfkiel. *Estate Planning Made Easy: Your Step-by-Step Guide to Protecting Your Family, Safeguarding Your Assets, and Minimizing the Tax Bite.* 2nd Edition. Chicago: Dearborn Trade Publishing, 1998.

Rottenberg, Dan. *The Inheritor's Handbook: A Definitive Guide for Beneficiaries.* New York: Fireside Press, 1998.

Shenkman, Martin. *The Complete Book of Trusts.* New York: John Wiley & Sons, 1997.

Stolper, Michael, and Everett Mattlin. *Wealth: An Owner's Manual.* New York: HarperCollins Publishers, Inc., 1992.

Williams, Joan. *Unbending Gender: Why Family and Work Conflict and What To Do About It.* New York: Oxford University Press, Inc., 2000.

Williams, Roy O. *For Love and Money: A Comprehensive Guide to the Successful Generational Transfer of Wealth.* San Francisco: Monterey Pacific Publishing, 1997.

Web Sites

American College of Trust and Estate Counsel. Offers helpful consumer information on estate planning. *www.actec.org*

GovBenefits. A guide to government benefits. *www.govbenefits.gov/GovBenefits/jsp/GovBenefits.jsp*

The Inheritance Project. The Legacy of Inherited Wealth: Interview with Heirs, at *www.inheritance-project.com*

Save Wealth.com. A comprehensive consumer-oriented estate planning resource. *www.savewealth.com/planning/estate/index.html*

SavingforCollege.com. A guide to state-sponsored college savings plans. *www.savingforcollege.com/*

University of Minnesota. A guide for dividing personal property. *www.yellowpitplate.umn.edu*

Miscellaneous

Whiting, Ellen. "Controlling Behavior by Controlling the Inheritance: Considerations in Drafting Incentive Provisions." *Probate and Property*, September/October 2001, 6–12.

The following articles are available directly from the author, John Levy:

842 Autumn Lane
Mill Valley, CA 94941
phone: (415) 383-3951

"Coping with Inherited Wealth" by John Levy, 1990.
"Trust vs. Trust" by John Levy, 1991.
"An American Taboo, or Why It Isn't All Right to Talk about Personal Wealth" by John Levy, 1992.
"For Richer, for Poorer" by John Levy, 1998.

CHILDREN

Books

Baylor, Byrd. *The Table Where Rich People Sit*. New York: Antheum Press, 1994.

Brooks, Andree Aelion. *Children of Fast-Track Parents: Raising Self-sufficient and Confident Children in an Achievement-Oriented World*. New York: Viking Press, 1989.

Galo, Eileen, and Jon Galo. *Silver Spoon: How Successful Parents Raise Responsible Children*. New York: Contemporary Books, 2002.

Godfrey, Neale, and Carolina Edwards. *Money Doesn't Grow on Trees: A Parent's Guide to Raising Financially Responsible Children*. New York: Fireside Press, 1994.

Godfrey, Neale, and Randy Verougstraete. *Ultimate Kid's Money Book*. New York: Aladdin Library, 2002.

Kindlon, Dan. *Too Much of a Good Thing: Raising Children of Character in an Intelligent Age*. New York: Hyperion, 2001.

Molnar, Alex. *Giving Kids the Business: The Commercialization of America's Schools*. Boulder, Colorado: Westview Press, 2001.

Rogers, Fred. *The Giving Box: Create a Tradition of Giving with Your Children*. Philadelphia: Running Press, 2000.

Web Sites

JumpStart Coalition: A nonprofit group that promotes financial literacy in children. *www.jumpstartcoalition.org*

More than Money: Money and children, #9 and What Are We Teaching Our Children. #24. *www.morethanmoney.org* (or call, 1-877-648-0776)

Obligation: Removing Channel 1 from schools. *www.obligation.org*

Resource Generation: A forum for young people to talk together about giving and investing. *www.resourcegeneration.org*

Misc.

Coco, Linda, et al. *Children First: A Parent's Guide to Corporate Predators.* Washington, D.C.: Corporate Accountability Research Group. 1998

PHILANTHROPY

Books

Ostrander, Susan. *Money for Change: Social Movement Philanthropy at Haymarket People's Fund.* Philadelphia: Temple University Press, 1995.

Web Sites

Active Element Foundation.
www.activelement.org or *www.furture500.com*

American Institute of Philanthropy.
www.charitywatch.org

Council on Foundations.
www.cof.org (or call 1-202-466-6512)

Creating a Women's Giving Circle.
www.women-philanthropy.org (or call 1-608-270-5205)

Foundation Center.
www.fdncenter.org (or call 1-800-424-9836)

National Center for Family Philanthropy.
www.ncfp.org (or call 1-202-293-3424)

National Committee for Responsive Philanthropy.
www.ncrp.org (or call 1-202-387-9177)

Resource Generation.
www.resourcegeneration.org

Responsible Wealth.
www.responsiblewealth.org

Third Wave Foundation.
www.thirdwavefoundation.org

Tides Foundation.
www.tides.org

MONEY PHILOSOPHIES, RELATIONSHIPS, AND ATTITUDES

Books

Aldrich, Nelson W., Jr. *Old Money: The Mythology of Wealth in America.* New York: Allworth Press, 1996.

Collier, Charles. *Wealth in Families.* Cambridge, Mass: Harvard University Press, 2002.

Danko, William D., and Thomas, J. Stanley. *The Millionaire Next Door: The Surprising Secrets of America's Wealthy.* Atlanta: Longstreet Press, 1996.

Klainer, Pamela. *How Much Is Enough? Harness the Power of Your Money Story—and Change Your Life.* New York: Basic Books, 2001.

Needleman, Jacob. *Money and the Meaning of Life.* New York: Doubleday, 1991.

Willis, Thayer Cheatham. *Navigating the Dark Side of Wealth: A Life Guide for Inheritors.* Zanesville, Ohio: Equine Graphics Publishing, 2002.

Web Site

More than Money.
www.morethanmoney.org (or call, 1-800-255-4903)

Index

ABOUT THE AUTHORS

STANLEY D. NEELEMAN, J.D., is a professor of law at Brigham Young University, where he regularly teaches courses on estate planning and related topics. He is of counsel to the law firm of Parr, Waddoups, Brown, Gee & Loveless in Salt Lake City, Utah, where he practices in the areas of tax, estate, and business planning. He is an academic fellow of the American College of Trust and Estate Counsel and is a co-author of several books and articles relating to estate planning.

CARLA GARRITY, PH.D., is a child psychologist who practices with a multidisciplinary group in Denver, Colorado. For many years, she taught at the University of Denver School of Professional Psychology. More recently, she has devoted her time to writing and consulting with schools around solutions for children experiencing distress due to divorce or bullying.

MITCHELL BARIS, PH.D., is a practicing psychologist in Boulder, Colorado. In addition, he lectures and leads workshops throughout the United States and Canada on developing healthy family relationships. He is the author of numerous books on child development, families in transition, and family discord.

Books from Allworth Press

Allworth Press is an imprint of Allworth Communications, Inc. Selected titles are listed below.

Your Will and Estate Plan: How to Protect Your Estate and Loved Ones
by Harvey J. Platt (paperback, 6 × 9, 240 pages, $16.95)

What Money Really Means
by Thomas M. Kostigen (paperback, 6 × 9, 240 pages, $19.95)

Spend Your Way to Wealth
by Mike Schiano (paperback, 6 × 9, 208 pages, $16.95)

Estate Planning and Administration: How to Maximize Assets and Protect Loved Ones
by Edmund T. Fleming (paperback, 6 × 9, 272 pages, $14.95)

Feng Shui and Money
by Eric Shaffert (paperback, 6 × 9, 256 pages, 69 b&w illus., $16.95)

Legal Forms for Everyone, Fourth Edition
by Carl W. Battle (paperback with CD-ROM, 8½ × 11, 308 pages, $24.95)

The Secret Life of Money: How Money Can Be Food for the Soul
by Tad Crawford (paperback, 5½ × 8½, 304 pages, $14.95)

Winning the Divorce War: How to Protect Your Best Interests
by Ronald Sharp (paperback, 5½ × 8½, 192 pages, $14.95)

You Living Trust and Estate Plan: How to Maximize Your Family's Assets and Protect Your Loved Ones, Third Edition
by Harvey J. Platt (paperback, 6 × 9, 336 pages, $16.95)

Old Money: The Mythology of Wealth in America, Expanded Edition
by Nelson W. Aldrich, Jr. (paperback, 6 × 9, 340 pages, $16.95)

Retire Smart
by David Cleary and Virginia Cleary (paperback, 6 × 9, 224 pages, $12.95)

The Retirement Handbook
by Carl W. Battle (paperback, 6 × 9, 240 pages, $18.95)